Gender Dimensions in Leadership

Reflections, perceptions and
perspectives on inclusivity
– for executives and coaches

S E Drijfhout

D1712067

DEDICATION

To every human being who believes that expertise, compassion and the ability to include define good leadership.

Every man not afraid to share power and influence with women.

Every person of whatever gender identity, who can define their purpose through their own lens and not that of the world's.

The Covid pandemic has been a brutal stress-test of leadership, and many who imagined themselves commanding leaders have found their one-dimensional assumptions utterly inadequate for the circumstances. Broadening the leadership debate to bring in crucial issues of power, purpose and ethnic diversity as well as gender, Sarah Drijfhout's timely intervention ranks as an essential guide for leaders to an unfolding post-covid, post-#MeToo, post-BLM world.

Simon Caulkin, Editor, Global Peter Drucker Forum, London, United Kingdom, The Observer's Management Columnist for 16 years

Exceptional in-depth review of male/female leadership inclusivity issues in organization culture facing global institutions. A must read for Investors, Boards, CEOs and all managerial personnel in the workplace. The reader will gain greater insight into their own leadership style, family values, ethics, interpersonal and business behavior. These factors have major influences on one's leadership and management style, traits, character and its overall effectiveness with both male and female throughout their leadership career.

Dr. Alan E. Cremer Ed. D, Founder Cremer International, Lecturer Harvard Medical School, Department of Psychiatry – Retired Cambridge, Massachusetts, United States

This book (and the coaching) compels me to hold a mirror up to myself, as I try to be a better leader in my current and any future role. Critically, I also find myself holding that same mirror up to every leader and senior stakeholder I work and interact with - this is now my benchmark. The book is a call to action for authentic leaders with the emotional intelligence to 'get this', to take charge to take care of their people, their clients and themselves. That's never been more pertinent than in the uncertain, brave new world in which we find ourselves post-C19 pandemic. My hope is that the issues tackled in this book spark the honest, game-changing conversations leaders need to have.

Deborah McCormack, Head of Early Talent, Pinsent Masons LLP, Glasgow, United Kingdom

Sarah Drijfhout has written a very informative and comprehensive book on the importance of gender in leadership. A wake-up call for the stereotypes encrusted in our way of thinking.

Professor Dr Angela Maas, First Chair in Cardiology for Women at Radboud University, Nijmegen, The Netherlands. Dutch Women's Council Representative to the United Nations

Why is it that - after all these years - women are still underrepresented in senior leadership positions, and what will it take to ultimately and finally make this a non-issue that doesn't need "fixing"..? "Gender Dimensions in Leadership" is an insightful, fascinating book that offers fresh perspectives and leads the way to addressing female leadership representation as a self-evident necessity. Sarah Drijfhout takes a deep dive into underlying cultural and psychological barriers. Once these barriers are brought to the surface and understood, she offers research-based practical guidance on successfully addressing the challenge. Definitely a "must read" for men and women that believe in the value of gender equality and diversity in leadership.

Professor Dr. Ruud Kronenburg, Professor of Marketing and Organizational Development, ICD International Business School, Paris, France

Sarah's book is an important contribution to any initiative about diversity and inclusion. She takes a conversation that can be uncomfortable for most male leaders to have and makes it easy for them to become part of that conversation, while helping their organizations become stronger in the process. Her framework is elegant and powerful, and every leader needs to learn it and share it if they intend to remain relevant.

Andrew Neitlich, Director, Center for Executive Coaching, Florida, United States

Sarah Drijfhout brings together two of the most important topical issues for leaders, gender equality and emotional intelligence. Gender Dimensions in Leadership shows how both of these key topics provide opportunities for leaders to engage and lead every member of their team in an inclusive, unbiased way. Rich in research with practical self-reflective coaching questions.

Deiric McCann, Head of International Development, Genos International, Dublin, Ireland

If you are serious about being an advocate and an ally for women in leadership, you will enjoy this book. It is well researched, smartly written and loaded with facts to help debunk and expose the myths, limiting beliefs, and misperceptions that have fueled gender bias. Similar to other matters of bias, gender bias is an issue of the head and heart. This important work demonstrates that gender bias is adversarial to an organization's progress and success. To overcome gender bias, it must be viewed through the lens of our collective humanity. In short, this book helps make the case that men have a moral obligation, role and an accountability to help conquer this foe.

Craig Coffey, Founder and President, Way Maker Leadership LLC, Dallas, Texas, United States

Debugging unconscious biases is a formidable task. This book will successfully guide you through the process of creating a more inclusive organizational culture, building on effective leadership, fully aware of gender bias in leadership.

Antonio J. Morales, Professor of Behavioral Economics, Universidad de Málaga, Spain

Sarah Drijfhout has written a must-read primer for anyone considering leadership, particularly for those who are interested in the very delicate relationship between male and female styles. Her profound knowledge about psychology, behavioral dynamics, neuroscience, entrepreneurship and her practical experiences as well, provide valuable insights into why gender effects perceptions in leadership. It has binding power, is evocative and above all it is very relevant in these challenging times.

Dr. Kees Tillema, Managing Director, Het Zuiderlicht, Groningen, The Netherlands

Sarah's book is an important conversation catalyzer around gender equity. Articulating the true "pain points" of an issue goes a long way toward mitigating them, and Sarah's done excellent work in exposing some of the nuances that aren't often explored when talking about gender equity. For example, many treat gender equity as something women don't have, and must pursue to get what they want. Sarah insightfully explores the reality that men lose, too, when they lead in the absence of women peers. Sarah takes readers through a journey of deeper and clearer understanding of what we lose when we leave women, all women, out, before turning her attention to what we can do about it.

Daniel Juday, Inclusion Leader, Columbus, Ohio, United States

Global companies in different cultures struggle to integrate talent from all disparate groups. This book touches on all possible angles of diversity and inclusion – suggesting we can address stereotypes and biases, and indeed redefine "leadership".

Dr. Ashish Asgekar, Seismic Analytics Geoscientist, Shell, Bengaluru, Karnataka, India

I have known Sarah for just over two years, and I must admit that when I first met her, I viewed her from my own biases, thus resulting in an instant clash. Sarah chose to display leadership at that point instead of ending the relationship at that first clash, as I was inclined to do. She reached out to me and showed me how we could work through our differences, which is the essence of this book. There are many compelling reasons to read this book and if you want to make gender equality a priority goal in your organization, without alienating people and seek "to understand the invisible road blocks created by the gender dynamics in your organization's culture", then this book is a "must-read".

Thandeka Mlala, Human Resources Business Partner, Green Climate Fund, Yeonsu District, Incheon, South Korea

If you're really serious about making changes to your approach and behaviors, you need to use the content of this book to retune your mindset to build better and stronger organizations. Not only fueling a more inclusive environment but allowing you to retain and grow a more loyal team who can lead your business on an equal footing.

Michael Leake, Founder, Media Steps Consulting, London, United Kingdom

This book is about being your best self. It's not about male versus female. It's about being a thoughtful human being with an awareness of how society and our upbringing may have programmed us to think, feel and behave. You will get some great insights with the fact/data driven theory that really challenges you to question how you react and behave, not just as a leader but as a human, in different situations.

Peter Buckman, Senior Executive, Medidata Solutions, Alkham, Kent, United Kingdom

Gender Dimensions in Leadership is the must-have book for any leader of teams or organizations. Geared towards all genders, the balance of in-depth research and practical real-life application makes this the perfect resource for improving your inclusivity and taking your leadership to the next level.
Dennis Kight, Board Member, International Coach Federation, Dubai, United Arab Emirates

A profoundly empowering book that will make you reconsider who and what a leader really is. Commanding the attention of both men and women, this book breaks down every aspect of sexism and gender inequality at the professional level, and shows its readers how to build stronger and more inclusive corporations, starting with the way we lead. A timely examination of gender and race as they relate to leadership in corporate America. This book is a powerful call to action that challenges our societal norms and structures.
Dr. Robert Turner, PCC, BCC, Certified Executive Coach, Urbana, Maryland, United States

While Gender Dimensions in Leadership examines gender equality as its central theme, its lessons for leadership go way beyond that topic. Sarah Drijfhout's powerful messages are a clarion call for current and future leadership and go to the core role of the leader – to create inclusive, fair and compassionate cultures. Only by doing this will the true potential of organizations be realized. The responsibility to make this happen rests with us **all** and it needs to happen now.
Tim Ford, Performance Integrity, Leadership Advisor to Boards and CEO's, Sydney, Australia

Sarah Drijfhout strategically aligns her executive coaching skills with her research on gender equity to address the potential roadblock in some organizations created by gender dynamics. Her Inclusivity Framework is logical, not emotional, and designed to help leaders harness untapped talent internally and externally.
Robin Reininger, Founder and CEO hrthought. Senior Vice President Human Resources, MasterCorp, Florida, United States

This is one of the pioneer books to cover gender in leadership at such length and depth. Sarah Drijfhout has done a commendable job to help leaders develop a mindset to effectively bring in diversity across ranks to achieve the organization's vision.

Satish Karnam, PCC, Bangalore, India

While the focus on this book is gender dynamics, the overarching concept and tactics can be applied across diversity dimensions. It is exciting and highly relevant to see a unique approach to gender equality in the workplace that engages men in the process, not just as advocates, but as participants in exploring and evolving cause and effect across genders. That is absolutely critical to enacting real change.

Stephanie Beljon, Senior Director, Employee Relations, Stryker, United States

Sarah Drijfhout is a change accelerator. Her finger on the pulse of success-by-inclusion is educated, intuitive and experienced. If leadership (and current culture) are to advance, she is a worthy guide with a balance of strength and compassion. This book is a must read for leaders: for men, women, and anyone who wants to make our world a more effective, and better place.

Peter Andrew Wolf, Founder, The Wolf Leadership Institute, San Francisco, California, United States

Including everyone and finding a way to appease the individuality within the group, enables the team to become high functioning because everyone feels comfortable and confident. This book helps all leaders understand the needs and abilities of their workforce and evaluate those assets that are best suited for certain roles. Gender aside, everyone has unique gifts and abilities. Leverage those and your teams become winners.

Michael Harte, President, Harte Group, Pipersville, Pennsylvania, United States

This book touches a really relevant subject. Not only for the corporate businesses of this world. But also for smaller businesses and organizations. Getting more women in leaderships positions often is seen as goal in and of itself, overlooking the importance of selecting people based on competences. With this book Sarah Drijfhout gives men and women insight into the mechanisms behind the gender dimensions in leadership. This helps us understand each other better and value each other for what we are capable of, disregarding gender.

Tim Verver, Team Manager, Urban Planning, Sweco, Groningen, The Netherlands

Sarah Drijfhout does not have a gender axe to grind. She wants collaborative success for all individuals who bring intelligence, dedication, drive and an earnest willingness to put aside their ego (or their submissiveness) in order to learn and to succeed together in their endeavors. Gender Dimensions in Leadership is a must read for men and women who wish to grow, be self-reflective and learn how to accomplish more together. After all, "the whole is greater than the sum of its parts."

Elizabeth A. Clement, Executive Coach, retired psychotherapist, Newton, Massachusetts, United States

This book is an important contribution to the thought process of any leader who wants to affect change. The skilled use of organizational science and practical steps had me embracing the 'bottom line' business case for breakthrough actions rather than incremental steps.

Commercial Insurance Executive, New York, United States

This is a roadmap for change. Through the lens of gender bias, Sarah demonstrates how the same current social constructs affect all who are marginalized. I am inspired by the insights and approaches she offers, notably, that while we need to unearth the biases that result in discrimination, men are necessarily invited in as key participants in change, demonstrating the very inclusivity and objectivity required if we are to move beyond our current state.

Thomas Bradley Cox, Leadership Pipeline Institute, Kentucky, United States

Gender Dimensions in Leadership is an invitation for leaders at every level to open the door to conversations that are needed in today's society. Every time we chose to engage in dialogue and expand our understanding, we take one more step towards creating an environment that we would be proud to have our loved ones working in.

Alyssa Snider, Chief Human Resource Officer, Empire Kosher and Free Bird Poultry, Greater Pittsburgh Region, United States

As a father of two daughters I suppose I have a vested interest in supporting initiatives which address the issues around gender and diversity in the business world. I sincerely hope, however, that my own leadership and management style supports and promotes all individuals with care, compassion and equality irrespective of my family circumstances. I'd like to think so, but just in case, I turn to books like "Gender Dimensions in Leadership" to keep this front of mind. Because this is where it needs to be and all men in business have a significant and undeniable responsibility to ensure that this is where it stays.

Simon Hawken, Global Sales Leader in a multi-billion-dollar technology company, United Kingdom

Gender Dimensions in Leadership is so right for this moment in global realignment. When the world of work and living is experiencing a rollercoaster ride of a lifetime, we are looking to leaders who take equity, service and direction with compassion and courage, seriously. This book advocates with reason, research and passion that leaders, men and women, need to be 'masters of inclusion'. People matter. Leaders matter. Global thriving matters. "Treating people kindly, fairly and humanely could just be the most innovative and competitive thing we can do". Essential reading for aspiring leaders and current leaders in all organizations, businesses and families.

Carrie Benedet, Founder Thriving Matters, Sydney, Australia

Most of us would agree that variety in thinking and acting is necessary to deal with complex problems. But in practice we see it's a struggle to realize more mixed teams. Sarah Drijfhout's book will help you to reflect on the different beliefs and perspectives people have on the paradoxes about variety. It inspires searching for solutions on a higher level than simple quotas and provides perspectives for needed power shifts.

Volken Timmerman, Consultant Organizational Development, The Netherlands

Sarah Drijfhout's book provides huge amounts of compelling evidence to back up what we at MyKindaFuture have always strongly believed, that 'Talent is everywhere, but Opportunity is not'. Diversity, Equality and Inclusivity is a topic much discussed and sought, all the more so as a result of 'Black Lives Matter' and the interesting link provided, through Sarah's work, to engagement leading to well-being, and well-being to belonging is a powerful one. All the more so as job performance is hugely impacted by belonging - high belonging leads to a 56% improvement in performance. What more reasons can you want to take advantage of this powerful piece of work!

Simon Reichwald, Strategic Lead for Talent, MyKindaFuture, London, United Kingdom

This book is for anyone who wants to go beyond simply asking the question "why aren't there more women in leadership?". Sarah's fresh perspective on gender diversity and inclusion in top leadership roles comes at a pivotal moment in our history where examining gender stereotypes and looking deeper into biases in the workplace for all, has never been more important.

Amy Hoidas, Director, Learning Development, Toronto, Canada

Gender Dimensions in Leadership addresses some important aspects of gender perceptions related to leadership…ones that we may not be aware we have! A worthwhile read!

Jeff Zegas, CEO, ZurichDavis, Inc., New York, United States

A GPS to Gender Dimensions in Leadership – online coaching course

The Gender Leadership training I experienced was very supportive and educational. I now understand both the visible and unconscious processes / biases that occur with this sensitive topic, along with recognizing the obvious and hidden difficulties you have to face when it comes to the promotion of female leaders. Thanks to your training, I am able to manage on a daily operative basis more effectively for female leaders, due to a thorough understanding of perceived signals and behaviors, as well as having a more informed view when choosing suitable candidates in the future. I believe every (male) leader should have profound knowledge about this relevant topic.
Claus Mühlfeit, Director, Creative Technical Textile Operations, Switzerland

I appreciated the diversity of learning options within the course, articles to read, the group coaching calls, assessments and self-reflective exercises. Specifically, being coached one-on-one by Sarah on personal issues that mattered to me, was really valuable. I could ask questions any time. It Was an eye opener to me that for years we all tried to change woman so they could fight and find their way to the top. But the solution lies within changing the system that was originally built by and for men and reinforced by societies' views of our gendered roles. It was so nice to have women and men in the group-coaching, as well as people from all over the world with different backgrounds, studies and jobs. They each had individual input and points of view. This diversity was so useful and enriching. As a Human Resource Manager, it was music to my ears to hear Sarah describe constructive ideas around how to create inclusive places. I gained many valuable insights into how we can maximize the input of the qualities of all employees and empower the teams they work in. Sarah is not afraid to ask questions and let them simmer in everyone's head for a while. She can also lead discussions in a relaxed way without steering it in any direction or requiring an agreement or answer too quickly.
Marije van Apeldoorn, HR Consultant, Counsellor and Coach, Groningen, The Netherlands

Having been a little dubious about attending the Gender Leadership Program, expecting that I probably heard it all before, I can honestly say that the time spent with Sarah, the team and on reading and discussing the recommended articles, books, homework, was both rewarding and enriching to me as a male leader and influencer of people. It reminded me how it can be all too easy to "go with the flow" when it comes to dealing with gender equality and diversity in the workplace. But now that I am better armed with awareness of meaningful real-life sub-conscious potential bias, it has now empowered me on how to highlight and help address the role that male leaders need to play in requiring and finding an "equitable selection process" to identify and promote the most competent talent in the workplace that has to be gender neutral - without any of the current legacy obstacles on gender bias that we all suffer, as that's the way it has always been. Thanks to Sarah and the GPS for Gender Leadership Program group for helping me become a better leader.

John Murphy, Former Chief Operating Officer, GE Capital Subsidiary, Ennis, County Clare, Ireland

I am a little blown away to understand the thoughtful intentionality that went into your pushing me to the front of the class last week. In my life I feel loving enthusiasm and support for and from women friends, as well as tremendous gratitude and support for who I am to many, if not most, of my female patients and for my steadfast support of women to feel strong and effective in their lives. But I can't say that I remember ever being so directly supported - i.e. pushed into the spotlight so that I can shine - by a woman before. I feel touched and a little teary to read your words and to feel the intention you put into your email a week ago. I agree with you so much about the importance of women actively supporting and believing in each other! The world would be a better place - a kinder and a fairer place - if more women supported each other to feel and act strong.

Elizabeth Clement, Executive Coach, retired psychotherapist, Newton, Massachusetts United States

I would highly recommend you, especially men, to take this course. You will walk away with a greater understanding of the challenges and obstacles that a lack of diversity lead to and you can create and identify ways to conquer and overcome them. You'll be more successful as an organization, and as an individual as a result.

Former HR, Cisco and IBM, Middle East (Male)

For Willem Jan, Gerben and William

Contents

Foreword

Forward-thinking business leaders around the globe today recognize that the task of building a truly diverse workplace is more than just a critical social goal or a necessary legal calculation. The evidence is clear, and has been for some time, that greater diversity at every level of an organization translates into better results across the board. In other words, when your talent pool more accurately reflects the world around you – one where women comprise approximately half of the population – your business will experience more innovation, increased employee engagement, and improved financial outcomes.

The question for leaders, then, is not whether to pursue diversity initiatives in the first place, but rather how to make them succeed in the face of entrenched attitudes and bad operational habits. In *Gender Dimensions in Leadership* Sarah Drijfhout makes a compelling case that one of the greatest diversity challenges we face – achieving gender equity in top leadership positions – can only be met by confronting the often-unconscious biases and judgements that inhabit each of us, men and women alike. Offering careful research, insights from global corporate leaders, and thoughtful analysis of real-world operational situations, this book is essential reading for any executive aiming to make measurable progress toward gender equity in the workplace, and to reap the benefits that inclusion will deliver.

Over the past years, I've had the privilege of talking with Sarah Drijfhout on multiple occasions during the creation of this work, offering my views on the diversity challenge in my role as CEO of DHL Express U.S. Like the book itself, our conversations always inspired me to think critically about the personal perspectives and assumptions that inform my own beliefs, and that more generally guide the way that businesses are built and run today. As you will read in the pages ahead, a truly strong and exceptional management team, one that rises above the competition, takes shape when the list of its potential leaders is broad and inclusive, and is not cut short by unrecognized stereotypes. Ultimately, for your business, the end result of prioritizing gender equity is that you will have recruited, hired and promoted the very best people for each and every position, regardless of gender, race, ethnicity, age, sexual orientation, religion or physical capabilities.

Importantly, *Gender Dimensions in Leadership* frames the discussion clearly from the perspectives of both men and women, specifically highlighting the role that men must play to realize change. As a result, unlike many books on this topic, it is designed to enlighten both sides of the gender equation, bringing each group together in a constructive conversation instead of driving them apart with polarizing assessments. Specifically, the book dives deep into an examination of the way that gendered expectations affect men as well as women, and it examines the particular challenges that men in leadership positions face under the weight of old stereotypes. At the same time, readers are brought to understand how unconscious biases impact the behaviors and sense of psychological safety for women, and how awareness must exist on both sides for change to occur. In the end, creating a business environment where more women operate in leadership positions requires adaptation and action from men and women alike.

Today, our world continues to become more global and connected, even in the face of difficult social and economic events. In this context, creating a diverse workforce is more essential than ever. Potential new employees, like customers, can come from around the globe, and their unique views, life experiences and interests can fuel creativity and collaboration in any organization. But this can happen only if they are allowed and encouraged to flourish. At DHL, we are in the business of being global, and so establishing diverse teams has long been fundamental to our mission. Like many companies, we have implemented initiatives to promote diversity in hiring, recruitment and succession. For instance, to help combat the effects of bias and to boost confidence among applicants, we have established an interview and hiring process that involves a diverse panel of reviewers, so that the unconscious biases of any single hiring manager can be put in check.

But at the end of the day, what matters most are not the programs in place, but the results attained. As you will discover in the following chapters, the job of achieving gender equity in company leadership does not usually fail due to lack of effort or intent, but instead due to a lack of understanding. That understanding begins at the personal level, and it requires each of us to examine and assess our own personal views and biases when it comes to gender and diversity. It requires us to question how we have come to define good leadership, how we judge personality traits, and ultimately how willing we are to improve.

So, with all that in mind, let's get started.

Greg Hewitt, Chief Executive Officer of DHL Express, United States

August 2020

***

In the six times I have presented at the Women's Basketball Hall of Fame induction ceremony, I have heard dozens of inspiring women take the stage and tell their story. They often emphasize the importance of a champion—such as a friend, family member, or coach—while also acknowledging in some way the challenge a woman faces playing a sport that is historically viewed as a "man's game." It is a logical concept: to overcome systemic barriers often requires a champion to develop hall-of-fame caliber performance. Talent and drive alone are often insufficient. There is a learning here for business.

Gender bias is a human issue—not a women's issue. The current pace in business to reach true gender equity is wholly inadequate yet the demand conditions have never been greater. We live in a world with a host of environmental, social, and governance problems and we need 100% of our talent pool included in the serious game of changing the trajectory. To that end, we need MANY more fearless champions of gender equity and we need a playbook. Sarah Drijfhout's book is such a book. It is neither threatening nor guilt-inducing. It is insightful, data-driven, practical, and inclusive. It is a book for champions irrespective of gender.

This book will help you and your organization understand the unconscious and invisible, identify the essential, build your leadership pool, and engage with stakeholders more authentically. If you are already a champion of gender equity, Sarah's book will help you refine your thinking as well as your ability to communicate and lead. If you are not one yet, I implore you to get a copy and start the phenomenally worthwhile champion's journey.

David Golden, Alan and Ruth Harris Chair of Excellence, College of Business & Technology, East Tennessee State University, Tennessee, United States

Introduction

In October 2017 a prestigious leadership summit takes place in Paris. Business thought leaders have come together from all over the world. They represent some of the most respected voices, innovators, academics and CEOs in the business management space.

On the first day there are small, round table discussions. One of them is about 'how to show up as a leader'. There are four contributors for this particular round table. Russell, among them, is particularly well known. The others less so, but all four have interesting perspectives on human nature. And they each have different perspectives on the behaviors necessary to be successful in the corporate world.

The chairwoman, Alina, begins the meeting, explaining her first language is not English and for all to bear with her. She then moves on to introduce the four contributors, one by one. Apparently, this intention to introduce seems to get lost in translation. The first woman Alina introduces, a women's leadership 'expert' named Sandra, decides that that's her cue to start diving into her topic. After a polite minute or two of indulging this, and a lot of uncomfortable shifting in seats, Alina manages to stop her. She re-iterates that she wishes to introduce everyone, before moving into any discussion.

Some noses, it seems, are put out of joint at this point. Sandra tries to deflect the embarrassment she appears to feel, as if Alina has made the mistake. This subtle maneuver makes Sandra look rather foolish, at least to some in the room, while many are frustrated by Alina's apparent lack of assertiveness. These are the subtle first signals of sexism. These are the subtle signs that women in leadership roles are quickly judged, quickly penalized and quickly feel targeted.

Enter ego

Each contributor provides some background as introduction. The thought leadership 'celebrity', Russell, then begins to split the attendees into pairs. He wants them to discuss the topic of self-management as a leader between themselves. The attendees hadn't paid good money to do this. They'd come to listen to four thought leaders talk. But apparently Russell decides his celebrity status gives him the right to self-appoint as leader, and to determine the course of the meeting. Not only that, but it quickly becomes a meeting about Russell and nothing else.

Alina and the other two contributors, who are men, wonder what their role now precisely is, as they patiently wait. Fortunately, group members speak up, saying that they want to hear from all four of the contributors. Alina again is able to get things back on track. Thankfully. The other two quieter men share some fascinating insights on leadership.

A little later a female attendee makes a valid point about a lack of females in leadership as a comment for the contributors to provide an opinion on. Rather than hearing her out, Sandra decides to interrupt her. This is beyond ironic coming from a women's leadership expert, when you consider how much we know about the fact that women often *are* interrupted.

So, in the space of an hour many behaviors and two distinct leadership styles have been exhibited. A domineering one. And a considered, inclusive one, which enables many more ideas to be discussed. The styles themselves have been demonstrated, despite gender.

What we expect in leaders versus what we *should* expect

At the end of the round table discussion half of the group are completely bewildered by the behaviors they've just seen. The other half appear to be quite eager to accept that someone needed to apparently take charge because the chairwoman's pace, style and caring attitude did not meet their own expectations of how a leader should 'show up'. This almost 50/50 split has been well researched. Almost half the population will self-select louder, more confident, taller, usually white, male leaders. This is despite the fact that they may not have the expertise required in the given situation.

When an attendee later asks Sandra what her take on the bizarre behavior by Russell was, she doesn't know what he is talking about. She simply thinks that Alina is not assertive enough and "you have to be assertive with big egos like Russell's".

How the meeting went was surely Alina's call, as chairwoman and hostess. But it got stampeded by a strong, male ego. And he was enabled by a women's leadership 'expert', who was of the school of thought that focusses on what women need to change in their behaviors to be heard, rather than, on what men, with big egos, may need to *not* do, so they can be. And half of the group condoned this behavior and thought Alina should have presented differently. Fixing women is something of the flavor of the month.

What's fascinating about this cameo is that while half the group perceived the chairwoman as not competent, the other half were completely shocked by the behaviors of Russell and Sandra. For this half of the group the, 'celebrity's' and 'expert's' behaviors, undermined any credibility the duo might have had before the round table began. Some of the male attendees afterwards talked about how they'd heard stories about this kind of treatment of women from their wives. This event had finally brought it home to them.

What it brought home to us was that saying and doing are two entirely different things in the corporate world. We couldn't have come across a better example of how much of the current advice out there to individuals on how to show up as leaders usually forgets some key elements. Those elements are the social context, the behaviors within the group dynamic, and how your gender plays into your perceived and expected role within that dynamic. It was also a lesson in how important the leader's role is and what the group themselves should be aware of, yet very often are not. And ironically it highlighted that it's very often thought leaders' ideas that provide superficial solutions which fail at reaching the deeper issues at play in the gender dimensions in leadership discussion.

This book therefore explores leadership through the lens of gender at the individual and social context levels. Most specifically it looks at the challenge in getting more competent people, who happen to be women, into senior leadership roles in the corporate world. It also looks at the challenge of getting men who *are* actually competent into senior roles.

A book for leaders of all genders and intersections, not only women

In part 1 we talk about the positive results that flow from gender equality. We explain the plethora of research that demonstrates that equality is good for us all. Gender parity leads to more successful, profitable businesses and thriving communities and societies. It leads to workplaces of happy, engaged people, who by definition feel free to be authentic, creative and innovative.

Specifically addressing the question - why aren't there more women in senior leadership positions to effect policy and change? — Gender Dimensions in Leadership exposes many of the biases and myths surrounding women *and men*, women in leadership, men in leadership, and our false assumptions around what makes a great leader. Most crucially this book starts to address the conversation around how our over-identification with what society expects of us as men and women leaves many people in a space of fear and anger. This perpetuates opportunities for the few and fails to utilize vast amounts of largely untapped and overlooked talent.

While most books on gender equality tend to be read predominantly by women, this book has been specifically written for corporate leaders, who at this point are more likely to be men. Most CEOs of the Fortune 500 are currently white men, with only two male CEOs men of color. In 2019 only 33 were women, and only 2 of those women of color. Why do we mention color when we're talking about gender? To highlight that these numbers don't reflect the population, but one group. Also, that while we use gender as the lens, we must continually remember that inequality manifests beyond gender.

Let's get this party started

Vernā Myers, now Vice President for Inclusion Strategy at Netflix, coined the phrase "Diversity is being invited to the party, inclusion is being asked to dance". While inclusion is an essential part of this journey, there's something else that keeps slipping through the nets that needs addressing. Inclusion needs to extend to leadership. Daniel Juday, an inclusion consultant and former Director for the Ohio and Indiana Diversity Councils, wrote an article on LinkedIn about why Vernā's statement wasn't entirely true. He articulated that the larger issue was around having the *power* for people to invite themselves and be part of the party committee.

Vernā gracefully responded to Juday's article, in agreement that "the need to re-imagine culturally competent organizational cultures, where people who have been under-represented and marginalized are deeply integrated in the decision-making, shaping and planning, etc. of the organization," was hugely important. She reiterated, very sensibly, that it's a step by step process. Juday agreed, allowing that, "in lopsided power structures it is often necessary to attempt partial or incomplete advances." However, it seems that admitting they're partial steps is a big part of the overall process. Until these marginalized groups with their enormous talents are also leading, we can't hope to get fair representative influence. Once we do, we'll utilize the talents of more and better serve the needs of all.

Giant leap for *human*kind, now

We think the time for a step-by-step approach might be allowing a lot of companies pay lip-service to an issue that's pressing and *possible* now. Yet we completely understand why Vernā used this diplomatic framing. Change is hard, especially for people who can't, don't or won't see the issues really at play.

Corporations want to be competitive, innovative and reap greater profits. There is a plethora of research showing that having more women in senior leadership roles can do just that. It seems having women in senior leadership roles is great for business and great for the workplace. With this in mind we explore the exclusion that's going on and investigate both how to get to the party, dance at the party and have more women and minorities be in charge of the party committee. Might leaders serve their organizations better by taking massive strides, *now,* to share that leadership? An increasing body of research seems to think so.

Beyond white feminism and patriarchy

While it should not be seen as a next step in a kind of hierarchy of first white men, now there should be privileged white women, and then later Black and brown people and then other minorities, it has nevertheless been the case that much of the gender inequality rhetoric has been focused on white women. This has been to the exclusion of other groups of women on this topic. Indeed, feminist theory itself is largely based on the white female experience, thus itself largely exclusionary in capturing the very unique and specific experiences of all women.

And much of the research into masculine ideologies has focused on patriarchy and the white male experience to the exclusion of others. In the discussion on equality *men* have actually been largely excluded. We seem to think equity is something women only need to fight for.

We need to recognize that everyone loses when we don't have equality. We need to understand that people, companies and societies thrive when we do.

We therefore attempt to use the lens of gender in a broader exploration that should speak to the hurdles for everyone, not just women, not just white women. Afterall inclusion needs to do just that, include everyone. We noted from our own research how much more is needed to both further research and better voice the needs of differing groups. This book, therefore, isn't focused solely on women, their issues and how they apparently may need to change to fit. This book also highlights issues facing men, while incorporating more nuanced issues facing certain sub-groups. Remembering that intersectionality is a central thread and relevant to everyone.

Effective dialogue and bridges

In the spirit of inclusivity there's no point targeting an audience of only women, or white women or even white men. However, when certain groups are seen as having higher status, and have arguably the most power, privilege and influence, it is these groups that we need to target more effectively in this dialogue. Because the balance of power and influence in many corporations *is* sitting in the hands of white men, their specific attention is needed. We need to build bridges to these men, not barriers erected through blaming rhetoric.

Issues with gender overlap many of the interests of all groups who experience biases and discrimination so this book should be somewhat relevant to everyone. Though many of the issues for Black, brown, disabled, older, younger, neuro-atypical, LGBT and many more minority sections' issues are different, most of the oppression is interconnected. It's ultimately about one dominant group over others.

We should also remember that bias at extremes has serious impacts on people's lives, all people's lives. The reader is therefore invited to insert the identity of their choice where they may see the word woman/women/man/men/gender and question whether the suggested strategies might still apply. Though not always, they can be relevant. The book has been written around some of the key issues that come up in the gender equality discussion and the chapters provide snap shots of these specific issues. These are the starting points for discussions we have within the 'GPS to Gender Dimensions in Leadership' coaching course we run for corporate leaders.

In Part 2 of the book we talk about feelings, and the things we keep avoiding. We begin with an exploration of gender and expose the myth that we are so very different for what it largely is, a myth. We look at our current belief systems and values, specifically talking to the issues around identification with what it means to be male or female. Crucially we ask how much of this conditioning is at odds with ideas around equality, specifically in leadership? We look at the psychological effects on men when they view themselves and others with gendered expectations. This focus on men helps us understand why the often-unconscious expectations we have of boys and men actually *serve to prevent* more women coming into leadership roles.

Men and women are often perceived as very different in our society. However, in one review of many meta-analyses there were found to be negligible, small or moderate differences between men and women in terms of communication, cognitive ability, personality and social traits.[1] Most recently in a meta-synthesis from hundreds of studies sex differences were mostly found to be small.[2]

Human beings are actually hugely adaptable, and while human biology renders some obvious physiological differences, we see all human behaviors can manifest *despite* gender. We use studies from neuroscience, psychology, sociology as well as case studies from the business world to help leaders understand this as a crucial point. For too long the stereotypes associated with a given gender have created limitations and expectations on individuals, and this issue became clear in our own research, which we also share in this book.

7

The Driftwood Inclusivity Framework

In part 2 we also introduce the Driftwood Inclusivity Framework we developed. This framework helps individuals and organizations start to track how biased or inclusive they actually are. Based on that, they can determine the type of culture they're likely to be creating, and target what they can do to change that.

The rise of emotional intelligence

Part 3 begins with an exploration of the concepts of belonging and uniqueness. We map gender norms to Maslow's hierarchy of needs to better understand the nuances of this complex topic, and its effects on people's psychological well-being. Diversity, Equality and Inclusivity (DE&I) work cannot be done in a psychological void. Fairness, a sense of uniqueness *and* a sense of belonging directly link to people's levels of well-being. People's levels of well-being directly link to their levels of engagement.

It is in this way that we provide a framework for assisting leaders in increasing their own emotional intelligence (EI) on this topic.[3] Research has found that leaders with higher emotional intelligence have higher rates of engagement in their teams. Capgemini, in a 2019 study, found that 78% of executives believed emotional intelligence was a "must-have" skill.[4] It also cited that the demand for EI was likely to increase by 6 times over the coming 5 years. Self-awareness, awareness of others, authenticity, emotional reasoning, self-management and inspiring performance are all core emotional intelligence competencies.[5] They are all necessary if leaders are to create gender parity and inclusivity in their organizations.

If we look at leadership as a concept, we can see how our definitions of leadership have been influenced by a myth of differences in gender. In part 3 we delve into these outmoded beliefs and values around what leadership looks like. Part 3 is about the things we miss and the choices we oft-times don't realize we have. It's about recognizing that an update on these values and beliefs around leadership might better serve us. Using the lens of gender, we begin to understand that the traits we stereotypically identify in good leadership may have been largely flawed.

Stereotypes and unconscious bias absolutely limit our choice of leaders and our correct assessment of the level of competence in many of the leaders we choose. Corporate executives and organizations clearly need to update their beliefs and values if they are to show up themselves as well-informed leaders on the topic of gender. There's still an urgent need to break away from the many gendered myths that pervade in our society which limit both women and men. We need to find more outstanding inclusive leaders for our organizations. We believe that what will determine the most successful leaders in the next decade will be those who can become *masters at inclusion*.

HONOUR not power

This book also explores why power is a real problem in effective leadership, and the effect of the hubris syndrome on a leader's effectiveness at developing other areas essential in leadership, like compassion. It discusses the science behind the fact that the more power and responsibility a leader has the less empathetic they can become, and why this is a problem in inclusivity work. We expose the current definitions of success, business success and leadership success. We create a new vision of how organizations might consider running themselves to get the very best talent for the kind of success that goes beyond quick quarter end growth, and inflated numbers for a fast IPO bid.

'Strong' leadership skills have often been badly scoped with a bias towards dominance and assertiveness, stereotyped as belonging to males. Not only do we expose this as a dangerous preference in itself, but we simultaneously highlight qualities that good leaders need to demonstrate. High levels of emotional intelligence, the 'softer skills', stereotypically associated as more feminine, fall within this.

In part 4 of the book we examine the relevance of equity, social responsibility and transparency in today's corporate world, and the possibility for exercising gender-neutral leadership. Part 4 is about actions, the things we can do. Firstly, we need to recognize what actually happens to women through women's eyes not through our own assumptions. We bring suggestions for organizational development and for creating coaching cultures which do not focus on how women and minority groups should change themselves to assimilate, but instead focus on the behaviors of everyone and the organizations who represent them. We introduce the HONOUR framework. This can be used by leaders and their teams to focus on some fundamental key behaviors needed to create more inclusive work cultures.

Fundamentally, this book is a call to awareness and then action from all CEOs and senior leaders. A call to embrace the issue of gender equality and parity as an opportunity for real innovation. As ironic as it may seem treating people kindly, fairly and humanely could just be the most innovative and competitive thing we can do.

Well-being as a central anchor

In Part 4 we look at how the changing face of work can look and positively impact men and women. Investing in longer term, sustainable talent development plans will attract the best candidates, create engagement and lead to unbeatable results. At a politically and societally fractured time good companies are poised to step up to the plate to create socially responsible visions and missions to inspire their people, their customers, and their business goals, which will be centered around more than pure profit.

Obsessive workaholism, burnout, and preoccupation with presenteeism over work quality are just some examples of a work-behavior legacy which benefits no-one. Work flexibility will be a key focus, as will the move toward a more mindful and compassionate type of leadership. In the age of Covid-19 this has been forced onto the management agenda.

We challenge another issue in Part 4. Current strategies for assimilating women and minorities rather miss the purpose of diversity. There are two problems with most of the advice currently out there for women. First women need to make all the changes and assimilate. The advice is if they make the changes, 'lean in' more,[6] acquire confidence, let go of perfectionism, make better choices, say no to things, acquire executive presence, - the list really does go on, - then these issues they complain of won't exist.

This mentality maintains patriarchy, the idea that men are default leaders and, if women want to lead, that they need to adopt more stereotypically male behaviors. They need to be more like the boys to fit in and then everything will be fine. Breaking the so-called glass ceiling. But the advice out there focuses on these glass ceilings being broken by white women who assimilate to white male ways. Actually, we should be expecting equality and fairness for everyone, not demanding power for the next group in the social hierarchy, white women, through replicating stereotypically masculine behaviors.

The focus on women also exacerbates internalized sexism, making the victim responsible for the inequity and responsible for the solution.[7] The second problem with the bulk of advice currently in the market is that by default it says that the current way we work is fine, and trends towards a certain type of leader, which seems to reflect male stereotypes of strength, decisiveness and power. We focus on how to prevent exclusion, by de-emphasizing the need for these traits, as well as strategies to create inclusion.

We explore how the 'softer skills' coupled with emotional intelligence, mindfulness and purpose are gaining serious traction for those willing to create the most successful companies, where people are highly engaged and productive. We expose toxic masculine cultures and cultures where obsession with work is encouraged, as being as damaging for men as they are for women. We describe in chapter 10 how a roll-out of education and coaching on the gender dimensions in leadership can be incredibly valuable for leaders, and the organization's male and female leadership talent pool.

Parallels with bullying

Most organizational systems unwittingly create hurdles whereby women must be this, that or the other to fit, in order to be taken seriously. Formal and informal structures and individual and organizational behaviors lie at the root of the problem. It is exactly these structures that prevent other minorities from rising, and these behaviors which keep such structures in place. This dynamic also closely resembles that of bullying.

The bully rarely knows lasting damage has been caused and was just looking for some attention and to feel powerful. The victim is alone trying to fix something they internalize as their own fault while they *cannot* fix it alone. The group avoids and ignores what's really going on. What we know about countering bullying applies extremely well in the context of seeking equity for all in the corporate world. Far from tackling the bully or empowering the victim in isolation, the most successful antidote both for bullying and exclusion is to get the whole group involved.

The leaders who can 'show up' to *really lead* this endeavor in their teams will be the ones who solve the gender gap and inequality in senior leadership. We're not suggesting all corporations led by men are bullies, or that all women lower down corporate ladders are necessarily victims. What we are suggesting is that a traditional work-environment based on stereotypical male leadership styles, command-and-control management and archaic ideas of pursuing greater and greater levels of profit, power and status despite the personal and societal cost are just that, - archaic, outdated, and ineffectual. For men, for women, and for society.

In this spirit we touch much more on challenges men face in the gender discussion. As the book Un-skirting the Issues points out, there are 'well-intentioned men' aplenty who would gladly know how to address the issue of gender discrimination but are unsure how to.[8] The problem with the great majority of advice about gender often deliberately or inadvertently blames men for the situation. If much of what is happening is due to unconscious bias, then this is as misguided and misplaced as it is to blame women for their lack of confidence or for not 'leaning in' more. Such materials polarize the sexes into some unnecessary gender war which has no place.

We need men and women who are *masters at inclusion*

We should also bear in mind that stereotyping has as big an impact on men as it does on women, perhaps to their advantage in acquiring more roles in senior positions, with associated power and status, but often at a personal cost and burden of expectation that comes from being *required* to be successful and the leader. While much of the advice in the business mainstream and best-selling markets centers solely on women it condemns men in its silence about them, and by default continues to often place all men in the same misogynistic, sexist, patriarchy-inspired box. This does a great disservice to the many men and many women who need to be engaged together in the conversation around gender, fairness and ultimately who's going to do what for the greatest benefit to all.

Male leaders ready to approach this in a bold way will reap the rewards if we make women in leadership a business imperative, rather than an initiative. To do so we will need to have the courage to face our own biases and those of our organizations. Fundamentally, we need to address how over-identification with certain masculine stereotypes within leadership prevent growth and change, both in ourselves and the organizations we lead. We will need to explore a new definition of leadership. And corporations will need to create new organizational structures and flexible working options to attract and retain talent, because men want balance in their lives just as much as women do. The Peterson Institute for International Economics and Ernst and Young carried out a study of 22,000 publicly traded companies in 91 countries in 2016 that showed that companies with 30% women on the boards performed 15% more profitably than those that did not.[9]

Yet we know from studies of Western European countries where quotas have been in place that this alone is not creating the tipping point to getting more women into senior roles. Achieving diversity for its own sake, while laudable from a social justice perspective, may not be enough in isolation to see positive effects trickle down.[10] The observed 'golden skirt' phenomenon in Norway meant requirement of 30% women on boards in 2003 led to women holding board positions in bulk. The mandate's effect on an increase in the number of senior executive roles women hold, however, has been slow.

Policies creating inclusivity and educating on what non-discrimination means, what bias is, and how stereotyping effects everyone, not just women, are what are still urgently needed. Coaching on this goes even further by personalizing the issues for the individual and providing an ear to each person's unique challenges. It specifically focusses on psychological well-being as a central anchor. It helps leaders recognize bias and grow themselves personally and professionally. And coaching in mixed gender groups enables sharing, belonging and the creation of accountability for the whole team. We therefore end each chapter with a summary of the key points, some self-reflective coaching questions and considerations. This helps leaders become more aware of their emotions and leads to a plan of action and accountability. With this, leaders are more able to apply the knowledge proactively and practically.

This book is a call to leaders, real leaders. Those who show up to really lead their people, by their side not out in front. To those leaders let's stop with the step by step approach and get ready to take some giant strides!

Part 1

Results

Why Equality
Is Good For Us All

1 No Honeymoon Without Engagement

> The worst labyrinth is not that intricate form that can trap us
> forever, but a single and precise straight line.
> Jorge Luis Borges, Argentinian writer

If you are an exceptional leader you will likely have a diverse group of people helping you. Just as we know that people with the most diverse social networks are usually the most informed, we know too that diversity creates the most growth and innovation in teams.[1] We also know that people with the strongest (notice we didn't say most) social connections are the happiest.[2] Happy people are vastly more productive and creative compared to unhappy people. Social connection and belonging are essential to our well-being[3] because happiness is directly connected to that sense of belonging.

So, it becomes essential as leaders to challenge our beliefs about how included everyone feels within our organizations, and thus how happy they might be. With the current statistics on engagement so woefully low this challenge has become a business imperative. More worrying yet is our apparent acceptance of such statistics as 'just how it is.' When Gallup released numbers showing that engagement was now at 34%, hailed as somehow a success because it had risen slightly on other years, we have to question why we believe having less than a third of people engaged at work is OK.[4] Or rather, how is it that any leader would accept that having 13% of their employees *actively* disengaged, thus potentially sabotaging the company, is ok?

How is it that any leader would accept that having 53% of people disengaged, not caring less about the business or customer, ready to leave in a heartbeat, is somehow good enough? If such disengagement is costing organizations in the US what's estimated to be between $450-550 billion per annum[5] why would you not pull out all the stops to get these people engaged - and fast?

Maybe it's not all doom and gloom though. A recent Annual Employee Engagement Report, 2019, made by The Predictive Index reported on by Business Wire, a Berkshire Hathaway company, found that 71% was the overall level of engagement rate in the U.S.[6] Much better news, right? Yet it turned out that people were far happier with co-workers and their job, and far less happy with organizations and their leaders.

Nine out of ten times people still leave an organization because of their dissatisfaction with the organization, leadership and the overall commitment to people development. Furthermore, actively disengaged workers alone, which according to Gallup let's remember is 13%, were still estimated to cost US businesses $483 billion to $605 billion each year in lost productivity. One multinational in the study found that just a .1% increase in engagement was worth $100,000 in annual value. It literally pays to engage employees.

High engagement numbers are critical

If you're the leader of a large corporation with a large salary, bonus, other benefits and control over millions if not billions, your employees expect you to have a duty of care towards them. Your example and the behaviors you model *do* make the difference. Boards are realizing this more and more. We see it in company metrics and results, and we know it psychologically. As pressure increases on leaders to show not just metrics demonstrating diversity, but numbers which reflect job satisfaction and engagement, coming directly from a sense of inclusion, it has become essential for leaders to learn the skills to engage their employees. 75% of workers leave because of their bosses, so doing what you can to stimulate engaged, happy employees should be your number one priority and development goal.[7]

Since we know that feeling included and treated fairly directly impacts on well-being and productivity then as a leader you'll need to show up for this task. Creating a positive company culture, modelling inclusive leadership constantly, creating a culture where collaboration is the norm. Having leaders who understand what's going on with their people is essential. Inequality can have far reaching consequences, making people unhappy, socially disconnected and destroying engagement.[8]

The disconnect

The critical point being that, based on our research, there is a huge disconnect between what leaders believe are the reasons women in particular leave, and what the reasons *actually* are. There is also often a huge mismatch between the most effective people for leadership roles, and the types of people we select. And there is an almost non-existent dialogue recognizing that men too have specific gender challenges at work and that these too need recognition and support. Similarly, those of the LGBT community.

While you may not yet have a demographically diverse team, reflecting on the ideas in this book and actively seeking ways to create better collaboration and inclusivity *will* lead to growth in your organizations. The Wall Street Journal recently published its first ranking of diverse companies.[9] It found that the 20 highest ranking companies for diversity and inclusion had an average annual stock return of 10% over 5 years, compared to the 20 least diverse and inclusive, which had 4.2% returns.

The best leaders are the ones who will be able to harness the strengths and abilities of men, women, those who identify in some other gender way and minorities as an intersection of these. There is a powerful business case for actively engaging in the competition for women and minorities which currently make up 85% of the talent pool in the US. And to quote Warren Buffet: "If obvious benefits flow from helping the male component of the workforce achieve its potential, why in the world wouldn't you want to include its counterpart? ...We've seen what can be accomplished when we use 50% of our human capacity. If you visualize what 100% can do, you'll join me as an unbridled optimist, about America's future."[10]

How well an organization and its leaders will be able to engage female and minority talent will determine the most successful businesses in the coming years, but more importantly how organizations involve and include men in this will be highly influential in its achievement. 'Masculine' leadership as it's been presented for centuries has been under scrutiny for some time now. There is more need than ever for fantastic male leaders who can themselves rise above the stereotypes.

Masculine stereotypes so often require men to be the problem solvers, taking charge as their primary skill set, rather than stepping back and allowing others to contribute, while simultaneously acknowledging them for it. Stereotyping reinforces that men are supposed to be in charge, that it's expected of them. It also reinforces the stereotype that they don't always have the highest empathy or skills for collaboration as examples. These are two skill sets we also know are essential in effective leadership.

Knowing this we might question yet Buffet's statement of how many men have actually *really achieved* their full potential. As Buffet stressed "...an even greater enemy of change may well be the ingrained attitudes of those who simply can't imagine a world different from the one they've lived in." Why can't we imagine a world where more women are leaders, and where we search for better, more competent male leaders?

As part of the research behind this book we conducted our own study into what senior leaders felt were the key issues holding women back from senior roles.[11] To conduct the research, we interviewed in-depth a cross section of men, women and people who identified as gender fluid. The majority of the group were white, four of the females identified as African American, another female as Black South African, one male and one female as Asian American, and two males and two females as Indian. Their roles ranged from CEOs, senior

VP's, senior sales professionals, senior academics, scientific researchers and advisers.

The minimum turnover for the corporations was $450M up to $130B. The sectors where these executives came from included technology software, business services, freight, packaging, medical devices, pharmaceutical and biotechnology, chemical, advertising, professional services, academic business schools, social enterprise and the legal and medical profession. The locations of the executives were geographically spread through Canada, North America and Europe, with an almost equal split between both sides of the Atlantic represented.

The in-depth interviews lasted a minimum of an hour and many stretched to 2 and 3 sessions. The distinct questions asked were: Why are there proportionately fewer women in senior management roles? What would need to change for more women to take on leadership positions? From the extensive information noted in the interviews it was possible to draw some clear conclusions about how individuals and organizations view gender, stereotypes and the perceived barriers preventing women moving into more senior leadership roles.

The initial study we conducted uncovered generalities and perceptions about what was creating this unequal gender representation in leadership positions. Much of the feedback centered around the stereotypes that still exist around gender roles, and how problematic these can be to advancing women. The purpose of this research was to focus on gender as opposed to discussions on race, and other inclusivity and intersectionality issues including religion, disability, age, sexual orientation, and a whole host of diverse sections. But we know that differing intersectional aspects are inextricably linked with the unique experiences for every individual. We talk later, for example, on the fact that the experiences and biases a Black woman may face are unique to her, and not the same as those experienced by white women or Black men. By the same token the types of discrimination can be multi-layered.

Understanding intersectionality

Figure 1 summarizes a host of differentiators that can interplay to either include or exclude individuals. We can be certain it is not comprehensive, and there are even more factors that create very unique experiences for every individual who identifies more or less with the labels given them or that they give themselves. Gender then is an exploration of one small piece of the puzzle of why we don't have more diversity in most leadership roles and corporations globally. As we shall see however the issues around gender are interconnected with the similar oppressions and biases that differing minorities face.

We attempt to represent the other sectors in a general sense in our discussion while not pretending to have sufficient knowledge to talk to them individually in the detail they deserve and require. However, as stated earlier, we believe addressing many of the behavioral and organizational changes in the face of gender inequality suggested can contribute to solutions to the issues for other minority groups as well. Ultimately everyone is organized in some way by gender both by themselves and by others which makes it an over-arching theme for exploring aspects of equality. And because discrimination is entrenched in behaviors and therefore ultimately structures, exposing these structures has relevance to equality as a whole.

It is also extremely important to clarify where the original concept of intersectionality came from and what it may be seen to represent in more recent years. It was Kimberlé Crenshaw, a professor at Columbia and the University of California, Los Angeles, who came up with the legal term of intersectionality to describe how individual characteristics such as race, gender, or social class might overlap or intersect.[12] Crenshaw, whose work has focused on critical race theory, observed that the legal system failed to recognize dual discriminations in cases which involved Black women. As an example, in the case of DeGraffenreid v. General Motors in 1976 Black women were the first people fired in a seniority-based layoff system in the early 70's, because they had not been hired before 1964. While the Civil Rights Act was only passed in 1965 Crenshaw pointed out its

7

passing did not somehow create an end to all racial prejudice in the legal system.

With a persistent racial and gender wealth gap still to this day and underrepresentation of women and minorities in positions of power, policy making and influence, Crenshaw critically reasoned more than 30 years ago that discrimination continued to exist because legal and socioeconomic structures themselves were largely built on racism. Specifically, while the courts refused to open the "Pandora's Box" of minorities and continued to treat Black women as purely Black or purely women they specifically ignored the unique challenges facing Black women as a group.[13]

So, this was the origin and the intended meaning of intersectionality. However, it appears to have taken on different meanings in the last few years. The original meaning for Crenshaw and for us is about demolishing racial hierarchies, just as we should be gender hierarchies. The interpretation of what intersectionality means to others is almost an upending of this idea. That is, that it should somehow be used against those with privilege, in the hierarchy white males, and where they themselves now start to respond as the victim. For some, "intersectionality isn't just describing a hierarchy of oppression but, in practice, an inversion of it, such that being a white straight cisgender man is made an anathema."[14]

Where Crenshaw's focus was on deep structural and systemic issues of inequality and discrimination, it is more often interpreted in terms only of identity and representation. As Jane Coaston observed in her 2019 Vox article, "Crenshaw herself said intersectionality isn't 'an effort to create the world in an inverted image of what it is now. Rather, she said, the point of intersectionality is to make room 'for more advocacy and remedial practices' to create a more egalitarian system." But part of the latest interpretation, that it is actually about inverting the current power hierarchy, has certainly put the backs up of many of those still owning the majority of the positions of power. And interpreting it in this way can make enemies of many of the men who neither created these structures nor fully understand them themselves.

Intersectionality is about recognizing individual specific issues in order to tackle specific discrimination and bias that effects those individuals. It's about working towards fairer systems for everyone. As leaders, rather than being overwhelmed by this idea, we can choose to be inspired. We must recognize that equality means recognizing the Pandora's Box and renaming this box, Opportunity.[15] Afterall what got left behind in Pandora's Box was Hope.

Figure 1
INTERSECTIONALITY
MODEL

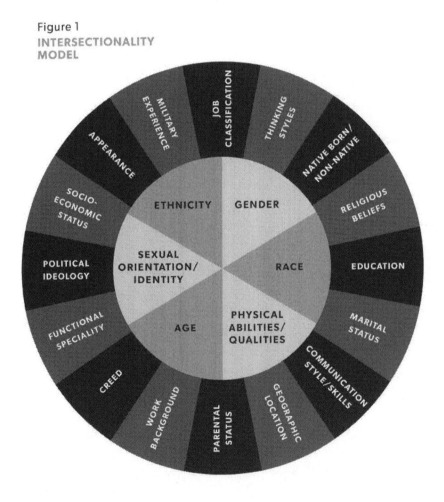

It's important to start your own exploration of what your biases might be, what you really believe and how these beliefs might be influenced by both conscious and unconscious thoughts. Before getting all defensive and feeling threatened, remember we all have bias. It's a protection mechanism in the brain for quickly sifting data, creating patterns. Having bias does not make you immediately a terrible person. Being in a leadership role, having massive responsibility for others, and *not* having a deep understanding about people, and your own and their bias is a liability, however.

Bias also guarantees we miss masses of opportunities. One of the primary duties that CEOs *should* have is to understand this and to learn the skills to be an inclusive leader. It should be high on every leader's personal development agenda to understand this subject on a deep level. As one of the senior executive male participants on our Gender Dimensions to Leadership program put it "leaders should have a *profound* knowledge about this. I've discovered it is so relevant to, …well everything!"

Test for bias, but be careful of biased tests

If we can agree all stakeholders when in such positions of power over others, such as executive leaders, need to understand bias, what things can we do? Possibly test for this, but with a huge disclaimer about the tests that currently exist.

One of the better-known tests on bias is Project Implicit at implicit.harvard.edu. Project Implicit is a non-profit organization and internal collaboration between global researchers interested in implicit social cognition - thoughts and feelings outside of conscious awareness and control. Its goal is to educate the public about biases and to provide a 'virtual laboratory' for collecting data on the internet. This test has to this point been widely used by millions of people and is often used by DE&I in organizations.

It is important to be aware of this test with some important caveats, however. Recent rigorous scientific research has determined that this test, and specifically the implicit race bias test, has neither sufficient validity nor reliability to be determined as objective. "A pile of scholarly work, some of it published in top psychology journals and most of it ignored by the media, suggests that the IAT falls far short of the quality-control standards normally expected of psychological instruments."[16] The reference in the footnote is not a read for the faint hearted. However, it *is* recommended. It demonstrates that this can be a complex, emotive topic.

While the IAT has been determined as both a useful tool for educational purposes and for measuring implicit bias in society, both these objectives have come under increasing criticism in recent years. What we ourselves caveat is that it cannot predict discriminatory behavior. Were such a tool to exist it would be a true gift for working in the area of equality. We also know that not every critique of the race IAT applies to other varieties of the test. We therefore make leaders aware of this. We use the existence of the test as a reference for discussion. Should people wish to take it, we add the important disclaimer that it is not regarded as the thoroughly scientific tool it once was.

You can find a gender implicit bias test on the Implicit Association Site. A test around women in leadership can also be found on the following link https://www.aauw.org/article/implicit-association-test/. This test has been set up as a collaboration between the American Association of University Women and Harvard University.

Rather than focusing on a test that measures reaction times which may or may not properly measure the existence or absence of bias, we have open discussions in safe small coaching spaces around the experience in taking these tests. We also hold personal coaching sessions about what the implications might be in terms of our own biases. This is where uncomfortable feelings can come up which leaders are encouraged to become aware of. This is how bias awareness can become conscious, shared and reflected upon.

Could the tool for discerning bias be as simple as being present and having positive open conversations? In our experience, yes. We believe that what we resist persists and denial of bias is to deny being human. We are unlikely to be either color blind or gender blind. Openness to the possibility that bias likely exists in some form is the gateway to enriching conversations, better understanding and growing beyond stereotypes.

Key Points

Inclusion = Happy People = Engagement = Productivity = Profitable/Thriving workplaces.

High engagement numbers are critical.

Inclusion starts with strong leadership. 9/10 employees leave because of bad bosses.

Women and minorities are being lost from the market. Their talents often remain untapped due to bias towards 'masculine leadership' and lack of awareness of their capabilities.

Modelling inclusiveness at all levels is essential to engagement.

Leaders need to properly understand intersectionality. It should not be seen as a way to invert the world we are now in. It should be used to eliminate discrimination, create true equality, thriving workplaces and societies.

Everyone has bias in some form. The key is to understand this bias on a conscious level and grow beyond it.

While tests for implicit bias exist in the marketplace, there validity has been challenged more recently. Bias tests can be a useful education tool, but they don't determine who is bias and who is not.

Safe conversations can be a valuable way to recognize bias and become self-aware of how it might limit our ability to think logically.

Self-reflective coaching questions and considerations

Have you measured engagement levels in your organization?

How engaged are the people in your organization?

What are your current turnover rates?

What is that costing you in terms of: time?

lost productivity?

increased overwhelm for others?

Financially?

To re-hire?

To re-train?

On the morale of your employees?

Are you managing to retain women employees?

How is the profitability and productivity of your organization?

What makes you feel uncomfortable in the gender discussion?

What would it mean to you if your gender biases were wrong?

What would it mean to you to become a more inclusive leader?

When uncomfortable feelings arise what can you learn about yourself?

Practice coming up with different possibilities around the person you see before you.

Get comfortable being uncomfortable. Learn to stay with your feelings of discomfort and try to understand them beyond the perspective you currently have.

2 The Business Case, Status Quo, Assimilation

Train people well enough so they can leave. Treat them well enough
so they won't want to.
Richard Branson, British businessman

The United Nations Sustainable Development Goal 5 targets gender equality as key to building peaceful communities and economic growth.[1] The World Economic Forum cites increased gender disparity due to marked reduction in women's participation in the labor force as detrimental to economic growth.[2] The World Health Organization Commission on the Social Determinants of Health found that those societies with higher levels of inequality, "unfair economic arrangements," have the worse health issues, crime rates and more social problems.[3] It concluded that "social injustice was killing on a grand scale". Leaders need to recognize that societies are created both in countries and in corporate entities.

It is proven that organizations that embrace diversity and inclusion will be more competitive in the coming decades and will outperform the companies that fall behind. A recent study showed that improving diversity in firms increased those companies' competitive advantage and prospects for growth, specifically demonstrating that companies in the top quartile for gender diversity "were 21 percent more likely to experience above-average profitability."[4]

This study also showed there was "a positive correlation between gender diversity on executive teams and two key measures of financial performance: earnings before interest and taxes (EBIT) margin and longer-term value creation, as measured using an economic-profit (EP) margin."[5] The Peterson Institute for International Economics created a paper examining the most profitable firms (6.4%> net profit) and showed that going from no females on boards to a 30% female share can create a 15% increase in profitability. It is not for nothing that measuring diversity is now becoming a key financial metric that investors and analysts want to see when making investment decisions.

While the argument for gender parity has been emphasized from a social justice perspective, as well it should, more recent research is now able to categorically link an increase in gender parity in senior leadership to better business results. We know that both corporate social responsibility and increased economic growth are regarded as essential to the effectiveness and competitiveness of corporations in today's market. The business case for successfully establishing more women in senior leadership roles has been made.[6] It's the real, deep work to achieve it that's the challenge for many corporations.

Gender parity leads to thriving societies

Though there seems to be a great deal of action around the subject of inclusivity, people don't appear to be doing it very well. While we have 50 years of laws behind us including equal pay provisions, the protections of the same rights for Blacks and whites, and a plethora of law purporting to promote women's rights we don't seem to be there yet. Indeed, the World Economic Forum suggested it would take another 99.5 years for the gender gap to close.[7]

This does matter. According to the World Economic Forum, "Gender parity has a fundamental bearing on whether or not economies and societies thrive. Developing and deploying one-half of the world's available talent has a huge bearing on the growth, competitiveness and future-readiness of economies and businesses worldwide." In terms of economic participation, the gender gap will take 257 years to close. It should be noted this was 202 years in the 2019 report. We'd suggest that any corporations who want to be

7

competitive in the global market and attract the best talent, irrespective of gender, probably want to achieve this faster than in 99.5 years.

According to the Gender Gap Report 2020 the so-called role model effect may well be helping close the gap in terms of leadership and wages. Having more women climbing the ranks provides a working model for others to follow. So much attention has been building about the course of women in the workplace over the last decade specifically, that has put the onus on organizations to make the changes demanded in the law. Yet there are two cautions to this promising sign.

The first is that lower down the labor force the gap is becoming worse again, showing that differences in compensation, for example, might actually be increasing, especially in developing countries. Secondly while this gap grows, we might want to question whether the increases that start to happen are based on sound merit or tokenism. The report specifically emphasizes that economic participation and opportunity are where the numbers are actually going backward. Why is this? It cites that women are doing more of the jobs which will become automated over time.

Not enough women enter the labor market where there are significant financial rewards, think technology or finance as examples. Women also have "insufficient care infrastructure and access to capital". So, women do not get the same opportunities. Nor are they tapping equitably into the economic benefits in the labor market. We also believe that the spotlight on women might be causing problems that aren't being seen. That we still have a bias to masculine traits, rather than leadership and talent being packaged in a male or female form might be more relevant. This bias to masculine traits creates further bias and a lack of inclusivity.

Including men is essential to women's equality

Whilst we've come a long way with the empowerment of women much of the rhetoric has disillusioned and distanced many men, and while it's logical for many to understand the arguments, our emotions tell us something else entirely is going on. Indeed, it's our emotions that can so often be at odds with the logic of gender parity. Studies are now coming to light showing that while companies have been keen to promote and create women's networks and discussions to empower women, they have simultaneously excluded men and created silos. For those with a truly inclusive mindset this should have been an obvious risk all along and has created an ironic black mark against a movement designed to liberate and promote the rights of women.

A recent study carried out by Thomas Reuters and Acritas, a provider of global legal market intelligence, found that women's networks within organizations were indeed more likely to create silos and that opening those networks up to men was a very positive development.[8] The report also highlighted how *unhelpful* coaching often ended up being and we have a very clear sense from our own research that the type of advice out there for women and men is flawed. Why? Because we don't understand the gender dimensions to leadership. Flawed, because fundamentally, most people do not have even a rudimentary understanding of the deep psychological issues behind bias. Nor behind people's motivations for playing out roles to adhere to certain cultural expectations. Coaching can be hugely helpful, but while people are biased and unaware about the gender dimensions to leadership it's more likely to do harm than good.

Most coaching given is very superficial. It is often non-applicable in the wider context of psychological distress and the effects of the threat of being measured against the stereotypes of one's perceived in-group.[9] These are often neither recognized nor fully understood. Stereotype threat happens when a person senses a common societal judgment might lead to them being found in some way lacking if they are perceived as conforming to a negative stereotype. It can also create anxiety leading to a failure in something they might actually be intrinsically good in. Examples include, women can't drive well, men are better at math, women should be in charge of childcare, men should provide financially for their families, women are not intrinsically 'built' for excelling in science, men make better engineers and business leaders.

It's particularly relevant in leadership. Men are seen as congruent with leadership. Women are not. Education and training on stereotyping, and how inaccurate it is, is essential for men and women who are coaches, mentors, sponsors and leaders.

For many people engendered in specific roles, inexorably linked to their ideas around what makes an effective man or woman, the feminist movement and push for women in senior roles has not just alienated but antagonized many people. Not just some men. The seeds of the feminist backlash still find plenty of fertile ground today.[10] And how we identify as individuals has a huge part to play in this. Non-bias aware males and other assimilated females not conscious of their own bias, are at most risk of perpetuating the current status quo, and becoming a part of this backlash.

When we assimilate, we become like the other. This is explained brilliantly by Dr Barbara Adams in her work on diversity.[11] While America is described as a melting pot, the culture dictates that the melting pot is homogenizing the majority to the ways of America. Adams sees inclusivity and diversity far more like a salad bowl, where people come with their own unique identity. We can see that this homogenizing has often played out in organizations where there may be one or two women who've reached very senior positions.

It's often, but not always the case, that some senior females have simply assimilated into the male 'way of doing things' rather than that they've necessarily been influencing in their own way. Indeed, these women might often self-identify with more masculine traits. This must be noted if we want to create more balanced systems and behaviors that reflect both masculine and feminine traits, values and ideologies.

Assimilated females can often be a block to introducing strategies for getting more females into senior roles and their presence can mislead their male colleagues into thinking that other females aren't interested in these roles. Meanwhile, junior women in organizations may see these senior females as assimilated, possibly 'yes' women, loyal to the males with power, rather than as people bringing their own set of unique characteristics and strengths to the role.

The queen bee phenomenon

A finding that highlights this situation of female assimilation is something termed the queen bee phenomenon. A Senior Finance Executive, female, we interviewed put it like this, "Driven women fall in the trap of being alone and don't bring other women along with them." One female executive described the situation like this. "I'd like to see more women support women. In our culture it isn't normal. There's a queen bee, and she wants to keep others out. She's a big deal and knows she's the unusual one. That's how they lose a lot of people here. They leave because they're fed up."[12]

Women who rise to higher positions, often but not always, break with their own group, and assimilate into the male group. Yet, rather than being seen as a behavior driven by being a ruthless, individualistic and unscrupulous female, and thus a further source of gender inequality, it's been argued that this phenomenon of senior women breaking from more junior women is a *consequence* of the presence of gender discrimination in workplace settings in the first place.[13] It's a maladaptive behavior that doesn't just effect women but is observed in other marginalized groups, individuals whom might themselves self-distance from their referent group.

A number of studies have been done to show how and why this assimilation behavior manifests. In one such study, when Surinamese Hindustani people in the Netherlands, who described themselves as weakly identifying with their ethnic minority group, were then reminded of something discriminatory that they had encountered at work they displayed similar self-distancing responses from the

Surinamese Hindustani group. This manifested in the same way that some senior women appear to do from other women.

When reflecting on how something discriminatory had happened that affected their emotions and had impacted their career the participants of the study were primed for remembering ethnic bias. Group members who identified more *highly* with their ethnic group saw the discrimination as a major issue. They were more likely to show favoritism to positive ingroup characteristics, conscientiousness in this case. Some of the members were more likely to try to improve the image of the group in this way. This is described in the study as a socially creative coping strategy.

Individual members who had *low* identification with their ethnic group were more likely to claim they were more stereotypically Dutch. Thus, they self-reported as more independent or direct, as opposed to the more highly identified Surinamese Hindustani. The latter were more likely to self-report as modest, risk-avoidant or unassertive.

Conscious of the social identity threat that being associated with their ethnic group might create for their own success, the low ethnically self-identified Surinamese Hindustani distanced themselves from that group by seeing themselves as different. They saw themselves more like the higher status group they were trying to aspire to belong to. Associated with the social group and the negative stereotypes of that group, these individuals tried to create identity separation, by "acting Dutch." The social identity threat of being viewed as like their ethnic group, and any associated negative stereotypes, stimulated a threat response to self-distance.

This behavior is seen as an individual's social mobility response. Affiliate with a group that is seen as more upwardly mobile by distancing from the group that's seen as disadvantaged.[14] This is part of the explanation given for why a large proportion of African Americans have a slight to strong automatic preference toward European Americans compared to African Americans. These individuals, under a social identity threat, will try to create upward mobility individually rather than be part of a group collective who move to fight discrimination in a different way.

Association with the privileged high-status group, white people, combined with implicit bias, which still has a massive impact against the low status group, affects everyone. Low group-identified individuals do this precisely because they recognize that in the working context being associated with your group is not conducive to success. Often companies fail to spot the risk of this happening and why assimilation is a key threat to true diversity, as is *assuming* that a given individual associates strongly with their referent group. That is why having a token representative from a specific social group where there is still a majority of one group does not in and of itself guarantee moves in the right direction for more equality. Nor does it guarantee itself a role model for others to follow.

It has been observed that as highly competent women progress in male-dominated organizations they can tend to adjust their self-presentation and leadership styles to fit better in masculine organizations. It's diluted forms of this type of behavior change we often see even *recommended* and presented in some of the popular media. People mistakenly assume that certain behaviors are the 'right' behavior for being successful. However, it would be truer to say it's the right behavior if you, as a woman, want to get on in a male-dominated work environment, or in a position of leadership. It won't necessarily lead to fairer, more equal and balanced work settings though. Nor will it lead to more women being promoted necessarily.

In this way, rather than adding to the diverse pool, some women tend to assimilate to more male norms while disassociating from other junior women, precisely because being associated with the female group brings with it an identity threat. That identity threat is that, while sexism and inequality exist, these women and other senior men may view other women in stereotypical ways. They may view other women as less competent and capable of leadership than they themselves and other men. Because of this risk some highly competent women don't want to be associated with this stereotype and so they self-distance. It is quite literally a threat to their identity to be associated with these other women.

Rather than being a weapon of sabotage in itself, self-distancing is actually seen as a protection for some successful women's survival and promotion. Of course, there may also be intentional female saboteurs. The queen bee syndrome has been extensively researched and presents as a further issue in the challenge around promoting the right people. It alerts us to the possibility that we may inadvertently be hiring 'yes' people, or people who may have narrow, assimilated types of behavior, similar to the homogenous group that might already exist. This can often, though of course not always, show up in situations where there is a token representative from a minority or as the only woman.

In one study done in an academic setting in Italy it was shown that, while there was no difference in the self-descriptions of the students regardless whether male or female, there *was* a difference among *senior* faculty. The study showed that among the faculty the senior females actually described themselves as being *more* assertive, competitive and willing to take risks than their senior masculine peers. They simultaneously saw the female students under them as *less* committed to their academic careers than their male counterparts. Interestingly the male faculty did *not* see the junior women as less committed. Individual upward mobility can *require* that the individual doesn't identify readily with their own referent group. In order to also distance themselves from that group they are more likely to attribute stereotypical views *to* that group.[15]

For the senior women in this study, for example, statements around having made more personal sacrifices, being more ambitious, and making the observation that other junior women were more wrapped up in their families and less ambitious, were voiced. Such statements raise two dangers. The first is that there's a binary even within leadership: you can't be a leader unless you commit all your time and energy to it, a psychologically highly detrimental strategy as we'll explore further. The second danger is there's a judgement again, a bias against another, unlikely to be based in fact. In this case bias against the junior group of women, the pipeline. It is reminiscent of the conversations and conclusions most men reached around why there weren't more women in leadership roles when we interviewed them.

Thus, senior women who have assimilated will deny there are structural disadvantages for other women rising and may actually block things such as flexi-time, quotas or additional training that might help either themselves or junior women. In this same study, however, it was found that these women will support policies which might help other *senior* women. So, it appears their own behaviors are very much steered by what they perceive as fair and right in their own narrative based on their own sense of identity. Perspective is highly relevant here. We need male and female leaders who can look at fairness from other perspectives besides their own. In other dimensions.

Understand how someone self-identifies

The research into the queen bee phenomenon makes a few interesting findings. Firstly, it is more likely to happen to women who self-identify *less* readily with their own referent group, signaling to us again that identity is a crucial ingredient in the gender parity conversation. Identity can transcend the sex of a person, and the stereotypical characteristics that that sex supposedly possesses. This is a key point for many people, including but not limited to the LGBT population, for example.

Another key point was that women who self-identified as displaying more masculine characteristics of leadership tended to have more subordinates. This added to the evidence that, rather than gaining greater feminine perspectives within the organization at the highest levels of leadership there was still a homogeneity, a hegemony towards the masculine. In other words, the more senior, the more responsible, the less feminine. Yet this homogeneity brings its own consequences – these women are often negatively perceived by those subordinates, with the risk of creating political and toxic cultures where junior women do not want to progress. And the isolation and lack of a sense of belonging for these senior women can indeed bring psychological distress for them as well.

In our own conversations with senior women some clearly made the distinction that in order to rise one must make sacrifices and make choices and that family, for example, is something that is not conducive to rising to the top. This tendency of some senior women to negatively assess junior women and those with families, determining that they themselves have made greater sacrifices, ties to the notion that this is not lending itself to discussions around diversity and inclusivity. It continues to endorse and legitimize the hierarchy. It continues to legitimize the separation of having family, with being leader, - but only if you're a woman. And it brings up again the issue that men have often been conditioned to seek greater and greater responsibility and status while, historically at least, simultaneously having less familial participation.

But shouldn't leaders be modelling better balanced lives, which in this instance includes spending time with family, yet might as easily extend to spending time on hobbies, civic and community participation, personal and professional development? Do we want stoical self-sacrificing automatons or humans with thriving lives as our leaders?

These studies also highlight a really key idea crucial to any strategy around creating gender equality. How people identify has significant effect on what strategic policy will work best to promote more equality. While we focus on the individuals with low self-identity to their referent group, we need to remember these are highly competent people. They are not necessarily deliberately sabotaging things. They are simply adapting behaviorally in a way that brings a degree of success for themselves individually. They have high expectations that if others want to climb, they also have to demonstrate the same merits and commitment. Yet their success comes at the price of distance from their referent group in a bid to avoid being stereotyped, and possibly wrongly limited.

The contradictory nature of this means psychological safety and well-being has still not been achieved. Pursuit of individual goals and separation carries psychological penalties. Myth tells us there are bitches who might be loyal to men more than women, missing the point that these individuals are more likely adapting to a system that is ultimately discriminatory and who are trying to make the best of it. Remember this queen bee phenomenon only shows up if the working context is one in which women are devalued and is one dominated by men; and it's not even a phenomenon just for women. Ensure that the culture doesn't *devalue* women or minorities. Create more balanced representation and equal pay. Tackle harassment seriously. Address the factors that make the work environment unfair for people and the maladaptive behavior of some highly competent individuals is likely to go away.

Positive distinctiveness, merits and dangers

By the same token the highly self-identified group cope by creatively focusing on the positive ingroup stereotypes, we could argue feminism in the gender discussion. In this group its members highlight positive distinctiveness, often the difference and the exceptionalism of women. This runs the danger of creating a binary. Highly self-identified individuals often exclude part of the referent group not so highly identified with them. It's part of the reason many Black and Asian women do not feel represented by the feminist movement, a movement that has predominantly looked at things from the perspective of a more privileged white woman's experience. It's also the reason why many white women *also* do not like the over-emphasis on pushing for women because they see themselves differently. They don't so readily identify with whatever 'being female' is supposed to represent. It's partly the reason that the LGBT community may also not feel represented.

The real challenge is how to retain a group identity, psychologically important to a sense of belonging and how to also have an individual identity which might be more strongly or less strongly identified with a specific group. It is all ultimately contextually driven and driven by what behaviors show up in that context. Pushing a movement based on the group identity by promoting the stereotypically perceived positives of that group demotivates those people driven by the desire to be recognized as being successful based on individual competence and uniqueness. And as we'll go on to discover recognizing both one's uniqueness and similarity with certain groups is essential for achieving a sense of inclusion.

Introducing uniqueness and belonging

This speaks to the need highlighted by Catalyst that true inclusivity requires both a sense of belonging and a sense of uniqueness.[16] Catalyst is a global non-profit that works with companies to accelerate women into leadership. Until organizations get a handle on how their individuals might identify, instead of assuming that if you're a man or woman for instance you identify strongly with certain masculine or feminine stereotypes, it is very difficult to have a sense of what it is that motivates individuals, and how they might feel they belong. While we constantly put men and women in gender-stereotyped boxes, we miss this essential point. Assuming that every woman is heavily identified with being, for example, nurturing and not ambitious is as problematic as assuming that every man is highly ambitious and competitive. And for some men and women their recognition as part of the group is less important than recognition of their individual merits. The truth lies somewhere along a spectrum. Everyone is unique.

Every person will be different depending on how much or how little they identify with being part of a group and how much they identify with being more an individual. Fundamentally the question becomes whether there is space for them to be identified in multiple ways? Here the value of recognizing how things intersect is also highly relevant and valuable. The construct of gender and assumed traits it conveys on us is hugely problematic if it doesn't give people the freedom to behave in ways other than those *expected* of their gender.

Belonging is fundamental

Probably one of the most important things we can realize as leaders is that human beings need to feel that they belong. Social connectedness is a primal indicator of health, and well-being. Women can be pretty good at picking up cues and realizing when they do not belong in a corporate leadership setting. It's often because they've not been accepted in that role. Similarly, any individual regarded as belonging to a minority group. So, it becomes critical to understand how individuals get their sense of belonging. We need to understand them as unique individuals.

It's one of the many reasons why many stop short of heading for that senior role. While people talk a great deal about lack of role models, as a key factor people rarely understand that at a very human level all of us need to feel like we belong, that we're part of the team. If the board room is full of white men, it might not be too welcoming for many women or minorities. Especially if the men treat them differently. If your differences are frequently pointed out in throw away stereotypical statements these have the effect of excluding when they included a certain other type. When a woman does not feel like she belongs there is always a higher risk that she will not want to partake.

If you're wise enough to believe in the intrinsic talents and potential of people, this is a huge loss. Junior women who may well be highly competent yet perceive that moving up the ranks might require them to break from their identity, which might more strongly identify with the female group, is just such a category. At that point 'leaning in' frankly becomes irrelevant. This feeling often gets missed in all debates around inclusivity, exacerbated by advice to change and find your voice as a woman. The voice, the unique individual perhaps already did, but no one was much interested in listening and there were poor leaders around who didn't facilitate the need to hear that voice. A feeling of belonging is one of the most fundamental human needs, and it is beholden on us as leaders to do everything we can to help everyone feel they belong. Group dynamics don't always facilitate inclusivity, but leaders *can* if they chose to.

Citing belonging and uniqueness as the two fundamental factors for success in making people feel included, Catalyst found that people who felt more included were more innovative, contributed more to their teams and saw similarity as a means of creating belonging and difference as a means to feeling unique. From the studies above we can directly see that people in non-inclusive work environments make trade-offs and these will be closely related to whether they see themselves as more strongly or less strongly identified with a given group.

Exclusion and inauthenticity

When teams exclude members those members in stark relief feel far less creative, are actively disengaged and neither feel they belong nor that they are unique. These factors create psychological distress in humans. There are further important distinctions to make here. Exclusion can lead to very negative feelings, a sense of anger, resentment, sadness. A lack of a sense of belonging can lead to a lack of being one's true self, an inability to be authentic.

This was the conclusion made in recent research done by two assistant professors from Columbia University, Michael Seplian and Drew Jacoby-Senghor. They interviewed 1,500 individuals including LGBTQ-identifying individuals, people from multiple racial groups and women working in male-dominated fields, capturing more than 17,00 incidences of identity threat.[17] These people came from a range of family environments, socioeconomic backgrounds, ideologies, cultures, education levels, and current hardships. These interviews captured a wide span of both identities and groups and are therefore quite exceptional. Most studies typically only take a limited number of identity groups and study them.

All humans need a sense of belonging which might be hard to achieve in full if your referent group is made up of another gender, the reality while men hold most of the senior leadership roles. But thriving societies and corporations need women and minorities in leadership roles too.

We also observed the situation in reverse in some of our interviews. Men too can feel excluded. For example, in one academic setting there was one male leader surrounded by women, who in fact did not feel there was an issue with women in leadership in his particular social context. With a lack of balance in favor of women having all the leadership positions he himself felt discomfort and exclusion.

In a different example, we spoke to one very senior female who explained that her husband was a stay-at-home father and that this had quite a significant impact on his self-esteem. He didn't see other father's around him, but he highly valued his role as the primary caregiver for the family. It made for a fulfilling but quite lonely existence. As we discuss in chapter 12, this is becoming an increasing issue for men, who want more familial participation.

So, men may also feel excluded in organizations where there are predominantly women, and in employment sectors traditionally associated with female workers. They face two issues, social stigma, and likely less pay than in traditional jobs for men, issues we'll shortly return to. But while gender bias around leadership competence still exists it turns out men are still likely to make more money than their female counter parts.[18] Access to economic power is still unequal.

At times there may even be quite incompetent women appointed to 'prove' that the company is trying to diversify representation. In one multinational company we interviewed more people talked of an internal conspiracy where they were certain that very competent women were being passed over, while less competent women were being promoted, only to fail. This created the result that the 'gender experiment' appeared not to have worked, keeping certain men in power. It is tempting to question whether these men were also keeping other competent men out. This situation was observed in two of the more male-dominated corporations where we conducted interviews. Its effect was to distill a sense of mistrust down the organization. More interestingly, these instances were reported and observed by men, and not women, as some might assume.

Assimilation and the inability to be authentic

We believe that in part we actually perpetuate inequality and lack of inclusivity by assuming men don't experience a lack of belonging and an ability themselves to be their authentic selves. In the interviews we conducted, as well as in our experience coaching men, it is very clear they more often experience the inability to be authentic. The pressure to show up and play up to certain male stereotypes, specifically in leadership, and to play down certain emotional or stereotypically feminine traits was frequently noted. In chapter 4 we specifically look at the masculine gender norms that influence this. We suggest that men too experience a lack of belonging and inability to be authentic in certain social contexts, leadership actually being a prime context where this occurs.

Assimilation itself can occur at an unconscious level, so primed are we to adapt to the social context. If, for example, as a woman you've asserted yourself and been very comfortable negotiating a high salary, which you've succeeded in achieving, you might have little sympathy or understanding when you hear that other women might struggle with salary negotiations, just as many men have difficulty sympathizing with this issue. Yet we know from the research that discomfort with salary negotiation is a widespread issue for women and can also be an issue that effects some men. And why would an ability or lack thereof to *negotiate* for salary be the only factor determining whether you should *get* more or less salary?

The gender pay gap is just one example of leaders not practicing what they preach when core values and credo's claim that the company aspires to being fair and equitable, yet we know that women only make $0.79 to every dollar white men make. Those were the figures for the uncontrolled pay gap published by Payscale in 2019.[19] It should also be noted that this is even bigger for women of Alaska Native, American Indian, Hispanic or Black ethnicity at $0.74 to every dollar white men make. Black men earn only $0.87, and Hispanic and Latino men $0.91 to every dollar white men earn.[20]

We'll continue to overstate this with no apology. Inequality is a human issue not a women's or a certain minority's issue. The gender pay gap often hides a bigger issue, the opportunity gap, summed up in the barriers that prevent women attaining the same status and high-level, high-paying jobs that proportionally many more men achieve. Many leaders appear to be blind around the reasons for this.

Key Points

Gender parity leads to thriving workplaces, economies and societies.

It is possible to accelerate gender parity now.

Access to capital and care infrastructures can accelerate equality.

The current spotlight on women may be sustaining inequality, exacerbating perceived differences, sometimes leading to assimilation to 'masculine' norms.

Queen bee syndrome is seen across gender and race and is a symptom of discriminatory and unequal workplaces. Inequality might be being perpetuated because of assimilated females and some of the current advice for women.

Identity threat and stereotype threat resonate with most people, while we have specifically focused on giving power to certain groups.

This threat gives a sense that they are judged by double standards, while not operating in an equal social context.

Leaders need to understand how employees identify as an individual, *and* how they identify with their 'perceived' referent group. This directly impacts whether they actually feel included or not.

Every person will be different depending on how much or how little they identify with being part of a group and how much they identify with being more an individual.

Self-reflective coaching questions and considerations

Is there space for your people to be identified in multiple ways?

Are your female leaders supportive of changing structures and systems to create more favorable environments for junior women to thrive and develop in?

In what ways do you recognize and honor the differing backgrounds of your people?

How equitable is your organization currently?

How can you objectively measure this?

Think equal pay, access to opportunities, clear succession plans, reward systems, flexible working.

How do you gain a sense of belonging and a sense of uniqueness within your own role as a leader?

Consider ways you might create a sense of belonging and a sense of uniqueness for your employees.

What assumptions might you have made around how you might achieve this?

What can you ask them as individuals to find out what is important to them?

Part 2

Feelings

The Things
We Keep Avoiding

3 What you don't see *will* hurt you as a leader – The Blind Spot

We are all in the gutter but some of us are looking at the stars.
Oscar Wilde, 19th century Irish poet and playwright

Sophie entered the elevator with the senior executive team of the NASA technology spin off. She was heading home after a grueling 20 hour stretch. Having been flown directly from the UK, she had attended the two-hour long interview in Seattle. This was held over dinner with 4 executives, three men and one woman. It had been generally enjoyable, talking about industry trends, the market, the opportunities.

Sophie highlighted what she'd achieved in her last role, strategized on where she felt she could bring growth to the company, and listened to the CEO, David, talk about the company's fascinating history and plans for future expansion. Then Joe, the Vice President of Sales, outlined the strategy for business development and mid-term plans for territory expansion. Rachel, Head of Operations and Kevin, Head of Marketing remained relatively quiet. David and Joe had concluded Sophie was right for the job and told her so, but did she want it?

Throughout the interview Sophie had a strong feeling about the company and opportunity. She would enjoy visiting the HQ in Seattle and knew she could build the company on the European side, having been the top salesperson in the number one company in the same market segment at the time. As she chatted with the group, casting her eye over a shoulder now and then to see if 'Bill' would walk in, - they had said Gates often came to this restaurant, - she hesitated.

Rachel and Kevin were less than friendly at best. While she might not have to work with them directly it was clear they did not like her or welcome her presence.

Her suspicions were confirmed when, in the elevator on the way down to the taxi back to the airport, she overheard them, - not difficult or subtle in an elevator you understand, - talking about how the last person to be employed by the company had also been "eye candy". It was a clear dig at her, clear in its aim, brutal in its delivery, divisive in its effect. The message she took away was that they had seen no talent in her, she was not welcome, and they would make her life hell.

A couple of days later speaking on the telephone to the CEO Sophie declined to take the opportunity. She told the CEO it was indeed unclear whether this might be the right move at this time, and she thanked him for his time and the efforts in making the meeting happen. What she really thought was she would be alone in Europe with very little on-ground support, and there were at least two people strategically placed who would be stabbing her in the back at every turn Seattle-side.

The tempting takeaway message from this is that Sophie didn't like the culture, but this was only partly true. There was something far more crucial going on in the thinking process that tipped this young woman's decision. And it was completely based on how she had viewed the CEO.

While all 5 travelled in the elevator it was clear Joe and David had not picked up on the snipe. They'd been involved in their own conversation at the time and had not heard Kevin and Rachel's dig. Though perhaps forgivable of itself it got Sophie wondering how much more these leaders might be missing of the toxic behaviors that were probably happening in the company. In the end her decision process came much more down to one of confidence in the company's leadership. How could Rachel and Kevin with this apparent lack of care and professionalism have even been appointed? This was not the first or last time they would do such things and frankly their unwelcoming behavior should have been obvious to David during dinner.

Sophie recognized she was not put off by the would-be colleagues who appeared to feel threatened by her. She'd dealt with this sort of undermining behavior by males and females many times, and that of itself was not a reason not to take the job, though it did get waring. No, instead she realized she was looking for more astute and emotionally intelligent leaders. Leaders who had a strong team behind them, and who were good at selecting strong candidates. Leaders who could spot bias and bad behavior. Leaders who could nip such unprofessionalism in the bud before it ever took hold or do damage. It was clear the CEO could not do this.

If David, and Joe also, could not even spot what to Sophie was explicit bias, how on earth would they ever have the sensitivity to spot implicit bias. Those tiny subtle behaviors that leaders of today have to be aware of to create inclusive workplaces. What other crucial behaviors were these leaders missing or allowing? What else might be undermining the sense of safety for individuals to challenge ideas and bring novel approaches to the processes and the business itself?

The gender of the players here is far less important than the roles they played. The leaders had demonstrated poor leadership by their ignorance of the social behaviors right under their noses. It had cost them the loss of some excellent talent in a technology niche where it was very hard to find good people. Sophie, as a consistent top-performer, had exactly the track record and skill set they needed.

Understanding others and modelling better behaviors

In gender bias it is very important that leaders are able to understand the mental states of others. In the context above it was clear that the CEO had no understanding of just how disengaged Rachel and Kevin felt to be so willing to sabotage this interview. How could he have missed how unwelcoming they had been to Sophie despite the fact they had sat having dinner together as a group for two hours? He had some serious blind spots in terms of observing and understanding human behavior.

Understanding bias is an important part of the puzzle in the gender dimensions to leadership discussion. But it is not the only crucial element for effectively leading. Being able to model inclusive behavior by being actively involved in observing the interactions between employees is one example of better behavior. So too is being able to select co-operative people, people strong enough that they do not feel threatened, irrespective of who comes into the company. This is an essential element for creating and leading collaborative, diverse and inclusive teams. Acquiring people who are open minded and inclusive themselves creates an atmosphere where others are more likely to be comfortable joining.

As Jim Collin's points out in Good to Great, a book we'll return to, it's about getting the right people on the bus.[1] Even more essentially inclusive leadership is about having the kind of leaders who understand at a profound level the impact that bias has on their own and everyone else's emotional, social and psychological state. It's about understanding how an awareness or lack thereof will then inform their decisions for better or worse. Inclusive leadership in the gender dimensions to leadership discussion requires leaders and their colleagues to have the psychological strength to investigate their self-identification with gender. Once leaders are aware, they make more logical, less emotional decisions. They make decisions based on fact not perception. They become far more skillful at emotional reasoning.

Recognizing sexism

While women may not always be regarded as silly and inferior as they once were, they are still, to quote Suzanne Pharr, "sexually objectified, and society gives tacit approval to pornography. When we internalize these messages, we call the result low self-esteem, a therapeutic individualized term. When we internalize these messages, we experience internalized sexism, and we experience it in common with all women living in a sexist world...supported in a society in which women-hating is deeply embedded."[2]

Sophie had indeed internalized these messages. Yet so apparently had both Kevin and Rachel who passed judgement on her so negatively.

Trying to belittle women by commenting on their physical appearance in an attempt to reduce them to an object is a classic strategy. Sophie felt victimized and questioned her own worth momentarily. However, a strong sense of self, an understanding of what sexism is, and a high confidence in her own self-determined goals enabled her to know she could succeed in the job. She could therefore ultimately determine that this company neither had the culture nor the leadership she was looking for.

The case also proves that it is not just men who sexually objectify women but also other women. As a culture our world is saturated with messages that over emphasize the importance of women's looks and sexual availability. In a white patriarchy context that culture equally overemphasizes a man's right and predisposition to objectify women. This predisposition that men apparently possess is in itself a stereotype. It has led to an oftentimes ineffectual approach to harassment, which has seen harassment complaint numbers largely unchanged in three decades.[3]

There are other perspectives here too. In our own research, for example, we heard from some men in technology who had a very different experience. While they were regarded very much as the nerds, the females in the same company were viewed as more socially articulate, and apparently more confident. One very senior leader cited these women as being the instigators of inappropriate conversations and games during social events, where they sexually objectified the men. In other research we know Black males are particularly objectivized for their physical appearance and as having stereotypical sporty and sexual prowess. Stories from Black men about how they too have been sacked when they rebutted sexual advances from white females, provide another example here.[4]

We know from other research that Black women experience the most sexual harassment, and the most penalties if they report it. One study also highlighted the contribution that the group dynamic makes in creating such situations, concluding that "women experienced more sexual harassment than men, minorities experienced more ethnic harassment than Whites, and minority women experienced more harassment overall than majority men, minority men, and majority women."[5]

We also know that the LGBT community experience high levels of harassment. A recent study done in the UK found that 68% of this community experienced sexual harassment.[6] Two thirds of this community did not report the harassment for a variety of reasons. 57% of those harassed thought it would harm their relationships at work. Four out of ten people didn't believe the perpetrator would be punished. One in four people didn't report this for fear of being 'outed' at work, underlining the general lack of safety this group feel to present authentically. Remember inability to present authentically relates directly to how much an individual is made to feel they belong.

What research on bullying can teach

These different perspectives tell us sexual harassment is not only a 'white woman's' experience or a problem that just women experience. This is a reminder again that the social context, hierarchy and structures are highly relevant to the types of behavior that might show up. It's also a reminder that each and every individual will experience bias and discrimination in a different way. And that leaders who can lead inclusively and fairly in these social contexts because they are switched on to the subtle behaviors going on, across gender and more sophisticated still, across intersections, are absolutely essential.

So just taking these few examples we already see that dominance and sexual objectivization is a human problem not just a women's issue. Yet more reason to argue that it is in everyone's interest to solve this and search beyond the gender binary and social hierarchy that can perpetuate harassment across gender.

It's dependent on everyone to neutralize any sexual conversation topic and any sexist behavior they observe. This is why both bystander training for all employees[7] and having a neutral ombudsman as a point for reporting complaints can both be good strategies for corporations to engage in.[8] It prevents the situation where the victim is more likely to be penalized, often in devastating ways, and the perpetrator mildly reprimanded in those rare cases where the victim's story is believed.

Many bystanders in companies think they are not part of the problem, but we know from research on bullying that it is not solved by targeting either the bully or the victim with interventional help, but only by helping the whole group. This is why actively teaching people about bias and harassment and remaining vigilant to their presence is essential. All too often leaders and organizations think they are not part of the problem, so it does not concern them. They are not tuned in to the fact that it may be going on, on some level, around them.

At the same time bystanders who may witness harassment or discrimination may not step in, usually afraid of the personal cost or any possible retaliation. Bystanders of bullying often think I'll keep my head down so I don't become the next target, or I can't make a difference anyway so why bother? Known as the 'bystander effect' it's a behavior that we see play out in many human interactions in both society and in companies.

What the research has found is that everyone's observation and calling out of bias, discrimination, and harassment can make a profound difference, just as it can to the presence or lack of bullying. You don't have to be part of the problem to be actively involved and essential in the solution. And because we all have bias, we actually *are* all unwittingly part of the problem. But the good news is we can all become part of the solution too, to everyone's benefit. Advocacy and accountability to each other within the group dynamic is key to this.

KiVa is the world's most studied anti-bullying program in schools.

It was developed at the University of Turku in Finland.[9] Research and evidence-based, its effectiveness has been scientifically proven in a number of large randomized trials. The KiVa system can teach us a lot about the power structures and behaviors that can have such a significant impact on individuals' well-being and engagement in the corporate context, as well as in the school.

Bullying is a group phenomenon. Research shows it is motivated by the pursuit of power, visibility and high status in the peer group. That describes aptly many a corporate culture. For that reason bullies need bystanders or spectators. These bystanders may reinforce the bully's behavior by verbal or nonverbal signals that are socially rewarding, sending the signal that this is socially acceptable behavior. They may actively support the bully. Other peers remain silent, but that silence sends the message to the victim that they approve of the bully's behavior, though these peers may not. [10]Courageous interveners are rare in reality.

KiVa's key message is that we all are responsible for our shared well-being. We need to all be courageous interveners. KiVa is actually an abbreviation for Kiusaamista Vastaan. This is Finnish for "anti-bullying." If everyone could be motivated to think of ways to help their classmates and peers instead of taking part in bullying, a large part of the bullying problem would be eliminated.

We believe if everyone could be motivated to think of ways to help their colleagues and their peers, inequality which affects us all, would also be eliminated. Instead of implicitly or explicitly supporting discriminatory behaviors which lead to unfair systems, we can prevent, intervene and monitor those behaviors. In order to do those things, we need to recognize corporate cultures which may implicitly or explicitly *support* discriminatory behaviors.

The Driftwood Inclusivity Framework

In our own research we created an Inclusivity Matrix, Figure 2, a two by two framework to help us identify if our organizations might

7

be demonstrating discriminatory behaviors and cultures. It can help us understand where we fall in terms of our own bias and in our ability to be inclusive. It has equal applicability to other types of bias, but we can apply it here to the topic of gender. Presence or absence of bias and inclusive behaviors impact us and others. Using the framework can fundamentally help individuals, teams and organizations understand where they fall in terms of awareness. That awareness determines how likely we are to do the conscious work that true inclusivity then requires.

There's a reason it's called the Driftwood (translation Drijfhout) Inclusivity Framework. Driftwood floats around the sea, aimlessly moving from place to place. Humans, with neither understanding of bias nor of the behaviors required to foster inclusive cultures, do the same thing. The sea is the environment, the social context. Depending on what's going on in that environment will largely determine the movement of the driftwood. The driftwood is an excellent metaphor for our reactivity, our human emotions. Anger, fear, ignorance, a scarcity mentality, pursuit of status, a need for power, a need to feel significant, a desire to belong, to be accepted, to be identified with certain values, a set of limiting beliefs, -many, many things can push that aimless driftwood back and forth between the quadrants of Homogeneity, Elitism and Tokenism.

In storms and times of particular turbulence we may move rapidly between these quadrants. Storms are the psychological distress human's experience. This psychological distress might manifest in men and women when we don't feel belonging or feel included. It's directly impacted by the environment and the levels of social support we feel we are receiving. Overwhelm, stress, a lack of autonomy all also play a role. Distress might also come from a perception of one's level of *social* worth, and how valued we feel by others. This is something different to *self*-worth, which is the intrinsic, non-wavering belief in self, one's own sense of worthiness. This self-worth should have no dependence on the opinions of others, and yet it does, because of our need to belong.

Unfairness, discrimination and bias create environmental psychological distress. Becoming aware of bias and proactively behaving inclusively are required in leaders to mitigate this psychological distress. By putting a rudder and a sail on that driftwood we set a clear course, despite the emotion. We have a vehicle for navigating the rough seas. The rudder is our intentionality; the sail our level of awareness. The course destination is the Egalitarian quadrant, where individuals feel they both belong and are valued as unique individuals.

The Driftwood Inclusivity Framework is highly relevant to the gender dimensions to leadership discussion. If you recognize your organization or yourself, as matching the attributes of Homogeneity, Elitism or Tokenism you can safely assume there is bias and/or some lack of inclusive behaviors being demonstrated. This is likely to be costing your business dramatically in terms of loss of talent, lack of

Figure 2
DRIFTWOOD INCLUSIVITY FRAMEWORK

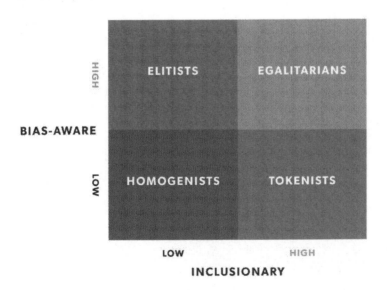

retention, low engagement, low productivity and minimal innovation. It's also a strong indicator that there may be more serious issues at play like harassment, gender pay gaps and discrimination in access to resources, sponsorship and opportunity.

Homogenists

In the bottom left quadrant, we have little awareness of our bias, and do not exhibit inclusive behaviors or have an inclusive organizational culture. We call this quadrant the Homogenists because our actions, or lack thereof sustain status quo and homogeneity, - all the same, all of the same kind. While in this quadrant people are likely to be running on autopilot, utilizing the limbic system, and relying on patterns to make quick judgements about others.

In the gender discussion we're more likely to box women into nurturing and men into strong, and if we see contradictions to this, for example seeing an ambitious woman or a man who acts modestly, react badly and make poor decisions about their abilities. We possess negativity bias around what people can and cannot do based on their gender. People make throw away comments about men and women and many of them may have no intention of changing their viewpoint.

Having this level of ignorance means that we alienate people who are more aware of gender bias and who will not tolerate such attitudes or feel engaged around such binary thinking. If perceived in a corporate leader this creates distrust and feelings of exclusion in employees. It might engender other people who are feeling anxiety and fear around their own identity and self-worth to follow these leaders.

Homogenists are unaware about the impacts of culture, environment, stereotype threat and bias on people and believe that there are clear, immutable differences between men and women. This is the essentialist view of people. Characteristics are biologically innate and immutable. Specifically, this is perceived between men and women, the men are from Mars, women from Venus hypothesis.

A homogenous group provides similar perspectives. While the culture may create some sense of belonging, it can stifle unique contributions. With a limited number of perspectives, there are less options and opportunities for real innovation. Homogenists are complicit in perpetuating inequality. It's the unconscious incompetence that Dunning and Kruger talk about, where everyone is subject to errors except me and it's this exact mentality that causes polarization in societies, politics and corporations.[11]

Dunning Kruger effect

In the Dunning Kruger study participants were tested on their ability to rate themselves on humor, logical reasoning and English grammar. They were also tested on their ability to rate others' abilities. It was observed that most people overate their own ability, and those who overrated their own ability by the most were actually also most *unable* to even realize their own lack of ability. The study found that "the same incompetence that leads them to make wrong choices also deprives them of the savvy necessary to recognize competence, be it their own or anyone else's."

While in the Homogenists quadrant we simply don't know what we don't know, and how limited our world view is. "*Our* normal is *the* normal". There can't be other perspectives worthy of our time. We are incompetent in assessing ourselves in our lack of knowledge or bias, and as crucially we are incompetent in spotting bias in others. In the context of gender bias, we are literally blind to the presence of bias. This has major implications about how we approach the topic of educating on bias for this group. Education is simply insufficient in isolation and may explain much about why the needle on this topic at a systems level in organizations is still slow in moving. Leaders must have the intention to learn. They must have a growth mindset, and an identity not too entangled in gender role norms.

Acknowledgement of bias at an unconscious level raised to a conscious level is the first step for Homogenists. Understanding how more inclusion and deeper, positive exposure to different perspectives can lead to even more conscious awareness of bias and its effects, is also crucial. Personal growth and development are key. People with more bias believe information consistent with their stereotypes and quickly dismiss information that challenges their bias.[12] More notably cognitive dissonance is strong here. People cannot consider things that may contradict their values and beliefs.

In an ever more complex world where we need leaders who can process complexity and make well-thought through, intelligent decisions, bias is quite simply an indication of a leader's inability to inclusively lead. While we may not be conscious of it ourselves other people will be.

Tokenists

In the bottom right we have people who are very *unconscious* of bias but may be intentional in their belief that women should have as much opportunity as men. We call these the Tokenists. Sometimes people hire a small proportion of women so as to appear to be symbolically hiring more women in leadership roles. Specifically, we see this perfunctory practice in under-represented groups and the practice itself gives the impression of equality, but without any conscious understanding of bias there is no real equality. More often these individuals hired might be seen as a symbol of doing something to improve equality, but while failing to address the underlying bias, others do not see this as real change.

Tokenists also blame something, pipeline, lack of confidence in women, when a quota initiative fails. It's the diversity part without the inclusivity part that is the bane of many a DE&I (Diversity, Equity and Inclusion) initiative. Unaware of our bias as to what we either perceive women to lack, or men to have the edge on, we are still more likely to choose a male for a leadership role. This bias demonstrates that we believe that women do not want leadership roles or didn't demonstrate sufficient contribution from past work to earn such a role. As Tokenists we believe we are doing everything we can to promote women and there simply aren't enough coming through the ranks. People in this quadrant perceive that family commitments naturally preclude these women from more senior roles. Expertise might be sacrificed for the sake of the apparent 'packaging' someone comes in.

Many intelligent people lie in the Tokenist quadrant. We think we believe in women's rights and independence on a logical level. In reality our behaviors demonstrate otherwise. Think about women in the group who readily default to the male as the leader, males who expect the women to arrange the office party, or men who dominate conversations, and are allowed by everyone else to do so.

The danger above all else is that the lack of collective acknowledgement that bias exists can create initiatives such as quotas for women being doomed to failure. Such initiatives may fail to get the quality of applicants through fair, objective measurables because the bias is still there, just undetected. Women are unlikely to pursue these opportunities because they know the culture is biased. Senior leaders will simply perpetuate the status quo and then say there's a pipeline problem.

Often people might be hired into positions packaged as leadership roles but in effect have no real power or authority. We saw this come up in our research when executives observed less competent women promoted to senior roles with no real power, while more competent women were overlooked. We also see this when more apparently confident men might be selected over other more competent men.

Tokenists lack a degree of emotional intelligence and social awareness which would incline us to think and therefore behave differently toward others beyond cultural gender norms. We may also be entrenched significantly in our own ego's need to assert the differences between men and women. This might be done as a means of self-protection and through a need to feel ourselves unique. We are not conscious of our own bias and really believe we see people as equal yet are likely to default to what we know. That is, often choosing male leaders over female. When a woman shows assertive traits and is ambitious, we don't like her. When a man is humble, he might appear to lack ambition or potential.

Tokenists may mean well on some level but unconscious bias means that some of our behaviors create inequality and a lack of inclusivity. We don't recognize this as a blind spot. Without information about the deeper psychology going on for men and women we also don't know what we don't know. Education around gender bias, self-awareness about beliefs and values and exposure to the research can be extremely helpful for us.

Ironically an enormous number of people fighting for a specific group's rights fall into this category because they don't consider things from another's perspective. They are biased in attributing given judgements and opinions to those individuals before checking and engaging in a healthy dialogue to see if it's true. The women's movement which has harnessed and done a huge amount to push the abilities, capabilities and rights of women has met many challenges in any attempts to engage men successfully in the dialogue of understanding. This is just one example of how an over-zealous insistence of one's own agenda fails to engage those with other perspectives. Also while we insist on just two perspectives, binaries, for men and women, we entirely miss the identity of people who identify with gender in some other way.

Elitists

People who exist in the upper left quadrant are aware of bias and make certain choices that reinforce that bias. They are non-inclusive. These we call the Elitists. As Elitists we are high on our level of bias awareness and believe there are immutable differences between men and women that dictate much of how society should run and what men's and women's roles within society should be.

We exhibit more maladaptive behaviors learned through a stronger internalization of masculine or feminine ideologies. Some women in this quadrant get their power from men, may feel inferior in some way to men, and often, though not always, defer responsibility and decision making to men. Their own identity is determined by their juxtaposition to the men in their life. Approval from men is a necessary fuel for their identity and self-approval. They often feel like they owe men something.

Some females in the Elitist quadrant may believe that women should know their place and might prefer to be liked over being respected when confronted with situations that create the double bind dilemma. That double bind for women is that if you're strong you won't be liked, if you're weak you won't be respected. Male elitists exercise their unquestioned belief in being superior and on a blatant conscious level. Men for example, might comment on how much they love women, but this can be seen in their objective view of women as somehow a support and aid to their own bids for power. It also shows up in those men anytime their behavior objectifies women. The obsession with women's outward appearance and verbal comments that accompany those judgements are typical behaviors of people in this quadrant.

Men in this quadrant are unlikely to surround themselves with smart women who they see as their equal. Men invested in a masculine ideology feel threatened by a strong woman who questions them or who might appear to have achieved more than they have. Her presence violates and contradicts their sense of self, how they identify as male, their understanding of cultural norms, and the natural order of people's roles in society as they see them. This is also the quadrant for dysfunctional meritocracies. Merit is not actually awarded to the best, but the one's *perceived* as the best. These meritocracies exist because of unequal access to opportunities and networks. There is an unfair playing field.

Some women who fall within this quadrant may be aware of their bias and break from the referent group, other women. They see themselves as unique and more aligned with men than women, placing other women in the stereotyped box of being inferior, sacrificing less in work or being too feminine to be impactful in a business context.

Their conscious bias is a maladaptive behavior, more likely driven by their individual aspiration to align with the perceived high-status group, men, and other senior women. The need to self-distance from the stereotype threat of the lower-status group, perceived as more stereotypically 'feminine' means these women tend to exclude other women, usually junior women, perceived as having more 'feminine' traits. This behavior itself is actually fueled by cultures of inequality as we discussed in chapter 2.

The belief system of Elitists is fed by neurosexism and every negative media image that portrays women as sex objects and men as intellectually superior and stronger. Sexual harassment and violence against women run rife in this quadrant mostly on a conscious level, though not always. Homophobia and the vilifying of sensitive men also exist in this quadrant. The silencing of women and the promotion of men as natural and default leaders happen here. Here sexism is internalized as something the victim themselves must solve. There is no recognition for a systemic problem, or issues in society.

Shaming and blaming rhetoric also proliferate in this quadrant. The notion that it's the individual female's responsibility to fix things by focusing on their own behaviors, with a complete lack of perspective on the social context, dominate in this quadrant. Unfortunately, a huge swathe of the business behavioral advice given exclusively to women contains the seeds of this mentality; that they must fix themselves. The advice given, rather than helping, unwittingly deepens the insidious nature of bias and sexism.

Egalitarians

In the upper right quadrant consciousness and intentionality work together to forge a path for women and men, and people who identify in some other way with gender, on equal footing. These are the

Egalitarians. People in this quadrant consciously discuss gender stereotypes and showcase the people who break from them, rather than aspiring to promoting models of tokenized individuals who fit the mold already existing. Honoring uniqueness in individuals, while creating a sense of belonging for all, sets these companies apart. Corporations with this kind of culture are great places to work and people feel they can bring their whole selves to work. Not just gender but other intersectional characteristics and differences are honored and respected.

Gender stereotypes and behaviors are recognized as things that can show up in anyone, and are hugely influential, and also changeable. There are no inevitable traits assumed just because someone is a man or a woman. Stereotypes are recognized, discussed and seen as largely illogical once people make the efforts to understand each other on more meaningful levels. The possibility for meeting and mixing with fellow workers from different silos and departments, and with other perspectives are all encouraged and facilitated in Egalitarian organizations. Egalitarians understand that gender does not lead to inevitable behaviors or skill sets within women or men or those identified in some other way with gender, though can have an influence in the form of identity threat.

The Egalitarian cultures recognize that all humans are hugely adaptable, change and develop. Fundamentally they recognize that change in itself is inevitable and healthy. These companies have growth-mindset cultures. Both males and females are represented in leadership equally and gender pay is equal. The new tribe is the inclusive, diverse group, not homogeneous or made primarily up from one gender, race, or age. People with physical constraints, differing socioeconomic status and many other intersectional demographics are represented at these companies. Leaders honor individuals' identities, while at the same time creating a sense of belonging at the human level.

For the Egalitarians people's self-worth is valued more highly than any perceived social worth in the social context. These leaders exhibit humility, not authority. They display happy high status,[13] the ability to blend without needing to be reminded of their higher social status. They are not insecure about their authority or ability being questioned. Indeed, they welcome challenge and differing perspectives. Because differences are welcomed everyone feels they belong. Leaders show inclusive behaviors in *small ways consistently*.[14] Quotas of male to female look fair, it's simply 50/50 as far as possible, and the right talent is in the right place, with a clear path of succession planning for every individual. Flex work is available to *everyone*. Rather than just having maternity or paternity leave, these companies have 'care leave' recognizing that their people may have all sorts of care commitments outside of work.

There is a high level of trust and engagement. Everyone has the opportunity to have a voice, share their worries and ideas. People feel safe and are able to contribute and share meaning and purpose. They are crucially encouraged to challenge the organization and grow personally. People feel they are unique therefore feel they can be authentic and will be accepted which creates a sense of belonging. Their sense of psychological safety and happiness has a direct effect on their productivity and creativity. Innovation, creativity and enhanced performance are natural by-products in this kind of work environment.

Limiting beliefs or evolving ones?

It should be noted that we can move between the quadrants perhaps more than we'd like to acknowledge and that with gender and identity threat constantly being recreated by our social groups, our experiences, and a multitude of media platforms, as examples, we are under fire to continue to re-align with our values and question the messages we are sent and send. That is why the act of inclusion and fairness need to be continually assessed. It is certainly never achieved in a one-off information seminar on bias. It requires attention and re-clarifying of one's own self-concept as a leader, and vigilance as a leader as to how those around us are being treated and showing up, and how we ourselves are doing so. This *requires* us to check in with our people and ask, never assume.

The work of creating inclusivity is the primary duty of all leaders of people. If we remind ourselves that 75% of people leave companies because of their bosses, and the number one reason for lack of engagement is a sense of unfair treatment then we remind ourselves of how essential this work is.

What's particularly helpful as we explore our bias is questioning how much of the time it takes us into shame and guilt or fear and anger. When we don't conform to the gender norm expectations that society dictates, we can easily get stuck in any of these negative emotions very quickly. If there is any sense that we may be being excluded, we may often be living in one of the less than ideal quadrants. By using a road map of awareness, we can see where we're at and where we might want to get to.

As individuals, teams and organizations it's in our interests to get beyond fear and to display courage in this work. Thus, self-awareness is key to understanding our own attitudes and the effects of stereotyping. It helps us understand other hidden biases that can influence our perceptions, the judgments we make, and how we act. It informs us about what we actually believe, and how that might ultimately be limiting. We can then make the choice to evolve in our values and upgrade our beliefs. Mindfulness of our bias will improve our decision-making. It will also lead to aligning organizational and personal values at a time when there is a crisis in engagement and leadership.

Once we can become mindful of our biased inclinations and behavior, we can then take the steps needed to model better behaviors that create more inclusion and much higher levels of engagement. More strategically and fundamentally we can better harness the masses of untapped talent that we miss while operating through a biased lens. In a global economy with such huge potential for social mobility it has become imperative to put human values at the top of the corporate and global agenda. So now we're more self-aware, and we may be more biased than we thought, what next?

Key Points

Leaders often miss bias and discrimination, both their own and other people's.

Self-awareness is key.

People need to understand what sexism is. It can be subtle.

Bias and discrimination are the biggest threats to your organization and people values.

Sexism is often subtle but can have massive consequences.

Everyone is needed to solve problems of bias, harassment and discrimination.

Research on bullying is instructive. The whole group is trained to be accountable for each other.

The Driftwood Inclusivity Framework can help identify levels of bias and inclusivity based on the type of work culture.

Homogenists: there's no conscious awareness of bias and no attempts to make a more inclusive culture.

Elitists: meritocracies are not built on a fair playing field. Bias is high and inclusivity is low.

Tokenists: symbolic attempts at inclusivity but bias is still present.

Egalitarians: people understand the presence of bias and make consistent, proactive efforts to include others.

Case study

Sophie interviews with the NASA off-shoot. How to recognize sexism, disengaged employees, and our own blind spots.

Self-reflective coaching questions and considerations

Where might you and your organization be on the Driftwood Inclusivity Framework right now?

How good do you think you are at picking up the emotions of other people?

How clear are you and your people about what sexism looks like?

What gender interactions might you be missing?

How bias aware do you think you and your organization is?

What efforts do you make to include others?

Who seems to act fairly and more gender inclusively in your organization?

What behaviors do they demonstrate that make them so?

Commit to one action that might lead you into the Egalitarian quadrant.

4 Patriarchy, Paradox and Pain - The Blind Eye

> Human beings are works in progress that mistakenly think they are finished.
> Daniel Gilbert, PhD, American professor of psychology

Plato in his Republic wrote a rather cryptic critique of how to create the perfect state. In it Socrates in conversation with Glaucon reflects that there are really no differences of significance between men and women, other than that women are somewhat weaker physically.[1] These days, two and half thousand years later, we can safely caveat that with 'some', and we reflect here on physical size and strength, specific physiognomy, not ability and talent.

It's worth re-emphasizing that meta-syntheses of many gender studies have shown that there are small differences between men and women in terms of cognition, communication and social traits. The gender similarities hypothesis ventured by Janet Hyde, a Professor of Psychology from the University of Wisconsin-Madison, based on the meta-analysis of 46 studies, found that males and females are highly similar.[2] A subsequent meta-synthesis in 2015 using 106 meta-analyses found that "findings provide compelling support for the gender similarities hypothesis, but also underscore conditions under which gender differences are most pronounced," recognizing that they "remained somewhat constant across age, culture and generations."[3]

There are not *large* differences in cognition, communication and social traits between men and women, there are *small* ones. But a myth of *large* difference, binaries about how men *are* and how women *are*, pervades. Our argument is that no person should be limited by others because of their gender, nor precluded from leadership because of bias and discrimination. Nor should people be elevated to positions of leadership simply based on bias around gender and this obsession with binaries.

While many assert the differences in sex and gender this book will not dive into the advantages and disadvantages of one over another. It will, however, talk at great length to the advantages and disadvantages of certain characteristics, traits, and behaviors. We argue that these are neither gender nor sex specific, just as the studies above have also shown, and yet these have become squarely stereotyped as being so in our culture.

As stereotyping is something of a cannibal, we discover how it feeds on itself and how stereotypes by their existence create stereotype or identity threat. When we sense we might be perceived through a stereotype this can create a situation where the stereotype becomes a self-fulfilling prophecy for both men and women. It can create "the real time threat of being judged and treated poorly".[4] To prevent bias we need to understand stereotypes on a conscious level, and the possibility of identity threat in a given context.

We focus on two questions: why isn't representation in the corporate world in senior roles equal across gender, and why is this a problem for everyone? While Plato might have held there was a difference in strength and virtue between men and women, he nevertheless recognized that women were equal to men in terms of their rationality and their capacity for occupation, acknowledging that women should be educated and allowed to work alongside men without differentiation. While exploring this latter aspect of being allowed to work alongside men, at all levels without differentiation, we specifically investigate the critical issue of gender in leadership.

Before starting we need to differentiate between sex and gender. Sex refers to the biological, anatomical, differences found in genes and bodily organs; gender, the social, psychological and cultural characteristics we attribute to males and females.[5] Much of the heated debate you'll hear in anecdotal form from your own people, the media, or the average ill-informed blog on LinkedIn, hinges around the arguments about traits being inherent and therefore unchangeable, based on one's sex. This inherency is referred to in psychology as *essentialism*. However, we know that gender is a socially created construct, influenced by environment and context, referred to as *constructivism*.

Gender role norms

The process of environmentally creating constructs is referred to as the *social learning paradigm*. Gender role norms have been identified based on this constructivist approach, and they are defined as socially and psychologically enacted behaviors that correspond to socially built ideas of masculine or feminine in a specific cultural context.[6] In other words people take them on to try to fit into a given social context. They are not as such *inherent*. Through this both men and women learn how to behave in the given social context. These norms are often changing and contradictory because culture changes, and psychological stress is often created when trying to adhere to these gender norms.[7] We also know that gender norms differ across race and ethnicity.[8]

It was white feminist thought that brought about the realization that little was known about how boys and men psychologically developed. What we have subsequently discovered over the last thirty years is how necessary and relevant understanding societal views of the norms of masculinity play completely into the topic of gender parity. What was notable in our own research was how little this had filtered into the corporate world and how a constructive focus on boys' and men's psychological development is still missing in much of the dialogue around the discussions on gender parity. We also noticed that in terms of the lack of understanding around female psychological distress the same could be said. However, the difference between the two is that there has been a great deal of positive dialogue around women's issues, but far less around those affecting men.

Make gender parity self-relevant to men

This lack of dialogue means some dangerous myths still pervade around what it means to be male and what we should accept and expect as a society from men. While the market, most especially in the corporate sphere, is saturated in terms of content produced by and for women about how to create gender parity, - what women apparently need to do or how systems need to change, - there is a paucity of information around the issues that men face in the gender equality conversation. There is also tellingly a paucity of male voices.

Without understanding equality at the male psychological level, we cannot hope to change systems at the corporate level. While men mostly *do* have the power and influence in the leadership stakes at the current time, we recall only 6.6% of CEOs of the Fortune 500 are women, for example, we need to make better attempts at understanding how to properly engage them as allies in the gender equality discussion.[9] We need to have tools much more far reaching than merely the suggestion that men sponsor women. If we want to get away from patriarchy, we'll need to do better than suggesting a system of patronage!

The development of masculine constructs has not only been detrimental to creating swifter gender parity, but as more and more research comes out in the last two decades specifically around men, shines a necessary spotlight on why attempts to create gender equality might be stalling. Men need to buy in to the idea of gender equality and what it means for everyone. Unless that happens it's unlikely that true equality will be seen as a positive societal development, but more likely a numbers exercise.

When Warren Buffet goes to events for women, he's usually the only man in the room. While most corporate leaders are still men it appears that they missed the memo on how to create gender parity. Or could it be that that memo didn't have the impact intended? Perhaps because we've mostly talked about women's issues and what women lack and need in that memo?

When we want to influence anyone, we need to think about the intention and the actual impact we're having on them specifically. We need to think about the self-relevance to men. All too often men have been made into the enemy rather than a valuable ally, because *some* men were indeed the enemy. With huge discrepancies in the power stakes, women paid significantly less than men, #MeToo and #TimesUp and a host of finger-pointing charges, we remain blind to the effect this has.[10][11] While stereotypes persist much of the powerful and necessary rhetoric nevertheless demonizes all men and has blinded others to the fact that not every woman is amazing.

Buffet's experience of being the only man in the room at events show casing the business success of women highlights the absence of men in this discussion. Everyone likely has gender bias at some level, whatever gender, and there are well-intentioned people and there are self-involved people, whatever gender. While doubtless unintended, the push for women in the corporate world doesn't appear to have created the investment from male leaders it necessarily needed. Why? Because no one thought much about male psychology and the social context they themselves are in.

In The New Psychology of Men masculinity is examined "not as a normative referent, but rather as a problematic construct."[12] In other words, it identifies problems created because of the forces of societal constructs which dictate what it means to be male and what it means to adhere to male gender norms. The paper reviewed the ideas of a gender strain role paradigm introduced by Joseph Pleck, a clinical psychologist and former Professor of Human Development and Family Studies at the University of Illinois, in The Myth of Masculinity, highlighting why conflicts are created for men in trying to navigate gender norms.[13]

In a world of increasing complexity even gender norms are under constant change and being continually redefined, and the messages they send to us as humans can be very contradictory. This creates a gender strain for males navigating their identity in the social context, and very specifically for men in the work context, because so much of what it means to be male in our society is linked to employment and leadership. Gender role strain needs to be acknowledged and is central to our discussion around inclusivity and gender parity. And we as leaders need to recognize that both men and women experience these contradictory messages.

Gender norms are personally internalized, observed in the behaviors of peers and observed in how leaders operate. From these observations, humans determine what behaviors appear to be 'successful' in the social context. Without the recognition that gender parity discussions themselves trigger such gender strain with the result that men have often shut down and women are rising in their millions to fight for equality in the workplace, there's a clear disconnect that needs to be addressed urgently. It seems to be another blind spot for everyone. Rather than ignoring it, adding a saturation of platitudes around how women suffer and how it's a man's world, while hypocritically sending another message that women have to change to be a little more like men, and the man's world needs to become more open to women, our equation is alarmingly off base.

Masculine and feminine psychological well-being

In more recent research we know that those who adhere *least* to either masculine or feminine roles but who instead combine these have far greater psychological well-being than those who identify strongly with one gender construct.[14] In a study into the well-being of men and women more tellingly still, it was concluded that the most relevant variable in the psychological well-being of both men and women was high masculinity, but crucially not without the absence of femininity. In this study in Spain 1700 men and 1700 women were asked to self-report in terms of how they viewed themselves as possessing traits perceived as masculine or feminine and simultaneously fill out a questionnaire on a psychological well-being scale.[15] The desirability of stereotypically masculine characteristics of independence, assertiveness, strength, individualism and ambition for achieving greater well-being in both men and women became very clear.

The study also found that for women's well-being, being purely a homemaker, having a manual labor job, not being in a professional occupation and not having high femininity were all linked to lower levels of well-being. For men well-being was linked to having a professional role and skilled non-manual work, as well as to having a partner and *critically to having high femininity*. The conclusion was that *adherence to traditional gender roles in isolation* will have a negative impact on well-being. Crucially men and women whose self-concept included both "masculine-instrumental and feminine-expressive characteristics" had the *greatest* well-being of all. This is an absolutely central piece of knowledge in working towards gender equality. Acknowledging it means we require a new approach to coaching men and women in the corporate world. It also demonstrates something of a cultural shift, which is a relevant piece in how individuals identify with gender norms.

Understanding the gender dimensions in leadership and the stereotypical expectations that associate leadership with masculinity we better understand the psychological distress, often manifesting yet often unseen, that affects behavior, well-being, and productivity in both men and women. This is key when we reflect that, on a societal level, men and women are expected to conform to certain traditional gender norms. By understanding this psychological distress better, we better understand how we can achieve gender parity and the mechanisms that will enable its realization.

Gender role strain

Joseph Pleck identified that historically it was viewed that males were psychologically healthier if they adhered to a set of masculine gender norms known as the gender identity paradigm.[16] However, these traditions of what it means to be male shift over time as cultures and society's shift, and are therefore in large part *not* biologically predetermined. Ideas of masculinity are dependent on the social situation. Furthermore, Pleck argued that a traditional view of masculinity was impossible to achieve and harmful to men's psychological health, and this he called the gender role strain. The gender role strain can be divided into three categories, discrepancy strain, dysfunctional strain and trauma strain.

Discrepancy strain is when a gender role expectation is violated, such as if a man internalizes that he should be a high earner or leader but isn't. Dysfunctional strain might be typified by corporate men who conform to the typified masculine norms, such as being highly competitive, having power over women or being emotionally constricted. Conformity to these may jeopardize one's ability to have work life balance or to express oneself in healthy ways, both in and outside organizations. And an assertion of one's superiority over women might lead to all sorts of maladaptive and undesirable behaviors.

Masculine norms like being self-reliant, not being emotionally expressive or vulnerable, and having a persona of toughness are all behaviors socially conditioned in many boys. We now know they are recognized to be psychologically harmful and create unhealthy behaviors, most likely also causing psychological strain. We can also begin to recognize that having had to suppress these emotional needs and vulnerability many men are not able to be truly authentic. Finally, trauma strain describes those men whose gender role strain has been particularly damaging. This might include war veterans, victims of child abuse, men of color and gay and bisexual men who fall into this category.

The authors of The New Psychology of Men concluded that beyond these specific groups the socialization of boys to the traditional masculine ideology is in itself inherently traumatic.[17] Levant, one of the authors, in a subsequent study on adolescent boys argues that the "intensification of sex differences and the resultant pressure to conform to the norms associated with adolescence" means boys are at risk for such trauma strain as well.[18] The socialization process that exists to create ideas of masculine norms is *itself* distressing – just think for example of a young boy being told he shouldn't cry. Humans cry, but it's environment and social dynamics that determine who may and may not actually cry.

There's a price to pay for those who may not, and it's universally taxing.

Discrepancy strain – the case study of Ed and Imani

Taking each identified strain individually let's expand on them further using a corporate world example. Discrepancy strain, when a man internalizes that he may not be measuring up in ways expected of him, might manifest as an internal dialogue, often unconscious, but one that can influence his behaviors. If, in a sales organization, Ed has internalized that he has to be the winner, needs status, but in fact appears only third on the leader board and didn't win the trip to the Bahamas, this will have an impact on his self-esteem. While we can shake this off as 'a get over it' moment, and we might perceive that he's fine with it, if he's bought into a high identification with certain stereotypical masculine norms, he's not fine. And we need to be aware of what the possible consequences of being 'not fine' might be.

Now let's say Imani won first prize, top salesperson, and the trip to the Bahamas to boot. Possibly inconsequential, but if Ed's also internalized two other masculine norms identified by Pleck, power over women and dominance, those have the potential to have undesirable consequences. A festering resentment against her, withholding of useful customer information, refusal to be cooperative on a joint global deal, any number of maladaptive behaviors can show up. And be assured these types of behavior show up in subtle and not so subtle ways all the time. With an array of consequences.

You as the leader don't see it, those blind spots you have, but Imani knows it, feels it. Maybe she can't put her finger on it yet, the ways Ed is undermining her, holding back on a key fact she needed to know. Communicating with the client which puts her in a bad light, not him. Maybe she can specifically cite something and tells you, but you don't take her seriously because you think she's being over-sensitive. Ed's a good guy after all. And by the way Imani's Black which means, according to the research, that her suggestions for leading this deal might be even less likely to be taken into account. The so-called 'double-jeopardy' of being both Black and female which some research shows means she's even less likely to be taken seriously.[19]

About those behaviors: you focus on Imani's not Ed's. We tend to hold women to a higher competency threshold, a phenomenon well-researched, and we are somehow more lenient on men.[20] Imani's angry because she knows Ed's withholding valuable information about the global client and is being vague over what he's agreed to with them. Imani suspects this jeopardizes the integrity of the next big deal for a short-term win. She can see a long-term relationship with this client, with more work in the pipeline. But only if her company doesn't compromise some conditions for initial work to land the deal quickly.

Imani hasn't even internalized the unfairness of your favoritism towards Ed and bias against her, but she will. And instead of focusing on what she's telling you about the subtle behaviors and cues she's picked up that would suggest this deal is a bad one, you can't get past the fact that she's angry, so unbecoming for a female. So typical of a Black female you think in your bias toward stereotyping her as an 'angry' black woman.[21] [22]

Imani thinks that maybe it's her. She gets the feedback to be more resilient, let Ed take the lead, to improve herself. This advice is actually code for internalize the sexism and racism in this context, but no one sees this, except her. It's all so subtle, hard to put a finger on, but possibly enough to already motivate her to start looking elsewhere. But is it that subtle? Really?

Suddenly, your top salesperson is planning to leave. And none of this you even realize, it's all so tenuous, under your social radar, and hidden by your unconscious bias. And she does leave. Oh, and the next irony? Ed gets promoted. Because even when these behaviors are not subtle, they're still not taken seriously, and these are the consequences. That 'subtlety' becomes conscious awareness if you as a leader better understand your own bias and those that disadvantage others. Now you've become conscious of your bias, but would you have been more likely to step in, challenge Ed, and put Imani out in front?

You just lost your top talent. Bad enough, but perhaps even worse you hired someone who's less competent than you realize. Oh, and that short term win you wanted, it came through, but the client got disillusioned by the lack of care. Ed appeared to be more concerned with signing contracts and the new-found status that his fancy new title gave him, than in the quality of the subsequent work. The problems that showed up that he didn't help to solve initially, have meant that the client's decided to go to the competition with the next contract. That pipeline Imani saw as needing nurturing, but that Ed assumed was in the bag, just dried up. Imani knew it needed cultivating.

Ed assumed the pipeline was OK because 'done is good enough' has been a part of his conditioning since birth. The long-term deal would need more than strong-arming a signed contract before quarter end to get subsequent work.

Variations of this scenario are the reasons women move on more often than men, but people assume it's because she wants a family, doesn't have what it takes (although these women invariably prove themselves more than competent) and that there's no pipeline. Experience this often enough and one might well tend to drop out of the pipeline, but as we'll address later be assured the pipeline is very full of competent women, and more competent men than the ones who often end up being picked for leadership roles.

Dysfunctional strain and toxic male cultures

Now enter dysfunctional strain. Things are about to get harder though their obviousness should make them easier to tackle. This one is blatant, at least it should be these days with all the conversation around sexism, harassment, bullying and misconduct. And yet, it's

7

often played down. Dysfunctional strain, where men adhere strongly to masculine norms such that their behaviors can have obvious negative effects on others, can show up in highly competitive male-dominated work environments.

Much has been observed about toxic cultures where "masculinity contest culture" exists.[23] Such environments encourage emotional constriction, the superiority of males, - but then within their own hierarchy, with the 'winners' at the top, which by default makes everyone else a loser. Any signs of weakness or sensitivity are scorned. The goal is to win no matter the consequences and far too many people get hoodwinked by this apparent demonstration of strength and determination.

The rewards are for the biggest closers, for example, in sales organizations where keeping to ungodly hours of dedication and putting closing deals before customer service might be the norm. Such cultures can be found across technology, sales, financial services, investment banking, the medical profession. In fact, all industries will have their examples. It's survival of the fittest, combined with show no vulnerability, that can build up this pressure to perform and keep performing, no matter the consequences.

This work ethic and the workplace environments it creates are the perfect breeding ground for bad behaviors such as sexual harassment and bullying to manifest. The culture pushes the requirement to continually prove you're on top of your game, superior, that it's all inborn and your right, more often as a male. There's no room for people to express doubts or admit mistakes so cover ups and laying blame at others' door are the norms, and 'trust no one' the company motto.

If women want to succeed in these work environments, they invariably do it by assimilating to the stronger masculine traits. These women will separate from other women who might stereotypically be seen as not having the drive, ambition, or necessary assertiveness. These women internalize the toxic culture, reinforced by messages that these cultures are normal and necessary, and if you want to get ahead in the corporate world you have to accept them.

Case study – Uber, explicit sexism

We're reminded most recently of the case at Uber when Susan Fowler, in a 2017 blog, described the culture and various sexual harassment incidents. When she complained to HR that she'd been propositioned for sex by her manager on the internal company chat, took screenshots to prove this (to all those who immediately leap to claim she made it up – a common retort when victims are brave enough to speak out), HR were unwilling to do more than give the manager a slap on the wrist. They justified that a warning was enough because he was 'a high performer'.

In other words, the company was prepared to turn a blind eye to what the sexual harasser had done. Fowler was given the option to leave that team, where her expertise and interest fitted perfectly, or stay, but to then not be surprised if the manager gave her a bad performance review. In fact, the HR individual suggested if the manager did give her a bad performance review that it would be Fowler's own fault.

This is not only the essence of what sexism is, making the victim responsible for the oppressor's behaviors, but it seems many people are simply unable to internalize that this male's behavior is maladaptive, unacceptable, wrong. Dominance and power over women, over any other human being, are NEVER acceptable in any situation, EVER. And yet not just the manager but the company were giving tacit approval to it.

Maladaptive behavior is assumed to be normal

Sadly, because so many people have internalized these as 'normal' male behaviors many people are unable to see the situation for what it is: a morally unacceptable abuse of power. And propositioning women for sex who are junior to us is a stereotypical behavior of a subsection of men, not something all men do because they can't contain themselves, another masculine stereotype.[24] It's not something men or women should accept as 'how men are', but it is a definition of masculinity that some men believe makes them male. So, for some men such behaviors are 'proof' they're a 'real man'.

Crucially as leaders we must recognize both in ourselves and others this as maladaptive behavior in some men, not its inherency in all men. And we must absolutely not turn a blind eye to such behaviors. Calling them out and making men and women accountable for calling them out as unacceptable is crucial to tackling the harassment problem in many companies.

Look no further than images of Hilary Clinton's face photo shopped in a Medusa's de-capitated head being held by Donald Trump as an accepted witty satire of the political debate and sold as online merchandise.[25] Or Angela Merkle being photo-shopped in a men's urinal. Juxtapose such things next to a male corporate event at a lap-dancing venue as a necessary 'treat' to 'close the deal' with their customers and it doesn't get much sleazier, with deep undertones of violence, dominance and the societal acceptability that 'boys will be boys'.

It should be noted that there are plenty of males who abhor such representations of women and these behaviors. But violating the perceived masculine norm that suggests it is normal male behavior to chase and dominate women, comes with a potential 'cost' for some men who do not. That is that 'if you don't condone this then you're not a 'real' man. For women it's the idea that this is somehow normal and "how men are" that perpetuates the insidious behavior and implicit acceptance of it.

In our research there were a number of men vitriolic in their berating of other men and labelling them as 'bastards' and as the main problem we have in the world. They felt very strongly that male dominance had everything to do with the problem that exists for women. And far from downtrodden these men who spoke up against those men in our interviews were highly successful leaders themselves. These are the men whose voices need to be heard. These are the allies that we need to recognize exist, and the voices of whom we need to raise up. Everyone needs to understand there is nothing normal or OK about sexual harassment or men asserting power over women, and that this is not 'how men are' although some men display such behaviors.

Clarity on values

A medical device company whose brand is family values and integrity yet condones its sales team's choice to take their most important surgeons to the red-light district, for 'a laugh', is completely complicit in this level of sexism. It's also very unlikely to retain much top, professional female talent. Companies need to look at their own behaviors and what values they claim they possess that they *really do model*. They also need to recognize when they don't model values about equality. Any behaviors representing one group dominating another, or objectifying men or women, explicitly condone sexism.

In the wake of the #MeToo movement only a few companies openly stood up and spoke vocally against sexual harassment and sexual assault behaviors, highlighting what was unacceptable in their company. Ernst and Young is an example of a company that had a high reputation for its work on creating more gender balance in the workplace and was one of the companies that immediately sent out internal videos to its internal staff condemning sexual harassment. In 2019 and 2020 Working Mother and Fortune had both named the management consulting company as a top place to work for women.[26] Unfortunately, more recently it was criticized again as just another company training its women on outdated sexist views. Employee complaints were received when it was uncovered that training from a women's executive coach had advice on how to pander and make oneself agreeable to men.[27]

The 'fixing women' rhetoric still abounds in a great deal of coaching and training. This is often because this work is approached from only one perspective: the perspective of women who have internalized sexism. Approaching things with an understanding around male psychology is certainly urgently needed. Additionally, an understanding that the traits of what might be considered masculine and feminine exist in all humans, brings new elements to the conversation. Approaching this as a collective group, advocating for human rights and psychological well-being, has a compelling effect on people in our experience.

Taking a proactive stand against sexual harassment has a very great impact on the morale of employees and sends a strong message of zero tolerance for such behaviors. It contrasts starkly with those companies who don't address it or acknowledge it. Sending such clear messages can have a massive effect on the trust and buy-in within a company. It will self-filter the most professional when its leaders show no tolerance or acceptance for sexism and harassment of any kind. But it needs to be done in combination with up-to-date reflections of equality, not as a guide to navigate the perceived whims or dangers of men. And simply hiring more women and then having more women in management positions is not enough in isolation.[28]

Let's be very clear, senior management positions where power is *shared* with women can do much to counter a culture which subversively condones sexism. Furthermore, harassment training delivered as a shared issue where everyone has responsibility to caretake for each other can be far more effective than the "forbidden-behavior training" it has often ended up being, to quote a recent article in the Harvard Business Review by Frank Dobbins and Alexandra Kalev.[29] The traditional way of training on sexual harassment has seen little change in the numbers of harassment complaints since the 80's with 16% of men and 40% of women saying they have been the victims of sexual harassment recently.[30]

Bystander intervention training where all people are treated as "allies working to solve the problems of harassment and assault rather than potential perps" has a far more positive outcome on reducing harassment.[31] It's precisely this attitude of treating everyone as part of the solution, rather than the 'women are victims and men are perpetrators' rhetoric, that we embrace in our own approach to educating and coaching on the gender dimensions in leadership. It's the KiVa method.

Anyone can be a potential victim of sexual harassment as we already highlighted in chapter 3. So, it's essential we consider men as also victims, as allies, and *not* just as perpetrators. And important to acknowledge if we are really striving for inclusivity, equality and real gender parity as leaders.

Endorsement of masculine, non-endorsement of feminine

In The New Psychology of Men it was concluded that the gender role strain for men actually *upholds* patriarchal structures, where men have the control over society and make the rules. Small wonder then that this shows up in the corporate world, just as it does across the rest of society. And something that we, as advocates for gender parity, should be paying far more attention to. We should also note that the cultural changes we see have meant that there is a closing of the masculinity-gap between men and women.

In one study it was concluded that there was evidence for "women's increased endorsement of masculine-stereotyped traits and men's continued *non-endorsement* of feminine-stereotyped traits."[32] This should worry us all. If we recognize that both masculine and feminine traits are necessary for psychologically healthy humans shouldn't we be promoting the benefits of the so-called feminine *in* us all?

Adherence to some masculine norms can literally lead to a 'psychic mutilation', as Roger Horrocks named it. There is something paradoxical in the fact that adherence to a patriarchal system, which implicitly if not explicitly puts men in charge, disempowers men psychologically and is the cause of a great deal of pain.[33] And if we are not careful it may do the same for women. "When women become like men society is doomed," is a quote we once heard, but are unable to trace the roots of. We believe its message is the one the study in Spain uncovered. Masculinity is great for us all psychologically, as long as we have the balancing attributes of femininity. If we don't, we may all be doomed.

The psychological well-being of our children

While we are determined to battle for the rights of girls, promoting programs like STEM and "ban bossy"[34] to help them fight against traditional gender roles and behavioral expectations, it's sobering to note that the clinical research shows that it has also been widely recognized that adolescent boys experience even greater, indeed "overwhelming pressure", to adhere to gender norms than girls.[35] What is being offered to *them* in terms of safe spaces where they can talk about their challenges in navigating what's culturally expected of them as boys and later men? How much might *that opportunity* allow them to step comfortably out of gender norm roles? In references to American culture, Holmberg wrote, "Our culture defines masculinity and femininity as binary opposites and forces a boy to disown the feminine."[36]

It should not be underestimated the impact this has on boys. A 21% rise in suicide in boys aged between 15-19 was reported in a 2017 study.[37] There are many factors which may contribute to suicide, but traditional gender roles have been cited as a contributing factor. The idea that boys and men should be independent, are more risk-taking and less likely to seek help may all be factors in the gender paradox seen in suicide rates. This paradox sees more males than females die from suicide in the Western World, although more recently we are seeing this gender gap closing.[38]

We also know that economic status and the impact of unemployment can have a massive impact on males. One study observed that for each 1% increase in unemployment there is a 0.79% increase in suicide.[39] Post-Covid-19 we can expect a drastic rise in the number of suicides. Had many leaders taken the risks of Covid-19 seriously and acted immediately, many other foreseeable events might have been mitigated. When leaders lack the competence to foresee the size and impacts of a risk, it has many dire consequences, as we'll explore in chapter 8.

It is interesting to note that China is the one exception to the gender paradox rule, where it has been observed that more women than men commit suicide.[40] The reasons for this can be directly related back to societal pressure on women to succeed in a specific gender role, that of female as home-maker. In China women are regarded as being completely responsible for keeping the family intact, while suicide itself is depicted as an appropriate method for avoiding disgrace, should they be perceived as not having achieved this. Avoiding shame can have a massive power over people it seems. And it's not specific to sex.

Further we know that LGB youth are almost 5 times as likely to have attempted suicide than heterosexual youth.[41] Reasons for an increase in suicide rates include discrimination and physical harm, housing instability, and the absence of support for their transgender or non-binary identity. Holmberg's assertion applies equally well. People are either forced to disown or make some other choice while we adhere to a cultural code of binaries in gender. The Trevor Project highlighted that the LGBTQ youth identify themselves in an incredibly wide array of ways in their 2020 survey.[42] The survey showed that LGB youth identified with more than 100 different combinations of terms to describe their gender identity. This demonstrates just how important a sense of uniqueness is for humans, and how we cannot refer to gender in binary terms alone.

Just as uniqueness is important, however, belonging is equally essential. Alienation and a sense of loneliness are known as risk factors for all groups in rates of suicide.[43] And we see here how both uniqueness and belonging show up as necessary factors in the psychological well-being of humans, irrespective of how one identifies with gender. Indeed, it's the binary that male female stereotypes create that seem to impact all demographics in limiting them, and sometimes in devastating ways. Mara Grunau, executive director for the Center for Suicide Prevention in Canada has pointed out loneliness effects everyone. The 'outwardly successful professional who has prioritised career advancement to the detriment of all else, including social relationships, may find himself "at the top of the pyramid, alone."'[44] We often coach professionals exactly in this situation, and adherence to gender role expectations has been a large contributing factor.

Levant's observations of how adolescent boys attempt to conform to expectations associated with the male role that creates gender role strain is instructive. In Levant's study on adolescents it was noted that the boys who get into trouble with the law for example, and who might display maladaptive behaviors such as anger, aggression or substance abuse were those who adhered to very stereotyped traditional roles of masculinity. These included having no fear (risk taking thus), hatred of homosexuals, restrictive emotionality, nonrelational attitudes towards sex, a focus on achievement and status, avoidance of femininity, aggression and extreme self-reliance. So, it should not be a surprise to realize that this carries on into adulthood for *some* men and has wide implications for conformity to gender norms in the corporate world.

It is adherence to expectations with aspects of the masculine role, in large degree, that ultimately effects how successful any moves to create more gender parity might be. And it has specific implications in leadership for everyone. Why? Because as we'll go on to discuss, leadership is squarely and stereotypically seen as a default male role, with a requirement for stereotypically masculine behaviors. This male issue becomes a human issue and is hugely relevant to the discussion on women's equal rights and gender parity.

The socialization process for boys and girls happens very early. While boys are discouraged from being emotionally expressive and vulnerable, but instead encouraged to be competitive and tough, girls are discouraged to assert, express anger or be aggressive. Girls are taught that emotional connectedness and relationships are paramount.

So, boys are taught to suppress the feminine and girls to express it. This socialization process begins already with parents behaving differently towards their baby sons than their baby daughters. As an example, it has been observed that parents will talk more to their baby girls than to their baby boys.[45] [46] Differences in treatment continue into the education and playground socialization settings, where peer groups, more often sex-segregated, reinforce these expected behaviors. Is it any wonder then that differences in treatment might lead to differences in behavior?

There is more and more evidence suggesting, for example, that the alexithymia (no words for emotions) often observed in males is a learnt behavior rather than an inherent one. And if we consider that anger, a more often observed male behavior, is actually a consequence of pent up, unexpressed emotion, the proof of learnt maladaptive behavior becomes compelling. Nor should we kid ourselves that anger is an emotion that men somehow have a monopoly on.

The damage from repression of emotion is not only psychological but also physical. While gender role conflict can lead to depression and anxiety, gender role strain is observed as leading to physical consequences, with cardiovascular problems as just one example, of many. Both present as issues for both men and women in terms of their well-being in the work setting and the often-contradictory pressures that success in the corporate world requires must be questioned.

Discriminating against caring men

Pleck argued that the failure to live up to masculine gender norms, which he observed most men are unable to do because of their contradictory nature, was determined by a few things. These include historical changes, the changing expectations of women and men, and inconsistencies within men's life cycle. He argued that not being able to meet all the societal expectations of what it meant to be male lead to low self-esteem and psychological distress. Providing the bread winner expectation as an example, he highlighted how this expectation that men be the main bread winner, which still pervades today, also meant they were expected to have less familial participation.[47] Both bring their own negative psychological side effects.

While most countries and corporate cultures are still slow to provide the same paternity rights to men as women, and men still earn more on average than women, these negative psychological effects should be kept in mind because they are actually *reinforced*. Society still sends the message that men *should* be first and foremost providers and leaders. Unequal pay for women is morally and economically unacceptable, and maternity policies are required if many women are to keep a foothold in their careers as a starting point.

Yet while it is clear corporations start to better understand how inequality effects women directly, we may be well served to ask additionally the question how does unequal pay for women hurt men? How does having minimal paternal rights impact men's read on what society thinks they should spend the majority of their time on? And how do these in turn then impact women's economic, social and human right to equality? Help with childcare? Help in the household? How do these messages to men reinforce the message to women that they have to choose to be married and have children, rather than lead? Not to mention reinforcing that there must be a choice and they cannot do both, while apparently men can? How much does the messaging to men reinforce the message that women don't have a right to pursue a successful, high paid, high status career in leadership?

While we continue to have a binary for people, while we continue to organize them by gender, we perpetuate the societal expectations on men to do just those things that damage women's access to power, status, influence and finances. And we marginalize those who identify with gender in other or multiple ways.

We perpetuate the either / or, all or nothing, sucker's choice.[48]

Key Points

People turn a blind eye to the role of power in assigning leadership roles to men.

Conformity or non-conformity to masculine and feminine norms have benefits and costs.

Much of the women in leadership conversation has been fueled by white feminist thought.

The white feminist lens now runs the risk of limiting our understanding of how to achieve gender parity for all.

There is an urgency to understand masculine psychology and differing 'norms' within minority groups.

Without understanding equality at the male psychological level, we cannot hope to change systems at the corporate level. While sponsorship is one key area, if we want to get away from patriarchy, we'll need to do better than suggesting a system of patronage alone!

Both individual and social contexts need to be better understood and considered.

Research shows people with a balance of masculine and feminine traits have the highest well-being.

The concept of gender role strain is introduced. 3 types of masculine gender strain have been identified: dysfunctional, discrepancy and trauma strain.

All three types of strain are recognized as traumatic for boys and men.

Tackling male attitudes in a braver way will help gender parity. The context of individual men must therefore also be considered.

While stereotypes persist much of the powerful and necessary rhetoric nevertheless demonizes all men and has blinded others to the fact that not every woman is amazing.

Gender constructs have a significant impact on our children.

Masculine gender norms might include power over women,

dominance, being highly competitive, independence, no fear (risk taking thus), hatred of homosexuals, restrictive emotionality, nonrelational attitudes towards sex, a focus on achievement and status, avoidance of femininity, aggression and extreme self-reliance.

Leadership is perceived as incongruent with women while we continue to prioritize masculine traits in leadership and perceive gender in only binary terms within humans.

While corporations remain slow in creating care leave and care pay equally, men are also discriminated against.

Case studies

Losing Imani and promoting Ed. Demonstrates the subtle, gender bias and additional intersectional dimension. It also demonstrates how easily we might hire incompetent men.

The Uber sexual harassment case demonstrates explicit bias and explicit discrimination.

Self-reflective coaching questions and considerations

What character traits might you have gendered?

How much are your beliefs tied into this?

How do they affect your behavior?

Exploring masculine gender norms which ones might be having a strong influence on what you believe or on how you show up? You can answer this irrespective of your gender.

Where do you see some of these masculine gender norms show up in the people you work with?

In what ways are they positive or negative?

How do they affect how you feel about other men and women?

What limiting beliefs do you have around men and women?

How do these beliefs limit or create opportunity for your organization?

Consider exploring the masculine norms and how they might get in the way of your leadership.

5 Myths, Martyrs and Monsters – The Blind Alley

I am telling you that your perception of ultimate reality is more limited than you thought, and that truth is more unlimited than you can imagine.
Neale Donald Walsch, American author

What are the relative merits of certain qualities which might culturally be determined as 'male' or 'female'? Don't all humans have the capacity for these varying traits? Might that belief bring out the best in us all? According to the study in Spain, crucially a country that could be argued has an intermediate place between more individualistic societies such as the United States and more collectivist societies such as Japan, the conclusion was that investing in gender ideals limits the whole development of human beings.

Yet cultural conditioning has done much to influence and determine the relative importance of gender in the power and influence stakes. Our belief in stereotypes, rather like the primitive parts of our brain, both limit and protect us in our modern world of hyper-connectivity, disconnected connectedness, urgency, and the need for short cuts. Our brain's use of stereotyping that often willingly, unquestioningly and sub-consciously makes snap-shot decisions about the capabilities of a human based on gender, and a multitude of other characteristics can, on closer investigation, be deeply, deeply flawed.

As leaders we have the responsibility to become far more aware of these snap-shot decisions. When it comes to stereotypes most of the populations' brains are still squarely fixed in the Stone Age. Those leaders most aware will recognize this because they see talent *objectively*. They know that gender is irrelevant to the existence of that talent. Yet such leaders are really rare.

Martyrs and monsters

In Suzanne Pharr's powerful book Homophobia - A Weapon of Sexism in which she suggests we imagine a world with no sexual gender role and where opportunity is not determined by gender or race, she exposes the real culprits of gender bias, both open and internalized. *Economics* is a central issue, becoming *aware* of what's unconscious is necessary, and the *superiority* of one group over another must be challenged.[1] The observations by psychologists of what being male culturally might mean clearly has a direct bearing on these. The implicit messaging of the masculine norm of having dominance over women. This can create the danger of boxing all men as monsters and all women as martyrs.

More powerfully still Pharr recognizes the interconnectedness of all oppressions and although this book is specifically focusing on the discussion around gender inequality it's messages should and must be applied to all minority groups underrepresented in the corporate world. It is incumbent on all leaders to check biases at the door. We must build much greater awareness of how these unconscious judgements, which must first become conscious, can grow into insidious break downs in culture, trust and communication if left unchallenged.

Pharr further identifies the real danger of identifying people's sexual identity with a moral code, pointing out that it should not be about *who* you affiliate yourself with in a sexual way but *how*. Is it a relationship based on power, violence and micro aggressions, about asserting the dominance of one over the other, or a relationship born of respect, love and growth?

We can examine work relationships in the same way. How do we affiliate with others? We should examine our motivations as corporate leaders and whether the relationships we hold are ones where we assert power *over* others or ones where we humbly lead and develop people with equanimity. Do we focus on colleagues as equals although having a subordinate role in the organizational chart?

By the same token we need to monitor whether employees are themselves looking for self-determination or to be 'carried' by narcissistic leaders. Is the focus on the right people with the right skills for the right job? Is authority being exercised in a good or bad way? And how are the relationships between peers functioning? Are they born out of respect and mutual collaboration, or is there in-fighting, politics, one-upmanship? Is there a superiority versus inferiority war going on, sexism or racism, exclusion or inclusion?

It is useful to reflect on how ineffectual command-and-control leadership is in terms of building trust, loyalty and engagement. Such a leadership style has dominance at its core, and its use instils dissension and disengagement in the people it tries to lead. Selfless leadership however, focused on the growth of the people and the organization, rather than on the expansion of one's own ego and the gratification of self-interest, builds loyalty, trust and highly effective and functional individuals. Know that diversity and inclusivity, well-handled, create success.

Belief in myths

Our journey continues then with the question what do you believe in? Do you believe men or women are weaker or stronger at certain things, one more emotionally intelligent, the other more assertive? One more caring, the other having a greater propensity to ambition, or power? Or do you believe everyone has potential in all areas of human existence given the tools and necessary nurturing? You notice we already try not to generalize, or attribute given qualities to a given gender. But the biggest likelihood is that you will already be doing that for yourself as you think through this exercise. Why? Because most people organize people and their perceived attributes through gender.

The great majority of people have challenges in visualizing women as leaders in a positive light, accepting them as leaders, and not looking to men to lead. Gender stereotyping and conditioning is probably single-handedly the biggest roadblock to creating diversity and equity in the workplace. An equitable share in power and influence is necessary for equitable growth and human flourishing. Remember gender parity creates thriving economies and societies. When everyone is at the decision table the right decisions are more likely to be made.

It is with one sentiment in mind that we approach the ideal of equality. Every human life has equal value and equal right to justice, freedom, safety, the opportunity to thrive, and access to economic prosperity. They also have the right to lead if they have the skill and demonstrate a desire to serve others. These are bold and beautiful statements but it's important to ask yourself whether *you* really believe them and what do they mean to you?

Gender is purely a construct, yet this is a concept that most people find hard to accept, heavily fueled by their own self-identification. Until we question our own understanding of the construct and how it can limit human potential, and let's be clear women's, *other genders and men's* potential, we are unlikely to be able to create and implement successful gender parity and therefore the growth and engagement our companies need to be truly great. Without effectively understanding the issues around gender we cannot effectively utilize the talent potential in our own organization. We need to be prepared to face the discomfort of realizing that discriminating people on the basis of sex and then attributing gendered traits to them is simply a slightly less offensive construct for sexism. Sexism shows up in many human behaviors every day.

As Pharr put it so well: "Patriarchy - an enforced belief in male dominance and control - is the ideology and sexism the system that holds it in place...the catechism goes like this: who do gender roles serve? Men, and the women who seek power from them. Who suffers from gender roles? Women most completely and men in part. How are gender roles maintained? By the weapons of sexism: economics, violence and homophobia."

As more rigorous research is coming to light, we know that men are also suffering detrimentally in terms of their own adherence to traditional notions of masculinity, and this has to be recognized in the discussion around raising women up into leadership positions. That's not a conversation that's taking place at the moment. That shared understanding that bias affects everyone and that that same bias puts the onus on men to be leaders is itself a huge barrier for women.

Placing your employees and leaders in boxes male, female and the many associated traits that gender apparently conveys on those then-boxed individuals stimulates a Pavlovian response in the primitive mind for order that the best leaders need to break away from. Where does the order come from? Our brains need to search for patterns. A given stimulus creates a given response. This is known in psychology as a fixed-action pattern and it refers to an animal's or human's built-in automatic response which can be activated by a 'trigger' feature, a stimulus.

Cialdini refers to this as the 'click-whirr' response,[2] the tendency to mechanically react to one piece of information in a given situation, rather than to logically think through an alternative response. In his 'click whirr' analogy he describes a study carried out in 1974 by Dr Michael W. Fox who observed that mother turkeys always respond to the 'cheep, cheep' call of their chick. If a polecat, even a stuffed dead polecat, is to be placed near the turkey mother she will attack it. However, get the stuffed dead polecat to 'cheep, cheep' by playing a recording of a turkey chick placed inside it and the mother turkey will respond as a devoted parent.

In Western culture when it comes to assessing and appointing people as leaders, most specifically, the built-in automatic response pattern is to label based on gender, and appropriate behaviors based on that gender. And the labels are male – 'click whirr' - agentic and in charge, female 'click whirr'- supportive and caring.[3] The click whirr appears to be based on forming a stereotype about someone.

We need to reflect on whether we've properly assessed the abilities and attributes of the person standing before us. Are we bias-aware and intentionally inclusive and objective towards that person? Or do we possess the cognitive ability of a turkey?

While identification with certain aspects of our conditioning can be powerful, it can also be limiting. That can cause both limitations and suffering to ourselves and those around us. The socialization process that defines and organizes us by gender influences "who you are, how you think and what you do," as Cordelia Fine, a Professor of History and Philosophy of Science at the University of Melbourne, put it in Delusions of Gender. What's more, "When the environment makes gender salient there is a ripple effect on the mind. We start to think of ourselves in terms of our gender and stereotypes and social expectations become more prominent in the mind. This can change self-perception, alter interests, debilitate or enhance ability and trigger unintentional discrimination."[4] This is an excellent articulation of what happens with stereotyping.

Like Copernicus, derided by all for suggesting the earth went around the sun instead of the other way around, could it be that the definitions of gender construed as existing in the brain and in our hormones are largely built from the outside in rather than the inside out? And ought we to open our minds now to the idea that men, women, and anyone who identifies in another way with gender, can very readily and easily have interchangeable traits, characteristics and skills which in combination can make them phenomenal leaders? We believe so. In fact, looking at the behavioral research, empirical evidence and very latest neuroscientific research we're certain of it. And every business leader who wants to be perceived as up-to-date and well-versed in the false assumptions and claims made about sex and gender should be too.

Multiple identities

The evidence shows that we take on different self-concepts

dependent on the situation we find ourselves in. These are the identities that Seplian and Jacoby-Senghor refer to in their study on belonging and inclusion. In a given situation therefore we have what psychologists refer to as an active self.[5] We take on different stereotyped identities in a given social context and have many different identities, therefore. In a given moment we might be a breadwinner, caregiver, single parent, divorcee, economist, homeowner, free spirit, winner, loser, academic or cake-baker. It is in these moments that we might well be susceptible to taking on just those stereotypes in our perception of ourselves. And it is in these moments when the stereotypes associated with gender can take a hold, affecting our behavior in negative or positive ways.

Taking this to its natural conclusion we see how priming on gender in certain social contexts, for example within work, might affect our own behaviors. The social context influences how we perceive others and how we are perceived by them. And just knowing how others might stereotypically perceive us can be enough to create more negative or positive outcomes. This is particularly salient when we learn about stereotypes for leadership which limit the scope and scale of skills needed based on gender. Fine puts it eloquently in the title of her first chapter, "We think, therefore you are".

Blatant bias

We think men are leaders often because we have given certain masculine traits precedence in our idea of what leadership is. We view women less as leaders because we see them in more supportive roles. We deem relationships as somehow less relevant to leadership than agency and problem solving. Why do we cite problem solving and relationship as examples? Because culturally and through stereotyping most of us see women as better in relationship building and men as better in problem solving, and so a binary is created.[6] And which do we see as a more important skill of the two in leadership? While we gravitate instinctually to thinking of men as the default leaders, we automatically prioritize certain 'perceived-male' skills, in this example problem solving, over relationship building. We often do this without realizing how little these traits in isolation themselves might be useful in good leaders. It becomes then less about gender and more about the skill or trait we've inadvertently given priority to, and even gendered. This is a key idea we'll return to in chapter 7.

For now, let us analyze the other extremely important concept that we wear different active selves depending on the social context. It's useful to describe some of the studies which demonstrate just how pervasive conscious or unconscious stereotyping can be in these contexts. At its simplest level we know that just having tick boxes for male or female already starts to gender-prime a response. For example, one study showed that when subjects ticked the box male or female as well as identifying as European American, the females were more likely to rate their verbal skills higher and their mathematics skills lower, while males did the reverse, consistent with social stereotyping.[7] In the absence of the gender priming box the results for self-stereotyping in verbal and mathematical ability were reduced. Such studies have significant relevance when we recognize the gender priming that exists in many recruitment processes, tests and assessments, when confirmation of gender is asked at the start.

The other side to this is that we also know that others reviewing these tests or assessments will also make biased decisions when they know whether the person is male or female. Famous studies which have shown how creating blind auditions for participation in orchestras, blind reviews of applications to gain time on the Hubble telescope or the blind assessment of computer-coders have all led to fairer, unbiased selections. [8] [9] [10] These, not surprisingly, increased female representation when taken seriously and acted upon.

Simultaneously, studies have shown that just changing a name on a CV from male to female and nothing else will have a profound impact on the likelihood of that person being employed, paid a fair salary, deemed as competent or even likeable.[11] And yes for leadership roles this will likely be detrimental to the female name. It's the same reason many women throughout history have taken on male pseudonyms or use initials, the most famous example in modern day being J.K. Rowling. Her publishers, anticipating that her target audience of young boys might not want to read a book written by a woman, suggested she use two initials instead of her full name, Joanne Rowling.[12] Their bias also blinded them to the fact that girls might also enjoy reading her books, which they did in their millions.

More compelling still are the studies showing that a reinforcement of stereotype before a given performance test will have an influence on the result of that test. Going further, *active verbal confirmation* that gender has *not been proven* to give any difference in results can then result in a lack of those purported differences showing up. When, for example, women were told explicitly before a test that there were no proven differences between men and women on certain mathematical and spatial skills no differences showed up in the results. This should give us much pause for thought.

Brains and minds

We know that it's a wide held belief that men are better at mathematical problem solving. This is another stereotype and a case we'll return to. We also know, for example, that stereotyping strongly enforces the notion that women are regarded as emotional and more empathetic than men. Men are regarded as more logical and less empathetic. Popular works like to depict and reinforce these differences and are spread throughout our culture to give cadence to such notions. From Men are from Mars, Women from Venus[13] to The Female Brain[14] and The Essential Difference,[15] such books and ones like them, where focus is on gender difference rather than similarity, have done much to create a hype. They've embedded the idea of differences in ability.

Such books use neuroscientific claims or language that reinforce gender stereotypes in ways that are *not* scientifically justified. Cordelia Fine refers to this type of literature as neurosexism. She, along with Gina Rippon, a renowned neuroscientist,[16] have done much to expose the flawed scientific research behind many of these bestsellers, proving instead that it's far more likely that a "gendered world will produce a gendered brain, rather than the other way around."

Case study - waffles or spaghetti?

In 2019 Yasmina and Tom attend a conference in San Diego on leadership. There are more than a thousand people present. A well-respected leadership authority is giving a presentation on the importance of hiring more women, and the need for their unique skill set. She's explaining how neuroscience has *proven* that the neural pathways and communication routes within a man's brain are linear, like a waffle. They are focused and systemize. In women, however, the fMRI images show that the communication pathways are abundant, resembling spaghetti. There are many connections between the two hemispheres of the brain.

This so-called 'hard-wiring', she explains, proves that women are more able to multi-task, empathize and communicate more effectively. As the audience hear this message many are nodding their heads in agreement. Yasmina and Tom elbow each other with a teasing wink. This is the definition of neurosexism. Fine describes this as 'the myth that just won't die'. Many well-intentioned people do not realize that they are actually reinforcing gender stereotypes that have *not been scientifically proven.*[17]

The mainstream thought that sex determines so much hard-wiring and immutable traits in men and women is pervasive, often appearing to be largely unquestioned by the populace. That certainly appeared to be the case in many of our interviews with corporate leaders. The 'hard-wiring' essentialist concept about our brains has been fed by a great deal of poor research over the years, much of which has itself been biased, highlighting more often small differences rather than the very common abundance of similarities. Differences get published and cause sensation, whereas the masses of studies that find no differences between the sexes in the brain do not. Something known as publication bias. More recent research, done with scientific rigor and a critical eye, has exposed many flaws and indeed this bias for publication of difference rather than similarity, within the brain.

It is this research and authority that leaders must familiarize themselves with if they don't want to be seen as ignorant and backward in terms of their assumptions around gender. To do otherwise will identify business leaders as cave men or cave women. In our research interviewing many corporate leaders, however, we've heard a lot of cave talk, showing that this information needs to be shared widely with leaders in the corporate world. But which book is a CEO, and more likely a white male CEO likely to pick up? Will it be cutting edge work on neuroscience? Will it be an easy read by a thought leader, likely in the CEO's social network? Often a thought-leader whose badly researched material and need for sensationalism that the 'finally-there's-proof-that-men-and-women-are-different so-we-can-justify-power-discrepancies-camp' clamors for? Or a thought leader who wants to demonstrate how superior women are by the same means?

Judging by many of our interviews with corporate leaders they are picking up on the sensationalist material. Gender superiority arguments are not helpful, and they are sexist. Sadly because of this some of the bad science, rather than the good science, proliferates in the corporate world. Many men in particular talked of the complementary and different natures of men and women. As Fine talks about in her book Testosterone Rex, support for the scientific idea that testosterone dictates the differences between men and women is 'extinct', in the science world at least.[18] However, in the corporate domain this is far from true. In our interviews we often heard statements that men 'naturally' want to lead, that women don't have the 'innate' desire nor the confidence to lead. We heard the rhetoric again framed in a white heterosexual narrative. Limitations created by baby bearing within a heterosexual relationship paradigm, apparently determine who should have power, lead and have access to economic resources. And who should not.

It makes great headlines to confirm the gender differences we see every day as immutable – feeding our need for order in a social context. It also takes away a threat to our identity if we've grown up in a world where at least implicitly men are seen as superior when it comes to certain roles, and women feel safe if they have a protector. It was particularly salient in the mind of James Damore, the Google engineer who suggested there were few women in technology or leadership roles because of 'biological difference'.[19] Yet it's deeply flawed, not just because it inaccurately portrays reality, but essentially because it stifles potentiality and latent untapped talent. Worse still it can demoralize and disillusion those whose talent had once began to burgeon.

It's much harder work then to spot the similarities and question the very unsound scientific basis of much of these types of hype around difference between the sexes as depicted in the brain. And of course, there are differences, but these are differences between people. It seems the clean, tidy boundary between men and women that people seem to need to gravitate towards to make their lives easier and simple in a rather complex world, are not so clean and tidy after all. Yet as a leader of people we believe this is essential work that we *must* do. Seeing people as unique individuals, *not* with assumed traits of a given group, is essential in this. We must go deeper and be curious if we are going to be an inclusive leader who will get, and keep, the very best people in our organizations, and get the very best from them.

Sex in the brain (not on it!)

The work of Daphna Joel provides a highly accessible example of how to interpret much of the work on sex in the brain.[20] Joel, a neuroscientist and Professor of Psychology and Neuroscience at Tel Aviv University, has researched sex difference in a variety of ways in the brain. Using fMRI scans of 281 brains she took the biggest presented differences between men's and women's brain structures.

Only 2% of these brains fell at extreme ends of either female end or male end brains; these brains having either so-called 'female-end' or 'male-end' scores. A further 4% of brains had 'intermediate scores' that's something between male and female but not of clearly one or the other. The rest of the brains, a whopping 94%, had their own unique features of both male and female, and a third of these had extremes of both male *and* female scores. Joel and her team observed that every human's brain has a unique mix of characteristics, concluding 'Most brains are comprised of unique "mosaics" of features, some more common in females compared with males, some more common in males compared with females, and some common in both males and females.'[21]

Collaborating with the Max Planck Institute for Human Cognitive and Brain Sciences, Leipzig and the University of Zurich, she looked at 1400 more brains, where the same pattern emerged. Subsequently comparing the wiring or connections between brain regions where general average differences are noted between male and female brains, she discovered that when looking at individual brains, 48% of all brains had both extremes of male-end and female-end connections, as observed in other studies. When presenting the final results Joel color-coded the results in green, yellow or white, depending on the strength of a given score – and the images created showed that all brains are uniquely colored with a combination of both male and female, a so-called mosaic.

Empathy

Moving away from neuroscience and to psychology there are studies that show, for example, that if differences in empathy between men and women are made obvious as a goal of the study, stereotypes will show up with women presenting as more empathetic. If, however, unobtrusive means are used to measure empathy no gender differences will present, and men are not viewed as having less empathetic ability.[22] Yet in the social context, and certainly in the work context, we see this idea show up with two important affects. One is that we assume women are better at empathy and generally in communication ability because of that ability to empathize. Secondly, while we stereotypically assume men are less empathetic, we inadvertently downgrade empathy as a lesser needed skill, while we operate in a patriarchy system where men still hold most of the positions of economic power in the corporate world. Yet we know empathy is also essential in exceptional leaders.

We see therefore how stereotypes work to uphold a system that doesn't reflect reality, doesn't reflect essential characteristics for leadership, and doesn't reflect best practice in organizations. At the same time stereotypes endorse a hierarchy of skills based on perceived necessity and create an apparent contrast between men and women which we now have the evidence to demonstrate are not based in fact. The binary idea of men as rational and women as emotional is supported in a hierarchy that, from a social order perspective, puts masculine as the more valued gender with an apparent associated skill set in leadership.

We have actually seen that people can be *motivated* to demonstrate a leadership behavior irrespective of the apparent propensity of that skill being more stereotypically male or female. Remember the earlier study where it was shown that if the subjects are not aware that they are being tested on their ability to empathize then *no* gender differences show up to demonstrate that one gender has more ability for it than the other. Of the many researchers who've carried out such studies, William Ickes developed a study to measure the difference in empathy in gender and concluded that there were *none*, contrary to popular belief, something we've already touched on.[23]

Subjects in couples were observed for a few minutes and then each was asked to report what they were thinking at given moments when they watched a video playback. Their partner was then asked to comment on what they thought the other was thinking. No differences were seen between men and women in the ability to empathize. Curiously, later studies however started to show differences emerging. It was then discovered that a slight change in the form had meant that again females had been *primed* to show up as more empathetic when the researchers realized that subjects had been asked to *self-report* on how accurate they themselves thought they were in determining their empathy.

The results demonstrate that motivating subjects might create a different result.[24] Women know socially that they are supposed to be empathetic and were therefore primed to self-report as being so. This subsequently influenced and created a difference in the study results. It demonstrated compelling evidence that women are *motivated* to show more empathy "when their empathic motivation is engaged in situational cues that remind them that they, as women, are expected to excel at empathy-related tasks."[25] Empathy is a behavior expected in women, and not being seen as empathetic as a woman may carry an associated social penalty for women, - not being perceived as 'nice', with the potential risk of subtle exclusion in a certain social context. These findings have been found now in multiple studies and a meta-analysis of studies. We can be confident in this conclusion, therefore.

The idea that motivation could create more empathy was tested further by Kristi Klein and Sara Hodges in another study.[26] The female subjects taking the test were asked to assess their own ability to empathize before taking the empathy test. In a second test men and women were told they would get money if they did well on the test. In the first test the women scored better than the men in empathy, replicating what was seen in Ickes' study, that women may be socially motivated to appear empathetic.

What was fascinating was that in the second test both men and women scored higher and crucially no gender differences in the ability to empathize were seen, proving that a difference in types of motivator for men and women is at play, rather than inherent differences in their empathetic abilities per se. So, the behavior was inherent, and it simply took a given stimulus to make it present. This has significant relevance to the social context of work, highlighting the need to properly measure attributes relating to leadership ability, as well as consideration of the types of incentives used in a given work context.

By dipping into research therefore, we can find much in the last few years that dispels the long-held myth that males and females are so very different from each other in terms of traits and *potential*, despite the swathes of best-selling information you may have read to the contrary, stating instead that there are a huge range of possibilities in every human being. When we think about men and women, we think about them having very distinct characteristics. When we talk about men and women, we often talk about them in very stereotypical ways. Men are bigger than women, women are more nurturing than men, men are better in math, women gentler, better at communication and empathy.

Yet these are usually comparisons of averages, or more often average assumptions. Indeed, in each of the examples above we have plenty of research to show these binary statements are untrue in given situations. We probably have plenty of personal experiences of it as well. These personal experiences we talk about on the gender dimensions to leadership coaching course.

The myth of math

For clarity on comparison of averages or average assumptions let's take the following classic stereotype on math performance. Just going to two different sources creates two very different impressions. Take the source, Mark Perry, described as a scholar, who wrote a Blog Post, entitled 2016 SAT - Test Results Confirm Pattern that's Persisted for 50 Years – High School Boys are Better at Math than Girls.[27] Showing the average scores of math between boys and girls since 1965 the difference appears enormous, if we look at Figure A, presented by Perry. Women are clearly inferior in this field of logic and problem-solving.

Now let's look at the suggestion from Hans Rosling, who asks us to look at the image differently.[28] Simply by changing the scale on the vertical axis, the original image the SAT College Board presented, creates a very different impression. In Figure B, with the vertical axis scale changed, the gap between girls and boys is almost gone.

Rosling explains that all too often our inclination is to look for the gap, he calls it the Gap Instinct. There's nowhere we appear keener to do this than in our comparisons between men and women. Often what appears to be a difference, referred to as statistically significant, can be a very small difference indeed. Statistically significant signals that indeed something is going on, but if it is only presented in terms of the difference between the averages, we can get a very skewed view of how big that difference is.

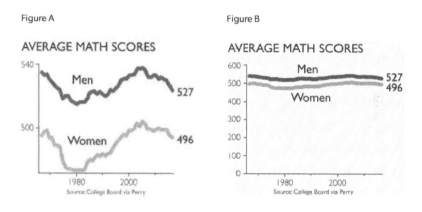

To illustrate the point let's take a third image showing the ranges of SAT scores between boys and girls, Figure C. Now, rather than this

Figure C

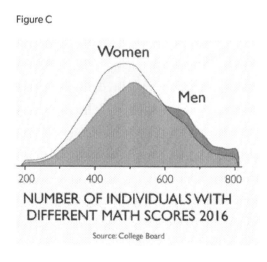

gaping gap in the apparent ability to solve abstract problems, there appears to be almost total overlap. As Rosling points out, "The majority of women have a male math twin: a man with the same math score as they do." Clearly, we can factually say there is almost no difference between men and women as distinct groups in math scores.

As leaders we need to be acutely sensitive to this danger of difference when assessing men and women. We should be homing in on what we do see, and what might be causing it. A few boys appear at the top end, and incidentally when observing other data from the SAT College Board, you will see that a few Asian girls' scores exceed the highest male math scores, a fact Perry decides not to include in his article, but one that does undermine his whole premise that boys are better in math. We also know that, on average, girls actually perform better through the year than boys, again providing us further information that certain conditions might be advantaging or disadvantaging everyone at certain points in time, and in certain social contexts.

At the beginning of a math SAT test everyone is asked to record their gender. We know that this reminder of gender can be enough to influence how much an examinee might be influenced by stereotype threat. What is that? That boys are better than girls in math. Perry seems keen to reinforce this bias as his provocatively titled article still remains the number one pop up if we do an internet search for 'SAT scores for boys and girls'. Ironically, we don't even need to put in math to find this biased article. It's right up there in the top spot on Google. Reinforcement of a stereotype *not* based in fact.

It's also important to note the SAT results of 2016 are different to many other years. Dig a little deeper. We only need to read a short way down the page written by the College Board on the results from 2016 to find, "Most data points in this year's report cannot be compared to those in previous years. Here's why: the redesigned tests are new tests based on the different specifications than the old tests."[29] So Perry has also been using data that is non-representative due to differing conditions in 2016 to other years. Hardly the unbiased, well-researched, factual information Rosling encourages us to look for.

So, in order to avoid this faux pas, just as the Brookings Institution did, we looked at data from 2015.[30] What *was* statistically significant? That Blacks and Latinos average scores were well-below average white scores, and that Asians' scores were higher than white scores. Indeed, one of the comments to Perry's blog pointed out that Asian girls scored higher than white boys, which as we've said rather undermines his whole claim on male mathematical superiority.

It confirms to us that there are far more factors than "inherency" or "natural ability" at play here. Racial oppression and inconsistencies in access to education, levels of encouragement, parental influence and stereotypes all have a huge role to play in creating inequality, and the success or failure in a given test. Gender therefore is often the lens that hints at inequalities that go way deeper when we look across race, ethnicity and other differentiators. It often highlights the deeply entrenched inequalities that exist at the systems level that preclude humans from realizing their talents.

Perry argues that there *are* gender differences. He argues that girls, though better prepared, fail when it comes to exam time. Although they out-number boys they still drop out of STEM faster. His rational for this? Boys are 'inherently' better than girls in math. He then contradicts himself further down his Blog stating, "the evidence shows that females are excelling in math and science in high school". Clearly then some girls are very good at math, so wouldn't it be sensible to encourage them in this? He goes on to describe the average difference in the SAT test as a "huge statistical difference," (which it is not) and as proof of "huge and persistent gender differences for math".

He concludes, "If there are some inherent gender differences," (...author insert) "closing the STEM gender degree and job gaps may be a futile attempt in socially engineering an unnatural and unachievable outcome." This last piece of wording is where the danger lies. One envisions little girls across the world scarred for life by being

7

forced to endure calculus. Are we to conclude that the girls who did very well at math are mutants?

Look a little deeper and this isn't what influences women when they leave STEM. It's lack of a sense of belonging and deliberate exclusion that makes them leave. Could it be that behaviors and the social context apparently affect boy's and girl's cognition, creating anxiety in females more often and reinforcing an idea of superiority in men? It's worthwhile diving into this a little further before assuming the age-old myth that it's all in the brains, the genes and the gender.

Robert Cialdini does just that as he explains in his book Pre-Suasion. Certain changes for SAT testing might significantly change any differences that still show up between boys and girls.[31] Research-based solutions to remove the stereotype threat, that girls are not as good as boys in math, might include the following. Girls taking the test separately from boys which removes the cultural reminder that they are assumed to not be as good as boys.[32] Assigning female math teachers to monitor the rooms with girls, which reinforces the role model effect, providing them a visual reminder that they can achieve as girls in math too.[33]

Taking away the 10 minutes up front thinking time, which focusses students on how to handle difficult questions, and instead using that time to focus them on self-affirming mindfulness can also be helpful.[34] Eliminating the requirement to tick a gender box at the start of the test, which in itself has been shown many times to create stereotype threat, is another example.[35] Applying these solutions in the context of race and ethnicity, unsurprisingly, has the same effect on positively influencing test scores for African American students.[36]

In some studies of populations these strategies have been shown to be beneficial, though it should be noted other studies have failed to replicate this. We should keep in mind that the replication crisis has made it difficult to replicate scientific studies and demonstrate the same results. This is specifically the case in the field of social psychology where it is notoriously difficult to reproduce the experiment in exactly the same way leading to the same results.[37]

Despite the challenge of the replication crisis there is little or no objective basis to believe that boys are better at math than girls, [38] and when there's no focus on gender we know girls normally score as well.[39] But overly focusing on gender has the reverse, negative influence in this situation for girls. Not only that but there's also been shown to be stereotype lift for boys, a performance boost gained when one is aware that the outgroup, in this case girls, is negatively stereotyped.[40]

Most recently a meta-analysis of 1.6 million students' grades was made to compare gender differences. The 2018 study published in Nature Communications concluded that the gender variability hypothesis, over-representation of males because of differences in academic achievement due to gender, was wrong.[41] Instead stereotypes, discrimination, harassment and backlash explained differences.

Finding the facts

Rosling is keen for us to see the facts for what they are. As his extensive work uncovered most people, including most experts, get statistically more questions wrong about the state of the world than the average chimpanzee in a zoo. Can anyone else hear Dr Michael Fox's cheeping baby turkey?

Rosling outlines that through these instincts we make a variety of misconceptions. By asking people and chimpanzees questions on a range of topics, - examples included global poverty, natural disasters, children's education, rates of crime, population growth, he showed that most people, even so-called experts, persistently scored as poorly as chimpanzees. He warned us that we have 10 instincts we perpetually use that give us a misperception of reality. The first is this Gap instinct, our propensity to find binaries.

There are three warning signs to the presence of the Gap Instinct, which Rosling refers to as "the comparison of averages, the comparison of extremes, and the view from up here". As leaders most

7

of our 'view from up here' experiences are filtered through our own identity, which prevents us from seeing what's really going on. There's a lot of 'view from up here' disconnect between male leader impressions and female executive stories in our interview data. These impressions are then also filtered through sensationalized differences between gender in publications and the media, and in people's own stories. Get the stories and experiences shared in education and coaching on gender dimensions to leadership and it's remarkable how quickly you can find that the majority of male leaders have a female leader twin, just as Rosling shows us in Figure C with math.

We also have to question the motives of the messengers. Has Perry simply misinterpreted the facts or is he deliberately misrepresenting them? His goal he makes clear – he wants us to stop forcing girls into fields they are apparently ill-equipped for. STEM is a male domain. Why is this so important for him to assert, when it clearly isn't true based on the data? It sounds like the sucker's choice, women should nurture, men do the logic stuff.

But based on the facts we clearly see in Figure C, there's a range of options here. It's not neat and ordered. It's certainly not binary. We know many male leaders struggle to promote women because of just this kind of binary mentality in corporate culture. Other men and women will also assert this gender binary narrative in some form. As we'll go on to discover it's very often because their own identity is strongly, some might argue, over-identified with either a masculine or feminine bias, with the assumed cultural costs or benefits that that over-identification brings with it.

We specifically juxtaposed three males here, Rosling, Perry and Cialdini, showing that it's not just women invested in the gender parity topic, who want to promote the truth. The scientists and social commentators, male and female, worth their salt are keen to see the facts. Corporate leaders must be similarly inclined. We must survey our people, find out the facts. We must understand our employees' experiences. Then we must think about creating the environment to cultivate the *talent* that cannot be tidily packed into male and female boxes.

The last decade has brought forth an enormous body of research in this area, with Fine's, Rippon's and Joel's work in the field of neuroscience most recently urging us to move beyond a binary view of our brains.[42] We need instead to see these complex organs as highly individualized and incredibly adaptable, just like people themselves.[43] While some might argue that they serve different functions, capacities and preferences dependent on the sex of the owner, we should remember that all behaviors show up in all humans. Functions, capacities and preferences appear to be highly individualized and universal in humans. They may simply be organized by gender depending on the environment and culture and be stimulated to show up more or less based on that environment.

Hearts

One final note. It's a great irony that for centuries scientists have been at great pains to show the differences in brains between males and females. Not so with the human heart, until very recently. While we associated heart disease and cardiovascular problems with men, very little attention was given to women. This has been costly. Only men were studied until the 90's, and it was assumed that whatever applied to them must apply to women. Contrary to the workings of the brain however, there seemed to be fewer political, religious, economic or sociocultural motives to invest in detecting differences in hearts.

Research over the last three decades has brought to light data showing that women's cardiovascular symptoms can present in very different ways to those associated with men. This often leads to misdiagnosis, which leads in turn to heart attacks more likely to be fatal in women than in men. Women complaining of symptoms different from the ones commonly associated with heart disease are still likely to be sent home, often being labelled hysterical. Yet levels of cardiovascular disease and morbidity are also the number one killer for women, not just men.[44] We also know that women, while living longer, may also be burdened with many more years of ill-health. Rigidity in following protocols and assumptions about what's going on with men being the same as what's going on with women are a huge part of the problem here. Inequality meant there was little interest in detecting difference until some astute female cardiologists paid attention.

Gender bias has meant that it seems scientists have been striving for centuries to show the differences in brains between men and women as a way to try and prove male superiority. It's ironic that they didn't spend so much time scrutinizing other physiological differences. Professor Dr Angela Maas, the first chair in Cardiology for Women at Radboud University, recognizes this all too well. As the author of the book A Women's Heart she writes of the systemic bias that leads to poor health outcomes for women with cardiovascular disease.[45]

She cites the biggest problems are misdiagnosis, because we now know women with heart disease have very different symptoms to the one's commonly associated with cardiovascular disease that men typically present. Not only this but the physiological processes of the disease manifest differently in women than men. Reluctance to accept that women's concerns are real is also a problem in diagnosis. So too is a lack of empathetic skills in doctors, or a willingness to believe women.

Cure care binary

Maas cites that the medical world is largely centered around the roles that follow gender norms. In The Lancet, 2019, a paper describes how gender norms can propagate negative effects. The "men cure, women care paradigm" is cited as part of the problem.[46] It's exactly this binary of roles and skills that also disempowers women and leads to far too few women being given leadership positions in healthcare, just as in the corporate world.

Leadership positions enable women to influence change, whether it be in science, health care or the business and global markets. This cure care paradigm is exactly what we challenge in chapter 7. We see how "taking care" and "taking charge" qualities are both required in leadership. However, it appears "taking charge" has the edge in the corporate world.

Now a Dutch Women's Council representative to the United Nations, Maas is well-placed to continue to raise the awareness around this important topic, at least in the medical arena. When we have greater equality in leadership roles, we'll see better outcomes both in business and in health. The UN sustainable development goals (SDG's), SDG 3 - improved health care and well-being for all, and SDG 5 - gender equality, both need to be acknowledged as hugely relevant in the corporate world.

Chronic stress and a low sense of well-being have been directly linked to the development of heart disease. We see the highest rates of burnout from chronic stress are among women in the workplace. Company leaders' awareness of gender bias and their recognition of the importance of well-being in the workplace and the impact unfairness has on that are therefore crucial.

Different or the same?

Perhaps we appear to contradict ourselves. On the one hand we argue men and women should be seen as far more similar than different. We do this in the context of ability, in terms of brains, our minds. Yet we also argue we need to see men and women differently, using hearts as an example. Assuming a one size fits all methodology or protocol, detrimentally affecting one group without all the facts, must be challenged. When there are differences between men and women, we absolutely have a duty to be open to understanding these.

The work of Londa Schiebinger, the John L. Hinds Professor of History of Science at Stanford University highlights this. A global authority on the history, theory and practice of gender in science she's pushed for the integration and analysis of sex and gender into research to better understand the differences and similarities between men and women for decades. Receiving funding from the European Commission's Horizon 2020 fund to further Gender Innovations and integrate gender dimensions into research.[47]

Schiebinger has observed that by fixing the number of women in the sciences, changing the structures of the institutions they are working in, and improving the knowledge we have to ensure we are working with the right data, better outcomes for *everyone* can be achieved.

The medical world has also been biased against men. Breast cancer, perceived as a women's disease, affects one in ten men. A third of osteoporosis cases, assumed as affecting mostly women, are men. Schizophrenia and autism are more likely to be diagnosed in men and boys than in women and girls, even if the only information changed on the symptoms list is the name of the patient. Infertility in men is increasing.

Inequality is a human issue not a women's issue.

Schiebinger's observations that levelling the playing field in scientific research will lead to break throughs and innovation can be applied equally well in the corporate context. The key areas we need to address in the corporate world are having higher numbers of women in leadership roles, promoting equality in the organization's structure, and measuring men and women in fair and objective ways.

Hearts *and* minds

Striving to understand differences *and* similarities for the purpose of creating improvements for everyone is a worthy goal. Arguing difference, *not* based in fact and using it to justify inequality must be challenged. If we stay in the dialogue and we strive to involve everyone, be it in communication, better studies or balanced leadership we'll achieve this.

To Joel's point we are all mosaics. We are all individuals. Society,

140

healthcare, corporations, governments all have an important role in ensuring equality in treatment and accessibility, be it to good health outcomes or economic access. Stereotyping people will blind us. Bias will delay us. Facts will get us there. Assumptions based on gender will not. Hearts and minds are needed in this important work. *Men's and women's* hearts and minds. No two are the same. We must continue to strive to understand differences and uniqueness. We must also recognize the similarities.

How over-identified you yourself as a leader are with your gender will have a great deal of influence on whether you really have the skills it requires to be a change agent for gender equality in leadership. But why would you even bother? Well do you want to get stuck in constructs of identity, or self-actualize into all that's humanly possible as a person and as a leader? It may well be there's a way to honor our own identity and that of others, *and* to explore the possibilities *beyond* gender identity.

Key Points

The weapons of sexism are economics, dominance of one group over another and homophobia, and the unconscious nature of bias.

We unwittingly prioritize masculine traits in leadership, because we more often assume men as default leaders.

Blinding assessments of people to avoid bias is essential.

Gender behavior is influenced by the active self, self-concepts and identity in given social settings.

We can motivate and stimulate the presence or absence of traits in people.

Creating psychological safety can significantly impact this. Rewarding people for showing certain abilities, despite gender, can also influence whether those abilities present or not.

Adherence to gender ideals limits humans. Stereotyping without consciousness is illogical.

Stereotypes around what men and women can supposedly do are pervasive.

Extreme binaries around logic ability and ability in communication still abound, but the latest studies find small differences between the sexes.

Most recent studies find any differences in ability across gender are likely to be due to stereotypes, discrimination, harassment and backlash.

Facts about innate gender difference, and the motivations of those bringing them, need to be challenged.

Neurosexism is the misrepresentation of neuroscience, claiming proof of innate sex difference in the brain.

We know that individuals' brains, like people, are a unique mosaic.

There has been historically a relentless push to strive to find differences between men's and women's brains, but not in other areas of physiology, until recently.

We need to strive to better understand differences and similarities in objective ways, to prevent inequality for everyone.

Case study

The pervasive myth of the female spaghetti brain and the male waffle brain

Self-reflective coaching questions and considerations

What are your relationships built on? Power and dominance or mutual respect and equality?

How do you observe how others' relationships function within your organization?

What are your own beliefs around male or female superiority or inferiority?

How is power and authority exercised in your organization?

What do you believe about men's and women's innateness?

What experiences have you had where men and women have stepped out of stereotypes?

What beliefs do you have around people's potential?

In what situations may you act in gender stereotypical ways?

Does this behavior make you feel authentic or inauthentic?

Consider a situation when you have been biased about someone's ability based on their gender.

What did you learn from the event?

Part 3

Choices

The Things
We Keep Missing

6 Uniqueness and Belonging, Needs and Norms, Self-identity and Shame

We all know the truth: more connects us than separates us. But in times of crisis the wise build bridges, while the foolish build barriers. We must find a way to look after one another as if we were one single tribe.
King T'Challa, Black Panther

To better unpack the complexity of the uniqueness and belonging needs it is useful to re-introduce Maslow's hierarchy. They have far-reaching relevance to the issues around the gender parity discussion.[1] As a reminder, the needs are loosely separated into material and spiritual needs. At the physiological level humans need food, shelter, warmth, rest. At the next level they need a sense of safety. We then move into the more spiritual levels: a need for belonging, a need for self-esteem and respect from others.

The highest aspiration for personal development, self-actualization, fulfils the need to be who we truly can aspire to be. Authentic self realizes its true human potential. As we explore the subject of understanding the gender dimensions in leadership, the hierarchy of needs can be extremely helpful in pointing out issues that come up for men and women, at given points along our psychological development as human beings.

Achieving psychological well-being

We make the premise that self-actualization encapsulates the notion that, as humans develop, they aspire to being more than societal constructs of what gender roles should be. Let's remind ourselves that those who adhere least to either masculine or feminine roles, but who instead combine these, have far greater psychological well-being, than those who identify strongly with one gender construct.[2] In the study into the well-being of men and women it was concluded that "the most relevant variable in the psychological well-being of both men and women was high masculinity, which linked higher rates of masculinity as the self-concept to higher rates of psychological distress."

This point is critical to consider when coaching men and women. It also has implications in leadership, when we still assign masculine stereotypes to perceived 'successful' leadership. Understanding the gender dimensions in leadership we better understand the psychological distress, often unseen, that affects behavior, well-being and productivity in men and women. People need to live their lives in thriving, fulfilling ways, aspiring to self-actualization. Research now widely supports the idea that adherence to gender norms can be counter-productive to this aspiration.

The ultimate human experience exists when masculine and feminine traits *both* manifest and flourish within the individual. But there are steps along the way to achieving that. Belonging and experiencing our unique identity, an identity that might simultaneously need to experience the satisfaction or adherence to certain more masculine or feminine constructs is a part of this. But not being limited to them alone is the ideal.

What often gets in the way of true gender parity without prejudice, which we suggest lies at the top of the pyramid in the self-actualization segment, is that gender can be so entangled in one's sense of self. Self-esteem is only reached when one feels one has fulfilled one's own model of what it means to be male or female, which makes up a part of the ego. However, contrary to Maslow's triangle, suggesting that we progress stage by stage in development, we actually need to recognize that all the needs are basic human needs.

This was also the conclusion of the Gallup World Poll run between 2005 and 2010. 60,865 participants from 123 countries were asked about their needs, which captured those identified in Maslow's original hierarchy. Ed Diener, who helped design the poll, subsequently analyzed the results with Professor Louis Tay at the University of Illinois.[3]

Social connection is essential

The study measured day-to-day feelings, both negative and positive, and concluded that the needs most linked to our everyday satisfaction involve the interpersonal realms. Examples are a need for respect and love. "*Societal need* fulfillment predicted SWB", (Subjective Well-Being) "particularly for life evaluation, beyond individual's fulfillment of their own needs, indicating the desirability of living in a flourishing society. In addition, the associations of SWB with the fulfillment of specific needs were largely independent of whether other needs were fulfilled." Social and community thus is *as* essential as basic needs. As Diener put it, "Although the most basic needs might get the most attention when you don't have them, you don't need to fulfill them in order to get benefits [from the others]". We can need shelter or food but simultaneously benefit from human contact and friendship.

It echoes the observations of René Spitz, an American analyst of the 1940's who coined the term 'failure to thrive'. He used this term to describe children separated from their parents and caught in terrible emotional grief because of that separation. John Bolwby, who studied European children left homeless and orphaned by World War II, observed that orphans well fed and sheltered would still die. But others given additionally love and cuddles would thrive.

Bowlby understood that emotional starvation was as debilitating as lack of physical nutrition and his work revolutionized the field of developmental psychology. His Attachment theory is the basis for understanding a great deal about how and why adults might fail to function effectively in their social relationships. Human beings are wired for connection and attachment. Threats to this can be devastating.

Diener and Tay found that income had little impact on day-to-day happiness. It was only significant in so far as it allowed access to basic needs. It's essential to keep this top of mind when we talk about pay discrimination and especially the wider implications economically for those discriminated against by the pay gap. While we can sit here as idealists, reflecting on how it's most important for individuals to achieve a sense of belonging and a purpose, the reality for a huge number of people, is that they are living from paycheck to paycheck. Tay's and Diener's findings do tie to the research, which has found that employees would rather take less pay and work in a happier culture. We should just carefully caveat that with, 'those that can afford it', would take a pay cut.[4]

Access even to purpose might be foiled where there's inherent discrimination and inequality. When corporations don't take care of the basic needs of equal pay, access to the same opportunities, and a workplace culture which ensures psychological and physical safety, first and foremost, values, missions and purpose become a nice to have for the privileged few. Systemic bias and discrimination exist in every organization where these inequalities are not tackled.

In Figure 3, even though we see Maslow's hierarchy of needs as a pyramid, we can infer all the needs are necessary at the same time. We invert the Gender triangle to depict that bias and discrimination might exist at every point of the hierarchy, except at the top in the equality section. Through the lens of gender, we can identify the type of gender bias that might be occurring. There is a large gender disparity at the basic need level. The gender pay-gap, and many more women experiencing sexual harassment than men, can be used as examples.

However, moving up the hierarchy doesn't mean this discrimination disappears. It may just become more subtle and implicit, and of course it may remain explicit. When we reach the belonging section, we might recognize a masculine *versus* feminine bias. Men are innately seen as this and do this. Women are innately seen as that and do that. This binary perpetuates inequality at the belonging level and continues to preclude women from opportunities and networks for future development, significantly in leadership development. In the uniqueness segment we see how masculine is often prized above feminine, and so this trend of bias continues.

Figure 3
MASLOW'S HIERARCHY OF NEEDS APPLIED TO GENDER EQUALITY IN LEADERSHIP

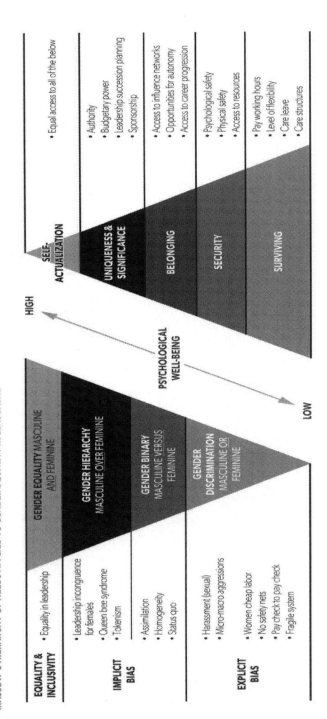

Importantly figure 3 inverts inequality. The concept is simple and elegant. If we make gender discrimination already non-existent at the basic levels on Maslow's hierarchy it has less chance for influence as we continue up the hierarchy of needs. Eliminating binary ideas and hierarchical ideas around gender significantly impacts the ability to create equality.

Self-actualization in leadership, as in human development, involves embracing both the masculine *and* the feminine. Then true equality is reached, psychological well-being, and a leadership style that encapsulates the broadest number of traits needed for success. Assuming these basic needs have been met, (and they often have not been) moving up the hierarchy list of Maslow, we can see that belonging and self-esteem will both be influenced by the social setting and the expectations of the individual. Making assumptions around where a person might affiliate, based on gender, will be problematic.

Self-identity and shame

Knowing this, are we and others prepared to look beyond social constructs of what being a 'real' man or 'woman' means? Brené Brown, a research professor at the University of Houston, working in the area of shame and vulnerability, has identified these issues powerfully as they relate to our gendered expectations. In Men, Women and Worthiness she talks at length to the point that, still to this day, societal expectations of what it means to be male or female shame us into not breaking from those expectations. To break away from those societal expectations can be hard. A sense of belonging, or an individual sense of our worthiness and self-respect, can be at odds.

Our desire to be more than just what culture expects of us creates conflict. Uniqueness and belonging can themselves be contradictory, if poorly understood in respect to gender identity. Yet both are essential. Fulfilling just what society, or the social context expects of us, is a huge problem for men and women. Why? As Brown explains, some shame is tied to us as humans, but much of shame can relate to how gender specifically organizes us, in terms of how we *should* show up in certain ways.[5] In psychological terminology this is called the gender role strain we talked of earlier. So, what does this look like in reality?

If you are a woman who feels strongly that being a good, present, selfless person *critically* defines who you are, you may not progress beyond the societal, cultural constructs of gender that expect that of women. The difficulty is this can often be quite unconscious. To give an example, it's why saying no to things, especially when it comes to helping and supporting other people, can be extremely difficult for women. It might be in their own interests not to over-stretch, and to have a sense of self not wholly defined by their relationship to others. However, by not being this selfless person people expect them to be they also run the risk of being socially judged and potentially excluded by others. It's a contradiction in psychological terms that forces choices, either of which may have good and bad consequences.

These psychological explanations need to be understood, to help women navigate the work environment. They help fully inform them on the possible implications and repercussions in choosing a given behavior, that's recommended by others. A Harvard Business Review article, Why Women Volunteer for Tasks that Don't Lead to Promotion comments section, highlights this missing psychological piece.[6] The article, valuable and well-written, explains that most people expect women to offer help, more than men, and to volunteer for non-promotable tasks. These women then appear too over-loaded for the promotable work. The consequence? They are passed over for promotion more easily than men.

Social penalties

The article crucially picked up that the group dynamic was also an essential component in creating this expectation placed on women to help. But it missed a further invaluable point. No one *forced* these women to offer to help and yet they still did. *Expectation* to help is not the same as *choosing* to give that help. As one person wrote in the comments section, the article answered important questions but not the one in the title. Why *do* women volunteer for tasks that don't lead to promotion? We get our answer when we understand the deeper psychological issues at play.

Women will be socially penalized if they say no and men most likely will not. If women step out of their gender identity role expectation, they'll risk being shunned by the group, and that brings other consequences. Saying no is just one example of many types of behavior that may serve women on their way to a sense of self-actualization. But saying no if you're a woman can carry penalties along the journey in a given social context. Helping women realize that there's actually a choice, *why* there's a choice and that those choices will *all* carry negative or positive consequences is incredibly empowering and helpful. And reflecting on the effects of masculinity, also a moving target, we'd do well to remember this is the case for men too.

If you are a man you may think that fundamental to your ego and sense of self is *how* you attain respect from others. We know that stereotypes in society, and in the corporate world, stress that men are, by default, natural leaders. So, some men's sense of self-identity and self-esteem might come from being seen as in charge and in a position of power. We see this often for corporate men who consciously believe they are fair and open, but unconsciously are tied to ideas of success being only achievable through status. For these men status means being at the top of the hierarchy. Being at the top of the hierarchy is in conflict with equality, however, if it has been attained on an unequal playing field. That unequal playing field is being selected *because of being male*, rather than because of skills, talents, and the effort that's been put forth.

It is also often contradictory to aspiring to full self-actualization and some men's *own* definitions of self and success. When we coach men, these personal definitions tie to deeper meanings of purpose beyond societal expectations. Very personal goals that may mean they are no longer responsible for bringing in the money. Such goals may not carry a title. They can often be hard to access for men who've spent their whole careers pursuing status. This fact is heavily underscored by the numbers of male executives we coach who have reached the top positions in their careers, are then let go, and then sit back wondering what they did it all for. They often have a deep sense of loss, wondering what legacy they've left.

Finding meaning and self-worth, beyond being the main bread winner for the family, beyond the title or perceived status they no longer possess, is psychologically challenging for these men. Loss of status can quite literally create a chasm in some men's lives. With their self-worth and identity being so tied to status, economic responsibility and being the leader, it can take time for them to uncover what's next. Having been so conditioned to look for status and power they continue to look for roles that embody these.

A bias toward some masculine gender norms means these men often forgot to create a strategy for their life, as Clayton Christensen, put it.[7] He observed that many of his former Harvard Business School classmates, who came to reunions, were estranged from spouses and alienated from their children. "They didn't keep the purpose of their lives front and center."[8] We very often observe this in coaching executive men and some women, who've dedicated their time and energy to career, and made little room for family, hobbies or other worthy interests.

Being at the top of the hierarchy is also at odds with creating equality to a large degree. It explains why many men would and do have difficulty accepting women as their leaders and not being in that role themselves. This is a crucial point. In self-actualized leaders we'd argue that self-worth is no longer attributable to who we lead, and whether others follow us, but whether we create other leaders. Self-actualization thus breaks away from stereotypes and cultural notions of what it means to be a 'real' man or a 'real' woman.

So how do we move to self-actualization? We have to recognize how constructs of gender limit us, define us and shame us if we break away from their narrow definition of how we *should* show up as men and women. And we have to recognize that they are contradictory, creating conflicts in personal and social settings such as work. We have to recognize that much of this is the reason that bias and discrimination exist at all. It's done to us, we do it to ourselves and we do it to others. Making sense of this with clients in coaching can have a profound impact on them, enabling them to internalize and create their own authentic path to success. In Brown's words, "If we don't claim shame it claims us." By claiming shame, we clear the path for conversations about equality.

The avoidance of "claiming shame" is so often deeply unconscious. It manifests in ways we don't consciously recognize as maladaptive behaviors, just to avoid its uncomfortable grip. And it's hugely relevant in the conversation around the gender dimensions in leadership. This is crucial to understand when strategizing on getting more women into leadership roles in the corporate world, achieving buy-in from men, and when leading teams to work inclusively and thus collaboratively together. Teams are often dysfunctional exactly because so many of these conflicting expectations of gender roles are present in the group dynamic, conscious and unconscious, and because ultimately leadership is still viewed as incongruent for females.

Telling women to be more like some men, by 'saying no', as an example, is simply erroneous, without this additional understanding. Men can say no and set boundaries and it is more likely to be respected. Women will be socially penalized more often when doing so.[9] And expecting men to step up to do more of the non-promotable tasks, without reflecting on why they wouldn't automatically consider doing them, is equally fool hardy. So, too, is giving them unequal amounts of praise and recognition if they do happen to step up and do those non-promotable tasks.

Coaching men and women, without understanding the deeper psychological drives, makes a great deal of coaching and advice superficial and counterproductive. You can advise a woman to say no to things, but the fact that saying no *may* carry a social penalty for her *must* also be acknowledged and discussed. That acknowledgement and discussion rarely takes place. Women who say no to things *are* more likely to get socially penalized, and this has to be recognized before they can determine their best course of action. To make a decision to set boundaries that frees them up to attain self-actualizing goals. Indeed, having a personal goal in itself can be more of an issue for women, since they've been conditioned from infancy to put relationships and thus others, first.

Men on the other hand are almost *required* from a young age to be agentic, which as we've mentioned already brings its own stress and pressure. It's often why they don't consider a strategy for their whole life, to reference Christensen, but heavily focus on career. Coaching corporate men to consider things outside of work, creating more balance and time for loved·ones, friendships and hobbies, as examples, can be equally challenging.

Allowing men to be vulnerable

When Brown did her work on shame, she originally didn't focus on men but only women. She tells the story of how at a book signing she was approached by a gentleman who challenged her about this. He challenged her to the idea that men are also not allowed to show shame or emotion because they also will be penalized. While we might think that what he meant by this was that other 'stronger' men – the bullies, the pushy fathers, the censorious teachers, the brutal coaches, don't allow these men to have emotions, he was driving at something else here. He made the point that women too rarely allow the males in their life to have emotions, to be vulnerable, to *not* have the answers, to *not* have to take the lead no matter what. He made an excellent point.

Social context again influences how far men and women are willing to take the vulnerable steps needed to step out of gender behavioral expectations, and what the risks might be if they do. This narrative is also strong in the heterosexual context. Roger Horrocks stated, "to become the man I was supposed to be I had to destroy my most vulnerable side, my sensitivity, my femininity, my creativity, and I also had to pretend to be both more powerful and less powerful than I feel."[10] As a psychotherapist who has dealt with many men in trauma and psychological pain he has recognized that boy's and men's cultural conditioning *creates* this paradox: "patriarchal masculinity cripples men".[11]

Many women, including the ones fighting for equality, indeed society as a whole, have been conditioned to expect, even demand that men lead. And part of the pre-requisite to leadership in the masculine context? That those men don't demonstrate the 'softer skills.' Remember from the discussion and studies on empathy, men are equally capable of these 'softer skills.' But stereotype threat can very easily stifle them. And as Brown has powerfully identified, inability to show vulnerability specifically, is a huge problem if we're trying to be effective leaders.

Needs and norms

James Mahalik, in particular, has done a great deal of research measuring the benefits and costs to men associated with conformity and non-conformity to masculine gender role norms and their levels of distress. In one of his studies men were measured on an assessment called the Conformity to Masculine Norms Inventory (CMNI). Mahalik could show that greater conformity to traditional masculine norms reported lower incidents of health promoting behavior, describing these health promoting behaviors as either inter-personally or intra-personally favorable.[12] In other words, adhere more extremely to masculine norms and you'll suffer psychologically for it as a male because many so-called masculine 'norms' do not fit as well with human needs. Human needs transcend the needs that masculine norms suggest that men have.

Just discussing the norms identified by Mahalik found in dominant culture in countries like the US, UK and in many western corporate cultures, creates a very good starting place for examining the stereotypes that men too are subjected to. It is extremely powerful to use in group coaching discussions around gender parity which we use in our own coaching work with senior leaders. The masculine norms Mahalik and his team identified were, winning, being emotionally controlled, taking-risks, violence, dominance, playboy persona, self-reliance, primacy of work, power over women, disdain for homosexuality and pursuit of status. They echo the list formed by Pleck and Levant in their earlier work. The implications of these norms present as great topics to discuss in small group settings. Many of them are at odds with concepts of equality. They also highlight the way perceived masculine traits take precedent over the feminine.

It's also useful to look at other research done by Mahalik and his team at Boston College, who asked the question, what is it that makes women feminine?[13] In other words, for our purposes, what makes them fit into the belonging and self-esteem boxes of Maslow's hierarchy from a gender perspective? Just as we have a list of norms for what is perceived as masculine, Mahalik created a list of norms for females which were as follows: nice in relationships, thinness, modesty, domestic, caring for children, romantic relationship, sexual fidelity and investment in appearance.[14]

In the discussion around leadership and expectations of how people should show up this list provides a great reference for some fascinating discussions around bias, stereotyping and how women are perceived and accepted as leaders. Brown's synopsis of Mahalik's work and what we expect of women? "Thin, nice and modest, and using all of your available resources in the pursuit of your appearance." Not exactly the messaging or mold for a great leader. And so, what happens? Societies, communities, corporations full of people who have also internalized this message unconsciously, if not consciously, also think women should be this way.

Leadership as incongruent to feminine norms

What happens if women step out of this very narrow definition? Derogatory comments about Theresa May's kitten heels, or Hilary

Clinton's and Angela Merkel's propensity to wear pant suits are the order of the day. They are socially penalized for breaking with social norms most often. They are called words beginning with 'b' because our binary thinking doesn't allow women to be leaders. Instead it organizes them in terms of how masculine or feminine they are. The tactics used try to demonstrate the incongruence between female and leadership. This is achieved by over-masculinizing these women, or by taking a shot at any feminizing features which signal they can't be taken seriously as leaders.

Our binary thinking doesn't accept that women are leaders in a society which still ultimately holds up some narrow 'masculine' traits as the blueprint for leadership. Why? Because we don't just have binary thinking in terms of gender roles, we also have hierarchical thinking in terms of who has power and who doesn't. Further there's a moral judgement of who *should* have power and who should not.

It's called patriarchy of course, but as soon as we talk about this word many men feel criticized and ridiculed, attacked, blamed and shamed, and they shut down to any conversation around equality for sure. And most of this anger, blame and shame comes from the fact that they were never allowed in the social context to be 'human' themselves. Gender organized in this binary fashion sends negative signals for everyone and gets people very defensive and angry all too often. Hurt people hurt people, and they exist across the spectrum of humanity.

Luckily most people are open to a conversation around leadership and what makes great leadership, even if they shut down on the topic of gender. What we have to realize, however, as leaders, is that gender and leadership are inextricably linked in people's unconscious in the ways we've just discussed. Until we immerse ourselves in the gender topic, we can't serve the quest of creating gender parity in leadership well.

A man who believes he has to be in charge is very unlikely to be comfortable with accepting a female boss as we've mentioned, nor will he be particularly invested in creating a pipeline of women leaders. Shame may well show up as he feels somehow that he is not fulfilling his proper role as a man in being the ultimate leader, if a woman is the leader instead. Remember in the case study of Ed and Imani where it can be even more subtle in informal leadership situations. This happens when we are unaware of how easily we default to the 'male as leader' paradigm.

This is crucial to understand because culturally this holds true subconsciously, though many intelligent people on a conscious level don't believe it to be so. Remember the Inclusivity Framework and how easily we can move between the quadrants, in and out of bias, and based on our willingness to include or exclude. It's this deeper psychology that keeps plenty of people locked in the Elitist and Tokenist quadrants, *if* they don't become either more inclusive or more consciously aware of their own bias.

A woman who continually says yes to everything because her fear of saying no will make her appear not 'nice', which we know is a cultural requirement of being a 'good' woman, is very likely to oversteer the boat and take on too many things. She's unable to say no for fear of the shame that may come from the judgement of not being nice. Worse still the social exclusion which may be a consequence of that. While we fixate on the idea that she *needs* to say no and drop things, we might coach such advice. However, on an unconscious level at least, something may be off for her. It's that saying no runs the risk of her being socially penalized, losing a sense of belonging, potentially a reduced sense of self-esteem. This aspect must be handled, recognized and made conscious.

Full psychological development is at odds with gender identity

Our sense of self is so tied up in the social construct of what our gender roles should be that those roles straight jacket us and make many of us behave in maladaptive ways we are not even aware of. This contradiction in who we are as humans and how we must show up as a given gender gives us a conflicted identity. This was identified in a

7

critical way for women by Dr Carol Gilligan back in the early 80's. Her research, based on interviews with girls and women, identified how psychology persistently misunderstood women's moral motives, commitments and psychological growth, and how being female stifled their voice in terms of how they could present themselves. She identified that for men and women our psychological development quite literally collides with the social construct of identity.[15]

In layman's terms we can only become self-actualized once we move beyond these narrow definitions of what 'male' and 'female' should mean, and what 'real' men and women *should* do. A healthy psyche resists the binaries of what men and what women *should* be and recognizes that self-actualization is the human voice which has 'masculine' and 'feminine' aspects, traits and behaviors. But a healthy psyche needs the support of other healthy psyches around it to make such a transition if it's to succeed in a corporate setting, or any other involving people for that matter. Remember uniqueness *and* belonging are both essential for creating inclusivity in any successful social group.

Penalties for non-conformists

It is therefore crucial to recognize that non-conformity to masculine or feminine gender norms also has negative consequences, while it simultaneously propels men and women to achievements of goals beyond what society deems to be right or appropriate for a man or a woman. Indeed, non-conformers in social contexts are more likely to experience group rejection. This has been identified in a large body of work done by social psychologists. A useful overview of this work can be found in a paper by Robert Cialdini and Melanie Trost, who conclude that "Any fully informed explanation of social influence must consider the characteristics of both the influence target and the setting, and the numerous ways in which they may interact."[16] A great deal of advice out there about equality and inclusivity misses this point.

Taking into account gender and other personal differentiators is important. So too is the hierarchy within the organization, behavior of peers and the examples of behavior modelled by leadership. Knowing that some people may not conform to aspects of either the group or the assumed behavioral norms of that group, we can see the contradictory nature of what might be required to create belonging, and what might be required to increase our self-esteem as unique individuals. Being able to be both simultaneously unique (different) and at the same time being able to belong (similar) needs to be given space and time. It is why this work on inclusivity can be so difficult.

As we identified earlier just being female does not mean you affiliate with your referent group or feel a sense of belonging with them. There were, for example, women we interviewed, who literally cannot stand the idea of joining a women's network. This is why understanding how someone identifies with the perceived norms of gender is really important. It is why it is so important to recognize the gender binary and hierarchy that exists and how it specifically interacts with leadership. And while we talk about psychological distress, we need to acknowledge that research has shown that exclusion and rejection cause pain similar or even more powerful than physical pain.[17] Small wonder people feel burnout when they experience unfair treatment.

We have plenty of research to support the notion that transgressing traditional gender roles results in people being negatively evaluated. Every gender reading this book can attest to that in their own personal experience at a point in time probably. But with the dialogue around gender equality focusing on the strengths of women, enabling women to feel empowered to some degree in breaking with traditional female gender roles, and a need for system changes as the most recent epiphany, we left men behind in the dialogue about their place and role in all of that. While the die-hard critics would say men have had their day, have dominated for years, had all the power, those same critics risk doing precisely what no one fighting for equality and inclusion should ever do. Focusing on one group to the exclusion of others.

We risk demonizing all men when only some men assert power over women, or pursue status no matter what the cost, or take unnecessary risks no matter who falls victim. But with the lack of conversation around men and their psychological challenges in the gender conversation there are few men interested or engaged in this, by now, over-exhausted-to-many-topic. For us all to develop psychologically as a social group we have to recognize that. And more importantly we need to recognize this. While the sense is that transgressing gender roles will result in a harsh evaluation for everyone, men who transgress gender roles may well be judged far more negatively than women who do so are.

Down-grading care work limits men's options in a rapidly changing world

This remains particularly pertinent in the workplace. Men don't jump into traditionally female roles. Less pay coupled with social stigmatization are seen as two of the biggest barriers to men taking on more pink-collar roles such as health care or teaching work. "Traditional masculinity is standing in the way of working-class men's employment" according to Andrew Cherlin, a John Hopkins public policy professor.[18] Cherlin argues that our cultural views on masculinity are behind the times in terms of their relevance to changes in the job market.

When we split out 'taking charge' and 'taking care' occupations and gender them, it really does have a negative impact. Double standards through a gender binary lens really do create twice the pain. They lead to men believing they don't necessarily have the caring skills to enter the care market, compounded by a society that largely says it's not OK for men to do such work. And they also highlight gender and race discrimination when men do take on such work. A study in 2016 identified the "glass escalator" effect. 'Taking care' jobs lead to higher wage growth and faster promotion for some men, but not for women. This was specifically observed in "more technical allied health occupations". [19] The study also found that hands-on direct care workers received lower wages. Minority men were more likely to be in these lower paid roles compared to white men.

While we gender-stereotype jobs and abilities, we give an intrinsically inferior value to perceived female roles. We down-grade the importance of such jobs, and ultimately down-grade care. As we are seeing with the current Covid-19 crisis and increasing numbers of the elderly needing care, as just two examples, how we reward our workers effects everyone. What we prioritize as important in our societies, effects everyone. How we prioritize 'taking charge' over 'taking care', and masculine over feminine, has wider implications for the presence or absence of thriving societies. It has similar implications in the corporate sphere.

The interpretation of Maslow's hierarchy in the context of gender will be pertinent to much of our discussion. It provides a great road map as to why the subject of gender parity can become so emotive and challenging for most people. To think of ourselves as self-actualized and above constructs of gender can come into direct conflict with our definitions of self, if those are deeply embedded in ideas around what it means to be a 'real' man or woman. Gender appears to dictate largely what occupations and roles we should and shouldn't have based on our sex. That can be very limiting, especially in a rapidly changing world.

A cultural view of masculinity makes it difficult therefore for men to break from traditional male jobs. But with a market shift in the types of skills now needed this is problematic. This is specifically observed in males who come from manual-labor jobs, such as machine operators, locomotive firers, vehicle electronics installers where jobs are projected to more than half within the next 5 years.[20] Rather than re-training for jobs they see as culturally not fitting with what it means to be men, many of these men wait for other manual jobs to come up.

Lawrence Katz, a Harvard economist, recently quoted in a New York Times article, described this as "looking for the job you used to have" and calls it 'retrospective wait unemployment'. These men do not want to re-train for a new occupation that might involve realigning with more stereotypically feminine traits, perceived in health care work, for example. He describes the issue not as a skill mismatch but as an identity mismatch. "It's not that they couldn't become a health worker, it's that people have backward views about what their identity is."[21]

It has parallels to the idea that most people think of themselves as having a fixed personality, and yet we know that everyone changes. Reflecting back on our lives most of us are very different to the people we were 10, 15, 20 years ago. But we attach a lot to the idea that we are consistent, have a fixed character, change little. It is this same mistake that we make when doing personality or executive assessments in organizations. While such assessments can be useful as a means of taking a point in time, they should never be regarded as presenting a fixed, unchangeable individual. At least, they don't have to be. More likely the case is that people become very fixed in their ways, habits and behaviors, as well as in their environment. This is often why habits seem so impossible to break and change. They can often appear to demand Herculean strength and commitment we just don't have.

It's this Herculean effort that makes cognitive dissonance such a powerful force. Most of us don't possess that degree of commitment. It's why we will even ignore facts to make *our* reality seem *the* reality. People on the low end of bias awareness, the Homogenists and Tokenists, will have an increased propensity for this cognitive dissonance. They tend to believe information consistent with their stereotypes of others, because the contradiction that other information might present, is too uncomfortable to rationalize.

Cognitive dissonance means we are more likely to dismiss information which is contradictory to our own beliefs, values or ideas, rather than to sit with the discomfort of considering other angles.[22] We argue that self-actualized individuals push beyond stereotypes, bias around gender and the mindless pull of cognitive dissonance. Egalitarians recognize that human potential goes way beyond the bounds and narrower definitions of masculinity or femininity.

Fixed mindset and fixed gender identity

Studies on compliance and conformity have been instructive in demonstrating just how far people will go in their behaviors to be seen to be accurate, to affiliate and to maintain a positive self-concept. People literally change their cognition and behavior to align with these motivations depending on their levels of need to be seen as consistent. But fighting for consistency might mean getting stuck. It also means we are unable to grow psychologically if we are determined to hold on to older beliefs and value systems. Assuming and assigning roles and capabilities for men and women based on a perceived immutable set of binary traits runs this danger. This is why the transition between the belonging level on Maslow's hierarchy, to self-esteem, to ultimately a higher state of self-actualizing, can be at odds.

The need to affiliate and be consistent might mean conforming to certain gender norms. This means people are less willing to question the status quo. It can mean we won't accept information that suggests that our own self-concept might be somewhat limited and limiting. Similarly, our assessment of other people or situations might be incorrect for the same reason. The need for a positive self-concept tied up within this need to appear consistent with past behavior compounds this. And if that high positive self-concept is too highly tied to the perceived ideals of what it means to be a 'real' man or woman, which we know are inconsistent anyway, self-esteem might be shaky. The assertion that people are a certain way, and that's the only way, in pursuit of a need to be seen as accurate, is itself problematic when it comes to shifting people and their attitudes in terms of their bias towards others.

Where do you think you currently lie on Maslow's hierarchy of needs as a leader, team member, or organization? Are you in survival mode? Do you have aspirations to self-actualize? What does that mean to you as a leader? How embroiled is your ego in the gender discussion? Do you feel threatened and irritated by the conversation around gender? How much might your people be identified with societal expectations around gender norms? How much might this be affecting their sense of uniqueness and belonging, their ability to self-actualize?

Let's leave gender behind for a while. Let's step into courage and curiosity for a moment and, rather than talking about gender, let's talk about leadership. We just can't guarantee gender won't come up again as you're about to find out.

Key Points

Gender norms can come into conflict with psychological needs.

A key one for men is that showing vulnerability may be socially penalized.

A key one for women is that being agentic may be penalized.

Both of these qualities are needed in good leaders.

Psychological well-being is dependent on belonging and a sense of uniqueness.

A sense of inclusion also depends on belonging and a sense of uniqueness.

Treating people differently based on gender leads to feelings of exclusion.

Understanding how people identify with masculine and feminine norms can be useful in understanding how gender might play into a sense of belonging or uniqueness.

Psychological development quite literally collides with the social construct of identity.

Experiencing the contradiction between gender identity, societal expectations and what women and men would want for themselves to self-actualize, may create a sense of shame.

Since masculine and feminine norms are to some degree based on hierarchy they need to be understood, in order to help solve gender inequality.

Down-grading care work limits men's options, and down-grades care work as less important in society.

Fixed mindsets lead to fixed ideas around gender binaries, and limit people's psychological growth and well-being.

Double standards in leadership, based on gender lead, to twice the pain in many organizations.

Self-reflective coaching questions and considerations

Consider how you affiliate with others based on your gender.

Consider what you may have assumed about how other men and women in your organization gain a sense of belonging based on gender?

Ask some colleagues how they regard themselves in relation to gender norms.

Ask some employees how they can feel a greater sense of belonging?

How would they like to feel unique?

What gives you a sense of belonging in your organization?

What gives you a sense of uniqueness?

What gives you a sense of significance?

Are there ways this significance may be in conflict with gender equality?

Are the ways you wish to feel significant in some way tied to gender norms? Do they limit you?

How do you perceive others might be limited by gender norms?

How easy is it for you to show vulnerability?

Consider the masculine and feminine gender norms in regards to yourself and those around you.

Consider a time when you felt shame because you were perceived as breaking a gender norm.

Consider one way your gendered ego might get in the way of your leadership and think of a way to overcome this.

7 Our flawed definition of Leadership - why taking charge to take care could be the middle way

To the brave barefoot woman, whose name I don't know,
but whose rational arguments saved me from being sliced by a mob
of angry men with machetes.
Hans Rosling, Swedish physician and academic

It is important to define what leadership is. This starting point will be fundamental, both to the process of challenging where we currently sit with our thinking regarding gender bias, and the conclusions we make based on that thinking. It will also lead us to understand why we may be co-creating yet more bad advice for female leaders and male sponsors.

Let us begin by drawing on two definitions of leadership, which demonstrate where there may be cultural divergence in our thinking. We shall use the term Level 5 leadership, which Jim Collins coined in the book Good to Great, as our ideal benchmark.[1] We shall also discuss the stereotypic behaviors *assumed* to make good leaders, in the 2005 report from Catalyst entitled, "Women Take Care, Men Take Charge: Stereotyping of U.S. Business Leaders Exposed."[2]

The extensive work and research Collins and his team did in Good to Great fundamentally invalidated what many in the West assumed to be the most effective leadership traits, namely confidence, dominance and assertiveness. What Collin's research "unexpectedly" found was that a "paradoxical mix of personal humility and professional will" were what set great leaders apart in the Good to

Great companies. "Level 5 leaders channel their ego needs away from themselves and into the larger goal of building a great company," he writes.

Stereotyping leadership

The key point, according to Collins, is that "One of the most damaging trends in recent history is the tendency (especially by boards of directors) to select dazzling, celebrity leaders and to de-select potential Level 5 leaders." This would tie in with the research that demonstrates that men will be selected on 'potential'. Women, by the way, are more often selected based on 'contribution.'

When most people read "dazzling celebrity leaders", it has been shown they think *male* and they think *white* most of the time.[3] So even our assumptions of what makes a great leader are generally biased, and as a part of that women and all minorities are being unwittingly precluded from leadership roles that they could be truly stellar in.

If we dig further into the findings of Collins', we note that humility is exhibited through "inspired standards, not inspiring charisma, to motivate others." It's the inspiring performance trait we talk about in emotional intelligence. It's about aspiring to excellence, which we'd argue is what companies demonstrate by making the effort to create new systems and processes, so that work contributions are objectively measured, and bias doesn't need to exercise its hefty influence. The results will speak for themselves.

Collins identified that Level 5 leaders had a professional will that created excellent results. They were uncompromisingly resolved to the task required for *long term results* (this is a key point). Most essentially, they looked at themselves if things went wrong, not at others, to blame. This refusal to blame others, in itself, is a key observation. These leaders accepted fully the responsibility of the task. They never used external excuses to pass off that responsibility.

At the same time, Level 5 leaders had humility. Collins further described this as "a compelling modesty, shunning public adulation, never boastful". Finally, these leaders succeeded by channeling ambition into the company, not themselves. They set up others to succeed in the future and gave praise to them and external factors.

While we pay attention to some of the most recent 'best practice' advice given to women to succeed in the workplace, we'd do well to keep Collins' observations front of mind. By doing so we can identify just how much of that advice suggests that women may be advised to assimilate to a standard that, by Collins' account, has failed in building the best companies. Collins' observations of the leaders of good to great companies echo the observations often made of women. These same observations are cited as what hold women back from further success. These are namely their modesty, propensity to take personal responsibility, putting others before self and their perceived conscientiousness (perfectionism).

It is useful to compare Collins' proven data with the list of leadership behaviors documented by Catalyst. The non-profit research organization highlighted those traits people perceive to be the common, necessary traits for a leader. According to the report males and females perceive males to be better at three essential leadership behaviors: problem solving, influencing up and delegating. While this perception predominates, there is a bias against female leaders, who are not perceived to be good in these tasks.

So, in society there is unequivocal bias not just as to the color and gender of a leader, but also for the *types* of behavior that that leader should exhibit.[4] To put it mildly all these biases may be rather limiting us, underscored by a populace belief that 'masculine' and 'feminine' traits are gender specific.

Leadership has no gender

The list of behaviors Catalyst cited is very comprehensive. The 'Take care' and 'Take charge' study done by Catalyst has shown that certain behaviors are stereotypically attributable to males in leadership and are regarded as atypical for females. There is a presence of stereotypic judgements in people's evaluation of females as leaders. These stereotypes and biases create the widespread perception that more dominant regarded masculine traits, 'take charge' traits, are what set great leaders apart. But this, only if they are men. We discuss this double standard for women in chapter 9.[5]

It is also worth noting that statistically, although these stereotypes persist, women have been ranked as more effective leaders than men in many studies.[6] While a competition of qualities and abilities between men and women is neither helpful or conclusively empirically proven, this fact should also prompt us to investigate and unpick these contradictions further.

The conflict in research points clearly to the fact that gender is not a reliable predictor on how a person will lead, and actual leadership behavior is *not defined* by specific gender. It is however stereotypically represented as such in the general population's perceptions, and this has huge implications for how women can realistically break into executive leadership roles. It challenges us about how much we value certain behavior traits. It challenges us to question why some of these traits may get downgraded in their importance, depending on what gender the leader is.

While the executives we interviewed could cite both male and female leaders they regarded as highly effective, there were mostly a disproportionate number of males to females in their career experience, especially as they climbed the corporate ladder. This latter fact demonstrates that women drop out of the bid for senior leadership roles at a certain point, more often at post-childbearing age, although the proportionate decline already begins at the first management promotion. Moving from entry level to C-suite female representation falls by more than 50%.

Yet we know women are also as ambitious, if not more so, than men.[7] Meanwhile, 50% of men think women are well represented in companies where 10% of senior leaders are women.[8] Does this demonstrate some men view women as lacking leadership ability, or that women lack interest in leadership? Or does it demonstrate that

Perry's blog got it wrong about male's superiority in math?

The studies on stereotyping are very helpful in explaining why we may be suffering when it comes to understanding and accepting our roles as leaders, and males or females *as* our leaders. As noted in the Catalyst research, stereotypes mislead us when it comes to leadership. "Inherent in gender stereotypes is the assumption that masculine and feminine characteristics (including 'taking care' and 'taking charge' behaviors) are mutually exclusive." There's that binary thinking showing up again. It's the either /or limiting belief that we expose in chapter 11.

To circle back to the Jim Collins' Level 5 leaders, this false dichotomy between women's and men's characteristics, has placed both men and women in inadequate categories for style and behaviors. It limits the range of effective behaviors within the workplace. While we focus on Collins, we do it specifically to expose the 'modesty versus confidence' argument in stereotyping. And as we've already explained with the Dunning Kruger effect, over-flowing confidence might more often represent a lack of expertise and skill. Modesty could well be a sign of a greater level of ability, both in men and women. We might do well to remember this.

Figure 4
KEY LEADERSHIP
BEHAVIORS

CONSULTING	NETWORKING
Checking with others before making plans or decisions that affect them.	Developing and maintaining relationships with others who may provide information or support resources.
DELEGATING	**PLANNING**
Authorizing others to have substantial responsibility and discretion.	Designing objectives, strategies and procedures for accomplishing goals and coordinating with other parts of the organization in the most efficient manner.
INFLUENCING UPWARD	**PROBLEM SOLVING**
Affecting others in positions of higher rank.	Identifying, analyzing and acting decisively to remove impediments to work performance.
INSPIRING OTHERS	**REWARDING**
Motivating others toward greater enthusiasm for and commitment to work by appealing to emotion, values, logic and personal example.	Providing praise, recognition and financial remuneration when appropriate.
INTELLECTUALLY STIMULATING	**ROLE MODELLING**
Exciting the abilities of others to learn, perceive, understand or reason.	Serving as a pattern standard of excellence to be imitated.
MENTORING	**SUPPORTING**
Facilitating the skill development and career advancement of subordinates.	Encouraging, assisting and providing resources for others.
MONITORING	**TEAM BUILDING**
Evaluating the performance of subordinates and the organizational unit for progress and quality.	Encouraging positive identification with the organization unit, encouraging cooperation and constructive conflict resolution.

Highlighted words depicted as 'taking charge' traits, 'masculine' behaviors

7

Non-binary, non-siloed systems intelligence

Beyond Collin's Level 5 modest and obsessive leaders there are other examples of types of leader and leadership that may also be successfully utilized at certain times. In Michael Maccoby's assessment, part of the failure in western management is the splitting of work roles into hierarchically ordered chunks, creating the situation of silos and a lack of collaboration. He further muses that western management's inability to understand or replicate what the Toyota system of "humanware" meant, reflects on this missing 'systems intelligence' piece. 'Systems intelligence' enables the development of a whole socio-technical-business system. It requires leaders, not just with high IQ, but the personality, social and technical skills to run them. High emotional intelligence captures a large part of this 'systems intelligence' piece.

Maccoby's theory is that this inability in the west contrasts starkly by an ability in Asia to combine Asian philosophy and cultural tradition. "Chinese philosophy is holistic, relating opposites like yin the female principle, and yang the male principle. The Japanese daimyo tradition of feudal knighthood combined the Way of bu (the arts of swordsman, archery, horsemanship) with the way of bun (the arts of calligraphy, poetry composition, painting). In the west both these arts and these gender energies are separated. Not only that they are organized in a hierarchy."[9] A clear example of how gender binaries separate characteristics, abilities, and powers. And a possible clue as to why corporations in the west struggle with issues around non-collaboration and non-inclusive work cultures.

When we interviewed the sample group of senior leaders, it was clear that the majority of the males and females had limited knowledge around what the precise issues are regarding stereotyping. Without the ability to be aware of exactly what was going on it was difficult to talk about and name it. Women had negative experiences and stories which they often related in broad terms. Males saw negative behaviors and consequences in broad terms. It all pointed to the issues around the double bind that women experience, which are born from bias in stereotyping.

Stereotypes, according to Catalyst, "by their nature create an invisible block to women advancing because by their very nature they are often not conscious and difficult to discern."[10] This would explain why, of the males in the group asked, most were unaware of what precisely it was that held women back. This led to the suggested easy go-to excuses like baby bearing, work life balance, and a lack of confidence. These are all factors which undoubtedly play a part, but they do not tell the whole story. These are the observable things, but it is often the results of the non-observable things, - unrealistic societal expectations, belonging or non-acceptance in a referent group, incongruity with adherence to expected gender norms, - that can have a very negative impact on women's behavior and leadership aspirations in the work place.

As one of the interviewees, a female executive, stated when asked how she felt gender might have impacted her in business she said: "You are damned if you do, damned if you don't!" she voiced the similarly used, but somewhat more desperately stated phrase used in the Catalyst study of 2007 on the double bind dilemma for women in leadership. This goes further. "You are damned if you do, *doomed* if you don't".

Men are largely seen as leaders by default, the "think-leader-think-male" mindset touched on earlier. Our conditioning goes so deep that "atypical leaders", women in our culture, who try to perform the traditional "masculine behaviors" are "damned if they do, doomed if they don't" if they meet this gender stereotype. Behaving this way is a violation of gender norms and women are penalized for it in numerous ways.

Gendering leadership creates a double bind

As another female CEO put it: "It's just a complete minefield. No matter what you do you'll either be disliked for being strong, or ineffectual if you are nice." "I have experienced a woman leader being extremely assertive, 99% of the time getting her point approved. However, she was seen as aggressive and not flexible with a strong personality," a male senior sales VP in a medical device company explained. This kind of feedback tells us that women are penalized for being strong, because their behavior does not conform to the gender norms in our society.

One male leader did say, "As men we need to challenge our own perceptions of what women are and hire more of them." He personally had an active policy of hiring returning mothers because, in his experience, they were very loyal and had a great ability to juggle different tasks. He facilitated their engagement by ensuring that they had the flexibility to work from home if they wanted to. This is evidenced in more companies, especially in the time of Covid-19, yet it does not prove that these companies are committed to opening *leadership* roles up to females.

A senior saleswoman in her mid-40's said, "I've been told I'm aggressive. If they'd said intense, I'd understand it, but aggressive I find offensive. Being described as a Rottweiler or a firecracker I find derogatory and negative." As she went on to explain "When you're in a culture where it's OK for things like that to be said, I don't want to manage the people." She gave thus her reasons for not progressing. This was a woman who had been the number 1 sales representative of a top 20 pharmaceutical company for the last 3 years in a row. Handling other internal projects, besides her main role, she should have been poised for promotion long ago.

If women are under attack for their behaviors this is hardly ideal for an environment that wants to groom the next set of senior leaders. Being called a Rottweiler, predator or bitch these days has replaced what being called a lesbian 20 years ago stood for. A threat to patriarchy, a threat to our constructs of what gender roles should represent. If women step out of the behaviors expected from them in a heterosexual gender role narrative, to Pharr's point, they still risk being labelled too strong.

Stepping out of gender role by being either too strong or too soft, neither being acceptable in a leader you can take seriously, is a constant problem for women leaders. 'Bitches' are a threat to masculinity because it's not their job to give the orders it's the men's. And that's a problem for everyone who's bought into a patriarchal system on some cultural level. It's also a problem for male leaders who demonstrate humility and a lack of 'charisma', yet who were proven by Collins to be the best at leading great companies.

If, as a woman, you're getting feedback from some sources you're too soft and from others you're abrasive, then apart from being very confused, you can probably be very confident that you're flexing well between the two styles women have to exhibit of taking charge and taking care in order to succeed. You can also be confident that the ones giving the feedback are the ones with bias. Yet the reality is that this is exhausting for women. If such behaviors and comments are given free reign it is unrealistic to expect that such things do not have a very negative impact on women.

Women drop out, or they assimilate to more masculine behaviors, in an attempt to navigate an unequal work environment. Rather than putting into question women's leadership style it may well be more useful to question the perceptions and the structures that currently govern our impressions and expectations. Organizations can and should lead in this questioning. Coaching is a highly effective medium for doing this. Questioning perceptions and limiting beliefs can quickly expose their unconscious presence, inadequate view of the truth, and dilute their potential for causing damage.

While strong leaders are often respected for passing tough but necessary policies, women doing this will be socially penalized in ways men are far less likely to experience. When you are constantly shunned by your referent group, or as you climb the corporate ladder, have no discernible referent group anymore, since your gender is not well-represented, your satisfaction and feelings of belonging and positive influence simultaneously diminish. This has been demonstrated in many studies, including A Great Place to Work study carried out in 2017.[11]

7

As women achieve higher levels of seniority their job satisfaction can fall, and part of this may be correlated to the fact that they are outnumbered by men. Many astute women slightly further down the ladder see the hassle ahead and consciously choose not to take the next step. One senior female salesperson communicated it this way, "but if I were promoted, I'd be alone surrounded by the boys' club. I like my current team much more." Comfort in a group setting, with people who give one a sense of belonging, is incredibly important. Discomfort, which might *appear* as lack of confidence, keeps talented females from leadership roles they could excel in.

Equality creates balanced leaders

What also came out in our research was that, where there were more females than males, the double bind did not show up so readily. A senior female scientific researcher said, "The department is lead mostly by women (in meetings men are normally outnumbered by women) who are really good at articulating what their vision is and demanding good results. There is a tacit understanding that you will behave similarly, without coming across as too aggressive (they will tune out), or overly passive (they will disregard you). Therefore, you just find your voice and make yourself heard." We need to understand that, when there is greater female presence, some of the behaviors that women appear to lack in less diverse companies show up much more prominently in organizations where gender parity exists, and where pay and status are also in line.

The wider research on this shows that where women start to see female leadership as the norm they quickly adjust mentally and behaviorally. They are far less likely to feel a need to conform to a traditional feminine gender norm. This indeed is the conclusion of the 2020 Gender Gap Report which shows that the 'role model effect' is having a positive effect on the increase in the numbers of women in corporate leadership. This demonstrates again that, while individual psychology and personal development play a part, the social context and social grouping behaviors are pivotal to creating this possibility.

While the double bind has been presented as a dilemma for women most people have missed the fact that men also suffer from a double bind of their own. In understanding gender dimensions to leadership it's essential we recognize that men too have been given contradictory and inconsistent expectations.[12] As Pleck explained these expectations mean that gender norms are problematic for men, both when they do and do not conform to perceived expectations of masculinity.

Pleck writes, "men are told that to be good citizens and good human beings, they should be non-violent and respectful of women; but they are also told that to be masculine means to "kick butt" and "wear the pants in the family." Extend this to the corporate setting and the average meeting, and we can see why men often dominate the conversation and push for results, without listening thoroughly to input. They are more likely to interrupt women, and compete for leadership positions.[13] Once such behavior is established as the norm, and even culturally accepted, it's small wonder that people take on roles in the group dynamic with, at one extreme, men steam-rolling, and at the other, women self-diminishing.

In our research when we interviewed senior executives men termed one of the major stumbling blocks to women moving forward was the female's own lack of confidence, while women referred to this as a certain fear.[14] As one female CEO stated it, "Women are afraid and will not go out into a man's world". We actually know what this fear is, a limited sense of belonging, combined with possible backlash and harassment for breaking into male domains. For the women interviewed there was a prevalence of careworn weariness about the topic of leadership, and painful awareness that *many* stumbling blocks stood between them and gaining the credibility they felt they deserved. The overarching perception was that women did not have the confidence to voice what they wanted or could do because it is a constant uphill battle trying to deal with the double bind.

Giving voice to these emotions and working towards ways of identifying what the psychological threat is, and facing it anyway through coaching, can be extremely powerful for women. And by navigating this conversation and being able to give worries and behaviors labels, helps women's own inherent confidence show up. Women's number one goal is to be heard in the leadership conversation. Tricky if you're constantly interrupted, spoken over or not actively listened to. Possible if the landmines are identified and the deeper challenges commonly occurring, mostly unconsciously, are identified and discussed.

Similarly, for men, if they become aware that they are interrupting, as one example, and analyze what's behind that behavior it can be helpful. Is there a perceived psychological need to show strength and decisiveness? Do they need to be seen as the hero? Is there a fear of breaking a traditional gender norm if they don't take the lead? Might there be the consequence that they will be perceived as weak?

What is the desired outcome for the meeting? To walk away being right, but with a lack of buy in from disenchanted people? Or to get the work done with happy, engaged colleagues? Simultaneously demonstrating respect for women, and the desired behaviors which make everyone feel included, by hearing their contributions in full, as an example, doesn't need to mean a man may or does appear less agentic.

The value of coaching

Coaching can give voice to all the unconscious behaviors and triggers that may be leading to undesirable, maladaptive behaviors. Behaviors which on the one hand might serve to reinforce gender role norm binaries, but which undermine relationships and opportunities for growth and trust. Coaching fulfills two fundamental jobs for women and men. It provides a safe place for their obvious needs to be heard and understood. Secondly, it supports them with a framework they themselves develop, which capitalizes on a behavior more commonly seen in people who want to grow and improve. That behavior is that they will look to improve themselves, before considering external factors. They will look in the mirror.

This is particularly important to create when we analyze how men and women receive feedback. It has been observed that there are some differences. There can be a tendency for women more often to internalize feedback and to look to improve themselves first. We believe this is partly a desire for self-improvement, but we also believe it comes from internalizing sexism as something they themselves need to solve.

For men it is often observed that they tend to believe improvements need to happen outside of themselves. It's been suggested that this might come from how boys and girls are conditioned. While boys might be seen to get feedback more often, they might tend to disregard it. This may well come from the conditioning to be more self-reliant and agentic, which encourages boys to be independent and self-determined. The masculine norm of competitiveness may also mean feedback might feel like a threat.

Girls are more likely to be socially conditioned to consider others, relationships as paramount, and to avoid challenging feedback, instead taking it more personally. Avoiding conflict may also be a factor. We might also recognize this again as internalizing sexism on some level. A greater fear of social rejection may also come into play because so much of what being defined as female means, is tied up with success in social relationships.

We should again be careful with generalizations on gender, however, and be aware this is not always the case. Nevertheless, in our coaching we more often observe that women want to work on themselves, and some men think others, rather than themselves, need to improve. Remembering Collins' observations, the 'looking first in the mirror' behavior that the best leaders demonstrated, is something to keep in mind. It reflects an observed phenomenon more visible in women.

Being conscious of the contradictory, inconsistent and all-pervasive presence of gender binaries in working relations and dynamics, can open up valuable dialogues for exposing these. Once recognized and discussed men and women can have a greater sense of self-direction over how they might deal better in a given work context the next time.

When asking another senior sales leader from a highly successful Canadian technology company what she felt were the main issues that derailed women she said, "Traditionally women are less vocal and poor negotiators. If women are not empowered to act or feel confident, we need to raise women up and ask, 'how do we help you find your voice?'" She had implemented a coaching culture within her organization, and this was helping females build their skills in negotiating, speaking up, and practicing influence.

We observe there are two necessary components in creating gender parity. Help individuals personally develop, but at the same time create the social context and the behaviors within the social group to promote and complement this work. That can only be done through involving men at every point and recognizing that men too have many challenges. To do otherwise is to run the risk of making the challenge solely that of an individual person to solve. In the realms of inequality, with sexism ever lurking, this is dangerous ground. So, when organizations ask us to come and coach their women for leadership roles, we politely refuse to do that in isolation, and explain why.

Insights from our interviews

In the interviews we conducted different behavior and treatment was observed in the process around career progression. Women wanted their work to be recognized and wanted to be asked if they wanted a new role. Men were far more likely to proactively ask for a new role than women. A senior female in HR said, "I see men ask for opportunities and it allows us to discuss career steps. Women don't and when I talk with them, they say they didn't want me to think they were unhappy or unchallenged, so they didn't want to bring it up. Growing uncomfortable with hearing no, and feeling greedy when asking, inhibits them, but not every leader will open that door for them."

This again demonstrates the two aspects to creating gender parity. Give women the skills to speak up, but also create the space to allow them to do so. Even more importantly, recognize this reluctance as a behavior which has served a purpose in an unequal world. Rather than expecting women to behave differently, show up as a leader and ask them proactively. The men interviewed assumed if women did not ask for a role, they did not want it. Once everyone understands the cultural and psychological basis behind why women often don't ask, it becomes incumbent on everyone not to make the assumption that they don't want leadership roles. It becomes incumbent on leaders to check before assuming. What is clear is that work done on all sides in terms of communication will close the apparent difficulties which get in the way of more women moving up the ladder.

When asked, "What do males in your organization think are the issues preventing women moving into leadership roles?" another senior female executive said cynically, "They don't give it a thought." The research ultimately highlighted the difference in the hurdles that face women and that face men. As one male Senior VP of a large chemical corporation stated when he and his team underwent some bias training at his organization, "guys often live in a goldfish bowl, it's not that they are intentionally dumb and ignorant." There is a very clear need here to help men understand what the issues are facing women and to help them out of the goldfish bowl. But in parallel both men *and women* need to understand what the issues for men are, that may be exacerbating the goldfish bowl effect.

There's also a very clear need to recognize that men too are limited by gender bias and stereotyping, and when we recognize this we work much more effectively together. Being expected to be the successful breadwinner and default leader, while being simultaneously labelled as having less ability for empathy and only able to approach things from a logic-based standpoint, all examples of the types of societal expectations and stereotypes men face, are just as damaging for men.

Taking care and emotional intelligence

As noted in the Catalyst report, many leadership behaviors are stereotypically associated with women. This presents an opportunity to look at these 'take care' behaviors. Where men need to improve in these areas they too can be coached to excellent effect, helping them also become more effective leaders. Men have empathetic skills inherently but stereotyping and fear of violating male gender norms can hide them from consciousness, as we discussed in the studies in chapter 5.

At a time when high Emotional Quotient is being seriously recognized as fundamentally important for leaders to have, the research showing that men are as capable of having empathy and insights as women, is also welcome and very helpful. Coaching on 'take care' behaviors might just enable leaders to more actively create organizations where diversity goes with the territory, and it becomes less likely they will select based on someone who 'looks like them'.

Clearly education around stereotyping and biases is essential but coaching can go further.[15] The McKinsey report Changing Companies Minds about Women stated that "it was important to change male mind-sets about women. This started by "changing their own mind-sets: all transformations start with self; leaders influence everyone else in the organization through their attitudes and actions." And it's an ongoing process.

You don't vacuum once thinking the house is clean forever. You also shouldn't put that vacuum cleaner in the hands of women alone. It's up to everyone to roll their sleeves up and clean. We are confronted by biases on a daily basis in who we meet, in the media, and in our own conditioning. The existence of stereotypes in gender polarizes people into rigid, false definitions.

Finding clarity on what a woman's goals are is essential. Coaching women on getting over limiting beliefs about asking for what they want and coaching them in these conversations can be invaluable. Yet having a better understanding that fear within the social context is far more at play than at the individual level for women, is even more essential. That fear is shame, experiencing the contradiction between gendered identity, societal expectations and what women and men would want for themselves to self-actualize. Strategies to achieve this might include coaching on role playing influence conversations where the woman uncovers, practices and then states what she wants.

Understanding the deeper psychological issues

Coaching organizations to understand the importance of asking all of their employees what they want next and developing a clear career path through coaching enables organizations to demonstrate their commitment. But having the sensitivity, emotional and social awareness around what inhibits these conversations is an essential skill many people lack. Addressing these deeper psychological barriers by coaches qualified in the psychological, sociological and emotional barriers existing in the gender dimensions in leadership discussion will make or break inclusivity drives.

A lack of this deeper knowledge is the reason most such initiatives have failed to this point. Having this deeper understanding of the barriers recognized and discussed has proven to be invaluable in helping companies develop succession planning, leadership development and high-performance cultures. Having these is likely to retain top female talent and competent other-serving men. Fundamentally understanding emotions and psychological drivers gives men a richer understanding that what they perceived to be the barriers for women were not. Armed with such knowledge they are then truly able to advocate for women.

Quotas alone won't work

The recognition of gender balance creating better decisions was highlighted by one of the interviews conducted with a CEO who talked about his own board which has 3 women and 4 men. "It is such a good sparring base for getting things done", he said. If a board of directors is made up solely of men, and if they are to demonstrate true leadership and shore their board up against the possibility of bias, they will need to be proactively willing to share that power, wealth and influence by ensuring a minimum of 20% representation of females.[16] 20% appears to be the tipping point number at the decision-making level that correlates most with a company's higher performance. Increase female leadership to 30%[17] and this can add an additional 6 percentage points to its net margin.[18]

A 'token broad on the board', for political correctness or because California just passed a law to say all corporations' boards have to have one female on them will not suffice.[19] That is ineffectual tokenism. In our framework the Tokenists have the intention to include everyone but still have unconscious bias. Just giving away places without recognizing biases is an insufficient strategy in isolation. We should keep top of mind Pharr's comment in this when she writes: "Tokenism is the method of limited access that gives false hope to those left behind and blames them for 'not making it'. It also builds resentment in those other groups now *not* being considered for positions through quota approaches." We've fought for a share in power, but there's still no equality. Good leaders need to do what it takes to get gender parity in senior leadership at the behavioral level right. Expose bias, actively include all genders and practice small inclusive behaviors consistently.

The misdiagnosis

We are currently experiencing unprecedented levels of burnout in the corporate world. The number one reason for burnout? Employees feeling unfairly treated. Unfair treatment includes everything from "bias, favoritism and mistreatment by a co-worker to unfair compensation or corporate policies."[20] A break in trust with one's managers, the executive leadership or teammates "breaks the psychological bond that makes work meaningful" states Gallup. This is particularly an issue for women and is largely the reason so many drop out of the running for senior leadership roles. Bias against women taking on leadership roles is still huge. The problem is most companies, most coaches, most HR departments, most media miss this psychological effect on women. But catching this key psychological effect is key to the problem and key to the solution.

More fundamentally than this most companies, coaches, and HR departments and most media actually misdiagnose psychological distress. This misdiagnosis is the favorite fall back for most leadership coaches helping leaders find 'leadership presence'. You'll read about it in most blogs on empowering women and the best sellers on what women need to do to be successful in the corporate world. You'll see it referenced in most articles on successful leadership. All these intelligent, well-researched, experienced, yet themselves unconsciously biased individuals, give another name for this psychological distress because they don't recognize it as such. Remember they also suffer unconscious bias, as we all do.

It means we tell ourselves beautiful lies about why women don't get leadership roles. This misdiagnosis of psychological distress and of identity threat has another label entirely. Another label that fools us all into thinking we need to focus our attention on women as individuals.

What's the mistaken diagnosis given to women most of the time? That women lack confidence. But lack of confidence or more often *perceived* lack of confidence, is a symptom – it's not the cause of fewer women in senior leadership roles. And addressing symptoms not causes doesn't cure the disease.

If you're brave enough to have come this far can you now deal with the ugly truth and tackle the disease?

Key Points

We often look for confident charismatic leaders, but research has shown that modest, other-serving leaders build great companies.

Humility and inspiring others to have high standards are crucial leadership traits.

We may stereotype leadership behaviors into masculine and feminine skills. By doing this we may downgrade softer skills and emotional intelligence, and too highly prize assertiveness, dominance and individual problem-solving.

Stereotyping leadership traits as masculine or feminine limits everyone. It also creates a hierarchy of roles, which can lead to silo thinking and less collaboration within organizations.

Being able to recognize and name these tendencies is an essential first step.

Gendering leadership creates a double bind for women, while it is seen as incongruent with femininity.

Creating more equality in assigning leadership roles can lead to more balanced leadership.

Perceptual and behavioral coaching for both men and women is very effective in creating behavior change and accountability. It works best at both the individual and at the group level.

Coaching everyone on emotional intelligence core competencies is highly relevant.

Understanding the deeper psychological issues for men, women and those who identify in some other gendered way is essential.

We perceive women lacking confidence, but this is often a misdiagnosis.

Self-reflective coaching questions and considerations

What leadership traits are most prized in your corporate culture?

What do you believe are the most important leadership traits?

How can you widen your leadership tool kit to develop traits you'd like to work on?

How can you create a coaching culture?

How might gendering leadership traits have limited your leadership repertoire?

How might gender norms have influenced a positive or a negative response to behaviors from others?

What traits do your team value?

What traits do they see you demonstrating?

How might measuring emotional intelligence help you better understand yourself and your people?

Consider how confidence or competence are assumed or might be missing in your people.

How might that be affecting the culture?

How might that affect people's perception of being treated fairly?

Consider brain-storming a new definition of leadership for yourself and your organization.

8 Confidence does not equal competence

I try to buy stock in businesses that are so wonderful that an idiot can run them. Because sooner or later one will.

Warren Buffett, American investor

Two groups are lost in the desert after their plane has crashed. Each group has a list of survival items they need to rank. One group is told to decide as a team on the importance of each item. The other group is told to choose a leader who will have ultimate say on managing the group discussion, the ranking of the items and the ultimate submission. After 10 minutes the groups are told how well the individuals are doing when their list is compared to that of a survival expert.

Something interesting happens with the second group. 45% of the time the second group decides *not* to choose the individual ranked as having the *highest expertise* about the task as leader. Instead they choose a new leader, usually someone taller, louder and more confident.

The first group, through conscious collaboration, invariably does well on the test. The 45% subset of the second group, who've decided to appoint a new leader, and thus to choose perceived confidence above competence perform the worst. Every year at Stanford University students are set this team building test, and every year the results show up again.[1] What we learn from this is that a lot of people are pretty bad at selecting good leaders. They will often select on perceived authority, confidence and the ability to persuade. But when it comes to results these things should never trump competence.

Competence is essential

Research has shown that the effectiveness of a leader of a group and that group's level of success will directly correlate to how competent that leader is and the position of influence they have within the group.[2] In a study done between Stanford University and the Erasmus School of Business in Rotterdam three different groups were set up. The first had an expert in the task who was also given a clear role as leader of the group. The second group worked in a collaborative way with no leader. The third group worked with a leader who had no deep knowledge of the expertise required in the task.

Comparing each teams' performance, the ones where the expert led did the best, followed by the collaborative teams, a nod to the power of inclusivity. Teams led by a leader who did not have competence in the field required did far worse. Taken together these studies remind us of Jim Collins' findings. We have a propensity to select charisma and confidence above competence and this can be damaging to our results. Combine this with our propensity to choose louder male leaders because of a bias towards perceived confidence and authority that men are stereotypically assumed as having, and we risk failing to access competence in females and quieter, more humble males.

The first study ultimately tests how good people are at recognizing good leadership. The results are sobering: 45% of the population are *not* good at this. As Tomas Chamorro-Premuzic has stated, we may be asking the wrong question with Why don't we have more women in leadership? and might be better served asking the question why *do* so many incompetent men become leaders?[3]

Case study - WeWork

If you want a real, larger than life example of this, look no further than the extreme of WeWork and its former CEO Adam Neumann. The individual and organization provide a stark example of the danger of choosing confidence and charisma over competence in a leader.

While Neumann smoked weed on his private jet, buoyed on a wave of apparent financial success from his high-tech working spaces for the actively mobile work force, the holes in his management and financial numbers became clearer and clearer. In preparation for an IPO, after an initial valuation of $90 billion by Goldman Sachs and $60 billion by JP Morgan, his company's valuation plunged to just $15 billion.

The public offering was delayed after general discontent with his management style gained attention. These concerns echoed from Silicon Valley through to the financial institutions of New York. Concern should be something of an understatement. Corporate governance could not quite believe the number of conflicts of interest within the company, while Silicon Valley laughed at the ineptitude and lack of detail in the IPO prospectus. This reportedly charismatic, ambitious force of nature, doubtless the more so because of his giant 6'5" stature, claimed revenues of $2 billion per annum while in actuality the company had losses of $1.6 billion annually.

All smoke (in this case marijuana) and mirrors, presumably the ones he enjoyed looking at himself in (but not in the way Collins' recommended leaders do so), Neumann appears to have demonstrated the kind of narcissistic behaviors we seem to accept in leaders. While proclaiming himself as nothing short of a demi-god, - in the past he's asserted he'll be president of the world one day and live forever, claims reported by employees who worked with him, - one has to wonder how such self-obsession reels people in. Sadly, such egotistical rhetoric does, however, as we know from research that narcissism does indeed attract followers.

We tend to be magnetically pulled towards strong, charismatic individuals. When Neumann had the apparent narcissistic gall to try to sell rights to the use of the word 'We' to the company from a private entity he owned for $5.9 million dollars it almost went unchecked. Luckily there is a God, it's not Neumann, and this attempt to personally profit at least failed. Unfortunately, many others however succeeded.

Focus on the company, not just the leader

But let's keep a clear head for a moment and try not to let our emotions run away with us. That's exactly what Nori Gerardo Lietz did when she suggested we put emotions aside and just look at the numbers, the objective measurables we propound as relevant in this book.[4] It seems the IPO prospectus, not unlike the man, played up to the positives, talking up short term perceived value, in this case something they called 'contribution margin', - free rental from landlords that would disappear over time and therefore be a future cost to the business. Simultaneously the prospectus didn't mention major expenses incurred. The ultimate lesson according to Leitz: "Any corporate leader with the intent of going public must let the company, not the individual, be the focus of attention. One needs to establish the corporate mission, lead by example, and let the company's actions, not the founder's verbiage, speak for itself."

Our point being, individuals rather wrapped up in themselves and displaying such confidence and charisma are unlikely to be the ones that run great companies. Collins' meta-analysis showed it and this case study proves it again. What Lietz observed was that Neumann took advantage of being an emerging company under the Jump Start Our Business Start-Ups Act 2012, which allows companies to apply for IPO with lower standards. For the most vigilant among you we'd hope you'd spotted that the standards of the company mirror the standards of the individual.

We see potential in both men and companies run by men far too readily, and in women who could very ably run companies, not readily enough.

For those of us who believe in a just world so far there's no happy ending to this, as there so often is not with these stories of huge wealth, arrogance, greed and the apparent confidence which veils the incompetence behind it.[5] Neumann, rather than falling, appears to have landed on his often-bare feet.[6] Receiving a payout of $1.7 billion just to get him out of the CEO role, while thousands of employees have lost their jobs and the value in their shares has plummeted, his

7

star continues to shine if at least not rise in the short term. Not only this but the severance package he received included an annual payment of $46 million dollars to continue to consult to the new leadership team at WeWork. That's higher than the total compensation of all but nine public CEOs' in the United States in 2018.

The pertinent observation to make here is this wildly over-confident, incompetent male mobilized thousands. And it was not just employees apparently swayed by his encouragement to party hard, drink tequila and smoke weed while at work - bizarrely not a red flag to a possible lack of personal integrity and propensity to squander company money.

Neumann also wooed the businessman Mr Masayoshi Son of Softbank, who ultimately bailed out WeWork. Was this difficult? Apparently not. Son purportedly promised $4.4 billion to Neumann within 12 minutes of meeting him and hearing his pitch. Something many a female led start-up enterprise can only dream of![7] It's surely a baffling display of lack of due diligence on the part of Son, and larger than life proof that charisma and confidence carry great, but illogical weight, when it comes to people's perceptions of competence.

When competence is not the priority

Blindness to competence is a real danger in 'blitzscaling', whereby a company's accelerated market domination takes precedent over the actual ability to be profitable.[8] In such stories there are so many enablers, not least the various venture capitalists and investment companies. For example, "the seemingly untouchable silver-haired leader of JP Morgan Chase, Jamie Dimon – now facing criticism for not seeing, or overlooking, the train wreck." This is how Eliot Brown reported the demise of WeWork, and one of the investment companies involved, in a Wall Street Journal article.[9] A train wreck that's been costly, with many employees being laid off over the years. More recently there have been claims of gender discrimination on a grand scale with Medini Bardhi, former Chief of Staff to Neumann, filing a complaint with the Equal Employment Opportunity

Commissioner, after she was demoted following each of her pregnancies.

When Bardhi returned from maternity leave, she was allocated a new boss, who was given her original job title and a vastly increased salary. In fact, $425,000 more than she had been paid. Gender pay gaps, stories of sexual assault, and lack of clarity in goals have all been filed against WeWork. These are the kinds of issues that pervade when incompetence reigns and women's rights are not protected. As the title of a piece in the Los Angeles Times by Sarah Greene Carmichael aptly states, gender bias and discrimination does tend to be an indicator of an incompetent organization.[10] Work on bias and end discrimination as leaders and you are deep in the responsible, competent work a well-managed company needs to do to be just that, well-managed. And profitable by the way, - something WeWork was not.

There's another take away to what we'd argue is an extreme example of the kind of hubris, mismanagement and abuse of power and money that's going on in a diluted form in many a corporate entity. Such stories and ways of supposed leadership may be under more scrutiny. Though we're sure most reading this story would have preferred to see a punishment rather than a pay out, there is at least movement by boards to hold CEOs and founders more accountable. It's on this point that other CEOs and leaders would do well not just to lean in, but to sit up and pay attention. There are increasing requirements to have more female representation on boards, equal pay and positive in-house survey results which prove that the organization *is* actually diverse *and* inclusive.

To those of us who have a strong belief in fairness and justice $1.7 billion and a non-executive role on the board for Neumann seem a little hard to swallow. Certainly, to the 150 workers at WeWork who wrote a letter to their bosses referencing "this story of deception, exclusion and selfishness playing out at the company's highest levels," there's little consolation.[11] And while these representatives claim, "We don't want to be defined by the scandals, the corruption and the greed exhibited by the company's leadership", - a cynic might ask how many of them enjoyed those tequila-fuelled office parties when life seemed good as an employee?

One can't help but be reminded of the fact that 45% of the population consistently appoint flamboyant, confident leaders, but this focus does not guarantee effective leadership. The point being, we all need to open our eyes to certain behaviors in leaders that should signal their ineptitude, and ask ourselves critically who's paying for all this? And is there competence behind the seeming confidence?

Remember Collins observation that there's often a propensity to select flamboyant, celebrity leaders and to de-select potential Level 5 leaders, simply because they may appear rather hum drum, serious and humble. Accountability is becoming greater, which shouldn't be bad news for those leaders doing the right thing. It just comes too late sometimes. But maybe not. Just as this book goes to press Neumann is suing Son for the $1.7B that he didn't pay him after all. Ironically, for Son's 'abuse of power'.[12] And Neumann's then?

Equality is a sign of good management

It's instructive to look at the WeWork concerns that matter to the workers now the bubble in leadership has burst. Their list of demands included that allegations of sexual misconduct and harassment should be taken seriously. They also asked that diversity and inclusion activities should materialize into real action, not just things to talk about. Finally, they asked that salary transparency should be surfaced to deal with systemic inequalities. If we as leaders are not doing these things proactively, the signal we are likely to send is that incompetence proliferates in our organization.

Remember Uber and how Fowler's concerns were brushed under the carpet by HR? And look at what happened to Uber just a few weeks before her infamous blog came out. #DeleteUber was a social media drive to encourage customers to delete the app and cancel accounts after the company was seen to be profiting from striking workers who decided not to offer taxi services in reaction to President Trump's travel ban.[13]

Deemed to be supportive of Trump's highly controversial executive order to ban refugees and immigrants from entering the United States, the bad publicity which resulted from Uber's unfair treatment of drivers as well as stories of a culture of sexual harassment massively battered its reputation. And it seems neither time nor a massive cash injection to build up positive PR does much to make the memories diminish as the company still struggles to rebuild its reputation two and a half years on.[14]

Want to convey the image that ours is a company that's competent and does really have an excellent work and community culture, not the ironic smoke and mirrors "We" of WeWork, (that was actually more about him)? Then doing these things will uncover those things. Follow Green Carmichael's advice if there is sexual harassment, pay gaps and pregnancy discrimination in the company. These should act as a strong signal to us of mismanagement, like "canaries in the coal mine", as Carmichael puts it. If we are not prepared to address them as leaders, we *are* mis-managing our organization - even if we don't skateboard bare foot with a tequila shot and joint in hand!

It brings us to another case study, but this time we'll use a female, Elizabeth Holmes of Theranos-fame. Holmes as a white woman was regarded as the darling of the venture capital world for a moment because she had apparently broken the glass ceiling. Holmes' story embodied many people's idea of the dial finally turning on fairer gender representation in the world of technology. Notice the common elements with Neumann, however. Other than being female the story is not dissimilar. Bold, confident in her self-presentation and self-promotion Holmes' claim was that the analysis of people's blood could be revolutionized to solve a multitude of health problems. Despite the dubious science she managed to raise $700 million in venture capital and run an operation over a number of years to develop this.

Everyone was turning somersaults that a female had finally broken into the Silicon Valley world. This had nothing to do with equality though. This was a white female infiltrating the power of white men and some women who were cutting a share of a dubious deal. There's a very big difference with this and equality. Holmes achieved this by using just those tactics that many of us fall for.

Holmes and Neumann simply represented players in systems where egos and greed might actually be the leaders of sense and soberness. Noticeably Holmes demonstrates just those traits that might have made her subconsciously more like the people whose money she needed. A very deep voice, tall, wearing turtlenecks not unlike those of Steve Jobs, the assimilation of masculine traits was duly noted. Few people thought to question the actual science, except for Dr Phyllis Gardner, a Stanford professor who was always sceptical of the claims.

The enemies again here are our somehow being reassured when we see a trait stereotyped as masculine, confidence. The case shows biases go beyond gender to traits that in themselves might not be the best to elevate. They are upheld by structures, power plays, and serious blind spots. These are compounded by travelling up blind alleys and turning blind eyes. People's hope for the next innovation in shiny charismatic, packaging.

One further difference. Certainly, critics laugh at Neumann, but Holmes is being hauled over the coals for her inadequacies and liabilities. We see here the double standard we apply to the mistakes of men and women. We raise eyebrows at him, but we want her blood. All of it, not just the one drop. Just as at WeWorks, there are many people involved in the demise of Theranos. We accept that raising huge amounts of capital on the illusion of a successful venture is part of the venture capital game.

Neuman gets away with it, with a tap on the wrist. Holmes seems to be being indicted for possible crimes that plenty of other people might surely also be privy to. But no, we put it all on her shoulders. Double standards really do cause twice the pain. And they certainly don't lead to gender parity, even in our social disapproval, as we explain in the next chapter. White men can fail but it not immediately be attributed to their sex, but them as individuals. For women who fail it's their sex that's relevant, not their individuality, and we make them pay hard.[15]

Some women lack safety, not confidence

What's fascinating about this topic around overarching ambition and confidence is how there's a flip side when we consider women. It's lack of confidence that's so often cited as a major hurdle for women going for senior leadership roles. But if we take onboard the evidence that women feel disillusioned and victims of bias then it should not come as a surprise that they may *appear* less confident. Burnt out employees exhibit lower levels of confidence. According to Gallup, "even if they stay," burnt out employees "typically have 13% lower confidence in their performance and are half as likely to discuss how to approach performance goals with their manager."[16]

Let's remind ourselves of the top three reasons for burn out: unfair treatment, unmanageable workload and lack of clarity in the role. Unsurprisingly we coach men and women all the time on precisely these kinds of issues. While bias is prevalent but still needs to be acknowledged on a conscious level by most organizations and individuals, the issues beneath overwork and lack of clarity of role can also be linked back to the distress felt by women.

Overwork can often exist for a number of reasons. First that high competency threshold is enmeshed in many women's work ethic. Women may tend to work harder simply in order to be seen as just as good, while knowing that any errors will be penalized more harshly and remembered for longer. The humorous-to-some adage that "women have to work twice as hard as men to be seen as half as good – luckily this isn't hard" while drawing scorn from some, and a knowing nod of the head by others, is only half true. It *is* hard and exhausting, judging by the higher levels of burnout found among women.[17]

It is also very common for women to be given extra support tasks as well as main tasks. Couple this with it being socially undesirable for women to appear 'not nice' by turning work away, even if they are already overloaded, and you create a lethal cocktail for over work. Now add to this a lack of clarity in the role, often caused by poorer quality feedback provided less often, and subjective job performance expectations, and this creates a very negative environment for many women.

Confidence *does not* equate to competence and while some men are perceived as having more confidence it does not mean they are more competent at senior leadership roles. And a lack of confidence does *not* equate to a lack of competence. This is why the default to a 'lack of confidence' in women, (and often men who appear to 'lack ambition'), as the excuse of why more don't reach senior leadership needs to be scrutinized much more closely. Responsible leaders need to do this. Bertrand Russell had it right when he said, "The fundamental cause of the trouble is that in the modern world the stupid are cocksure, while the intelligent are full of doubt."[18]

Unfairness becomes acute for some women over time and they are often unprepared to 'play the game' anymore. They often realize that they are only successful if they play to stereotypically masculine behaviors. This means that many feel a conflict between being authentic and being effective as individuals. Rather than being just another voice adding to the 'group think', invariably male and white, which already exists, they'd prefer to find their purpose somewhere else.

The Dunning Kruger effect is pervasive

It's very often the kind of driven confident personalities we want and think will set the world on fire, that can often think they are far better than they actually are at things. This lack of self-awareness blinds them to their own inabilities. We touched on this earlier, but the Dunning Kruger effect is real and does have implications in people's abilities to be self-aware. The results of Dunning's and

Kruger's study showed that people, often with the least ability, can end up in power because they are over-confident about what they can do.[19]

This over-confidence is often part of the reason we see big gaps between how high some people perceive their emotional intelligence to be and how low others rate them in demonstrating it. It's exactly the reason we should be sceptical of over-confident people and more open to modesty. Confidence just might be the ultimate red herring. The ultimate paradox. We're reminded of Horrock's assertion, "To become the man I was supposed to be … I also had to pretend to be both more powerful and less powerful than I feel".

We should also remember the lesson we learnt from the most current neuroscience. "The claim that science tells us that the possibility of greater merging of gender roles is unlikely because of "natural" differences between the sexes, focuses on average sex differences in the population — often in combination with the implicit assumption that whatever we think men are "more" of, is what is most valuable for male-dominated roles. (Why else would organizations offer confidence workshops for women, rather than modesty training for men?)"[20] Indeed, we should be asking this. Why do we?

Often in the DE&I discussion, where implicit bias is rife, people also don't know what they don't know, specifically the Homogenists. So, the Dunning Kruger effect is not only helpful in alerting us to the fact that apparent confidence might not be competence after all, but in fact might actually be a sign of incompetence. The Homogenists in our framework lack both awareness of their own bias and are low in their ability to include others. These might well be the same people who by definition have the least cognitive ability to see their own bias. We may actually be hiring these kinds of people both as our leaders *and* as the most incapable people to move the dial on DE&I.

Cultural Cognition Theory

Elitist thinking may be more detrimental still though. If we are in this quadrant our over-inflated self-view can be tantamount to "view from up here" thinking, to go back to Rosling's earlier analogy. In something called the cultural theory of risk, studies have shown that we tend to perceive risk in a way that *affirms our understanding of social structures and our place within them*. This can lead us to denying the existence of risk in certain situations, simply because that risk is replaced by a greater fear, something that might affect our particular advantage within society.

Kari Norgaard observed this manifest as socially organized denial operating at the country level. She interviewed inhabitants of Norway about how they reconciled the change in the weather and the obvious signs of global warming.[21] What she noticed was that many people appeared to be in denial about climate change, despite the fact that ski slopes had less snow in the Winter season, as just one example of its proof. This, in a country where many people's raison d'être is to ski, because there was historically always abundant snow.

Norgaard linked this denial to other advantages the country and social group had. The relatively newly acquired extreme wealth of Norway due to the discovery of oil and gas, and of course it's use, which ultimately leads to global warming, is one such advantage.[22] Regarding themselves as a population of intelligent individuals, who believe themselves to be globally responsible citizens, individuals appeared to find it difficult to reconcile that their own actions might lead to a threat to the climate. The resultant observed behavior was inaction to implementing policies to protect the environment. Not just inaction, the behavior extended to refusal to acknowledge climate change as a real risk. This is socially organized denial.

Dan Kahan, a Professor of Psychology from Yale Law School, has researched the cultural theory of risk. Put simply this theory states that people's perception of facts is shaped by their values. For these individuals, expert scientists are only perceived as experts if their research espouses these individuals' groups' position. They "are also more likely to accept misinformation and resist the correction of it when that misinformation is identity-affirming rather than identity-threatening."[23] In other words, if it suits their position, they'll acknowledge incorrect facts as correct, even if they are not.

There are a number of reasons for such denial, but sociologists recognize that it's rooted in social anxiety triggered when activities are socially stigmatized. If those same activities symbolize a person's world view, and their place in it, this stigmatization could lead to loss of status. The prospect of loss of status can create such social anxiety which blinds people to risk. So, to return to the country analogy, Norgaard argued that many people cannot reconcile both the need to prosper from the vast fossil fuel resource in Norway, and the global damage that using that resource creates. Denying global warming then is the strategy of choice. The experts' information doesn't fit comfortably with their day to day reality, so many Norwegians don't perceive the risk as real.

To quote Kahan, "Cultural cognition refers to the tendency of individuals to confirm their beliefs about disputed matters of fact (e.g., whether humans are causing global warming; whether the death penalty deters murder; whether gun control makes society more safe or less) to values that define their cultural identities."[24] This is the bias we find within our society and ourselves that may blind us to risks. But we need to have the humility to recognize experts who know more than we do and be open to that message, even if it challenges our world view. Incompetent leaders cannot do this. Competent ones can. Indeed, they ensure they have such people at the table.

The white male effect

It turns out this acceptance of facts from experts is an even greater challenge if you are a white male. "White male effect" is a gendered-racial phenomenon within the cultural theory of risk. Sociologists describe the white male effect as white male denial characterized as risk-skeptical white men.[25] We caveat categorically at this point, these are *some men, not all men*. These men characteristically hold individualistic and hierarchical power. They quite literally have a "view from up here", and they are looking down on everyone else, treating them accordingly, to protect their own self-interest.

A 2011 study into people's attitudes towards global warming revealed that 48% of conservative white men, described as "confident", were also confident in their belief that global warming won't happen.[26] Only 8.6% of the adult population shared their view. Meanwhile 98% of the world's scientists, the experts, believed global warming would happen. And according to the most recent data, not to mention the reported case studies across the world, global warming is happening.[27] Perhaps if a few more top people had a little more work life balance and stepped outside once in a while they might experience this firsthand themselves. As we'll discover in chapter 11 and 12 our persistence in choosing workaholics as leaders may not serve us well, for a variety of reasons, including them being out of touch with whatever exists outside the corporate bubble.

The data in the study observing white male effect further found, "conservative white males are significantly more likely than are other Americans to endorse denialist views on all five items". The five items were five indicators of climate change denial. It further found "that these differences are even greater for those conservative white males who self-report understanding global warming very well." We should remember, self-reporting as *being very good at something*, is a *common indication of low competence*. We should also remember these particular men think they know better than the experts. Clearly, on a logic level, this is impossible. Finally, though painful to some, we should remember almost half the population invariably choose these incompetent leaders, according to Stanford's annual study.

When we consider that 29% of these men also denied that climate change would *ever* happen, yet it *is* happening, the rest of us men and women, and however else we gender-identify as, *need to wake up and take action*. Many of these men have positions of economic power and policy-making power. We saw an example of white male effect and some high-profile men's denial with Covid-19's arrival.

While many of the most vocal deniers of the pandemic reacted too slowly to the need for immediate lock down, and now as this book goes to press, continue to do so in some form, cases have sky-rocketed in those countries. Beyond their high death tolls, these countries have disproportionately higher strains on health services, increased vulnerability in certain groups, domestic violence rates, inequalities in access to online education, not to mention huge unemployment rates, and economies in tatters, as *just some examples*. Indeed, many social issues have been impacted.

Poor risk assessment

Incorrect assessment of risk is the issue here. While some people assume risk is just the chance of something happening, people who can properly assess risk understand it is actually the *impact if* that thing happens. That impact itself has a further range of impacts. A pandemic is a grave event, with multiple consequences that need to be taken seriously, at so many levels across society. People good at understanding risk understand this. Sadly, self-interested types, who focus on little more than economic prosperity, are *not* among them.

More sadly still, many people, many leaders, cannot grasp the fact that climate change and environmental impact actually led to the pandemic. As we encroach on more and more wild habitats, animal diseases are increasingly likely to cross over to humans.[28] Eradication of habitats acting as carbon sinks is not just leading to increase in global temperature. It's leading to countless pathogens being unleashed from habitats where biodiversity is being compromised. While humans continue to intrude and destroy these areas, there is an amplification effect on the increase and likelihood of these diseases.

So, refusal to acknowledge one huge risk, and how that has been created, actually led to another. When things get very complex, as they do with topics like climate change, environmental impact, pandemics, interest groups, stakeholders and vulnerable sections of society, we need smart people at the table. Just to be clear we need *intellectually* smart people. Not business mavericks, who have no experience of anything else. But business mavericks, who have the brain to understand this complexity, are welcome and necessary.

Diverse and inclusive business mavericks, men and women, who can understand how the ecosystem of business itself impacts on society and the environment in complex and multiple ways, would be even better though. When we have diversity and inclusivity of all those impacted, with the intellectual capacity to deal with the complexity at hand, we have the right heads at the table. As we established back in chapter 4, those abilities are not specific to one gender, race, or any other demographic demarcation. Intellectually smart experts are very likely to be modest individuals who might rate their own skills as lower than they actually are. It's the Socratic paradox we should all look out for.[29] Which is why testing for cognitive ability in our leaders can be as necessary as testing for emotional intelligence. Both are essential in our leaders.

The risks of Covid-19 becoming a pandemic were huge and should have been obvious to any leader capable of perceiving those risks competently. It exposed many poor leaders, not just at the government level, but at the corporate level. Ironically many of these leaders claimed this pandemic was unprecedented. Since historically the world has had pandemics before, this is a naive statement. A well-read lay person, keeping abreast of science and health, has been aware for years that a pandemic is one of the major risks to the global population. World leaders, and corporate leaders, properly briefed and looking beyond their bubbles, would be aware of this threat too.

The situation in Wuhan, China, and the likelihood of spread if proper measures for containment were not urgently put in place, was repeatedly communicated by the World Health Organization. Yet world leaders, notably some white male ones, were in denial. SARS, MERS and Ebola were all dress rehearsals that came in quick succession, all occurring within the last 12 years. To a degree they were contained and mitigated. They themselves highlight the claim that a pandemic was an unforeseen event as an incompetent statement, not just by these world leaders, but leaders of many companies, and other institutions, apparently blind-sided by the idea that one could strike.

We have had 5 pandemics in 101 years, not two as many seem to assume. While the Spanish Flu pandemic of 1918 and Covid-19 have spread the most rapidly, there have been three other pandemics, Asian Flu (1957-58), Swine Flu (2009-10) and AIDS, which started in 1981 and which, while largely forgotten by many, still ravages lives today. Three coronaviruses in less than 15 years should ring a major alarm bell for any leaders competent and paying attention to interests other than their own.

According to Thomas Gillespie, associate professor of the Department of Environmental Sciences, at Emory University, "The majority of pathogens are still to be discovered. We are at the very tip of the iceberg. We fully expect the arrival of pandemic influenza; we can expect large-scale human mortalities; we can expect other pathogens with other impacts."[30] Vaccines won't help us in the short term with these challenges. Mitigating their impact by preventing their likelihood would be a better strategy. Taking care that we don't need to have the cure, would be the best approach of all. Taking charge by taking care. Caring now to prevent the need to cure later.

Notably in some countries the risks of the consequences of the pandemic were taken seriously. The facts were properly weighed, and immediate, uncompromising action was taken to lock down. In these countries the pandemic's damage has been lessened. The successful early lock down in New Zealand, Germany, and Thailand has led to a far lower death toll, and faster returns to economic movement. It did not go without notice that these were countries led by women. With so few women leaders at the country level, only 7% globally, we cannot say categorically, this proves women are better leaders. Nor do we believe there is any need to stoke a gender war. What we can see, however, is that the ability to properly assess risk in this particular scenario, may certainly have played a hand in their success. The focus on taking care of people and looking at the issues with a wide-angled lens, rather than through the microscope of economic interest, created an inclusive approach. Leaders who could see the potential impacts way beyond the economy alone, made far more intelligent judgements about how high the stakes actually were.

In stark relief countries with the most vocal leaders to initially deny the severity of the coronavirus, were all confident, conservative white males. Among these the United States, which, while having only 4% of the world population has 25% of the world's cases as of July 2020.[31] Notably Brazil and the UK, the former through bravado, the latter through lackadaisical half-committal, also have disproportionately high numbers of cases. And the effects of this incompetence, by these ironically named 'developed' countries will be felt for years to come.

Identity-protective cognition

Identity-protective cognition is part of what forms this denial. At its deepest roots, for some men, that is that being caring is not something to demonstrate but being tough is. Had these men focused on the immediate dangers of this particular disease, extremely contagious and asymptomatic in 80% of people, they could have mitigated more of its damage. The predictable exponential death toll apparently was less of a concern than keeping the economy running and staying popular. Yet the economies in these countries have been impacted far more seriously than in those countries where action was swift and uncompromising.

The massive stress placed on health services and on people's lives, rather than on the economy, ultimately would have mitigated some of the impact *on* the economy. Attending to the plight of the environment in the climate change issue is of similar concern. Protecting people rather than self-interest in remaining popular, while naively believing the risk of coronavirus not to be a 'real' one, has been costly.[32] These leaders misunderstood that not acting decisively, and not paying attention inclusively to all the groups who'd be impacted by Covid-19, would lead to more long-term difficulty. Yet they were blinded by short-term thinking.

Over-investment in masculine norms exaggerates a fear of failure, and likely leads to it

It's this same denial that means many men are uncomfortable around the gender parity in leadership discussion. Challenges to the status quo are something they want to avoid. This denial is also rooted in a fear of failure compounded by a fixed mind set mentality around what characteristics and values one should promote based on one's sex. This fixed mindset attitude can be particularly damaging. As Carol Dweck researched and showed, people with rigid definitions of themselves have a more exaggerated fear of failure.[33] So it makes sense that conforming highly to predominantly masculine or feminine gender norms might be fueling this rigid identity.

Weighing up risk and benefits for people's lives against material issues, are just one example of complex dilemmas that some men in power seem unable to resolve. This inability to properly see risk, while simultaneously making more often riskier choices, costs us all dearly. Some men may not believe that 'taking care' is the best way to deal with some of our problems. 'Might is right mentality' hijacks these men's thinking at this point. Indeed, it's the implicit structural superiority that *some men* have, that creates this right to might in the first place. Then 'Taking charge' at the expense of 'taking care' behaviors, becomes the arsenal of choice.

As Ben Hardy in Personality isn't Permanent wrote about people with fixed mindsets, "People don't want to deal with that kind of failure. It would put too big a mark on their identity."[34] Hardy explains why most people are unable to change and instead believe in the 'myth of personality'. We'd argue these myths are as pervasive around gender, as they are around other characteristics that we may believe we inherently have and are unable to change. Our over-investment in our identity, what that should apparently mean and represent, can be incredibly limiting. No where do we see it more clearly than in the binary fixed traits that we convince and reinforce to ourselves that men and women have. By doing this we may create both martyrs and monsters.

An article in Medium highlighted how 'white male effect' influences the gap between men and women, as being pervasive and widespread beyond political boundaries in our culture. "The gap between men's and women's perceptions of sexism, which after-all is a serious risk to women – economically, politically and socially, - is large on the left and the right".[35] 56.6% of men and only 34% of women think sexism is a thing of the past. Could white male effect be part of the explanation why we saw a discrepancy in our own data between men's and women's views on why there weren't more women in leadership roles? Clearly, yes.

The pandemic will likely look like a tea party compared to the effects that global warming will have on planet Earth.[36] It may well also look like one compared to other pandemics which are *highly likely to come and be more devastating*. We deny these facts at our peril. And unlike the effects of environment change, which some people may well be able to mitigate by affording to migrate, while others cannot, pathogens don't recognize wealth or human borders. Mitigating some of the devastating, and soon irreversible effects, will require robust, agile leaders who are competent in building bridges and putting the right priorities first. They also need to be competent, and we need to be careful in our assessment of confidence.

The inability to weigh risk continues to pose a huge risk to us all.

Good, competent, inclusive leaders have to recognize these dangers. We have to have the intention to acknowledge cultural cognition and the danger in putting our own interests, based on our own view of the world, as the priority. We have to have the humility to go into the difficult terrain of learning what our blind spots are, what the blind alleys are and what we may be turning a blind eye to. We need to recognize what our limiting beliefs might be. We need to be more aware of our own expectations around what being male or female 'should' mean, and whose examples we ourselves may be following for better or worse.

Long term success as a 21st century corporate leader will have a great deal to do with our ability to move into the top right quadrant, the Egalitarians. This is where we will be both inclusive and conscious of our bias. This is when we recognize the danger of identity-protective cognition, which is actually harmful, both to our own psychological health, and the wider social and environmental context. More and more employees and customers look for ethical, mission-driven, equitable corporations who *demonstrate* they have this Egalitarian mentality. They expect leaders to be able to properly assess global risks. They expect corporations to be thinking about climate change and environmental impact. They expect demonstration of care for the community. And they look for evidence in the engagement numbers. Not in the credo's and mission statements.

Talk is cheap. Questions lead to better results. Results speak for themselves.

Competence means being both able to deliver *and* being reliable in doing so. Often charismatic types talk a good talk but the deliverables behind the verbiage don't get done. False claims about ability are usually attributable to a *lack* of self-confidence, and actually if we cut to the core, self-worth. If people are arrogant or wrapped up in themselves, they rarely ask questions, so if someone is demonstrating a lot of curiosity and asking some thoughtful open questions it's a good indication that they're genuinely interested in people, rather than wanting people to be interested in them.

If you want to have strong leaders look for questioners and be one yourself. Similarly, if people are blaming others, enforcing their own agendas, it should be a very bad sign. All too often we seem to seek ambitious men who have an apparent vision. The Covid-19 debacle has exposed how poor these supposed visionaries actually are. Being visionary and proactive must include being able to adequately assess risk. It also means being responsible. Brave leaders take ownership for the results, *even* when they are bad. Cowardly leaders blame others.

We need to open our eyes and have the guts to recognize and call out these cowards.

The non-judgemental leader

To avoid charlatans, we must look for people who welcome and validate others' perspectives in a non-judgemental way. Be open to people who are willing to question things, not 'yes' people. Invite challengers who will offer other perspectives. And let's count ourselves lucky if we have people who repeatedly ask for feedback and strive to grow from that feedback. People who want and continue to grow are the wise ones. "Remember there is nothing noble in being superior to your fellow man. True nobility is being superior to your former self."[37] It's an irony that even this quote seems to have been falsely attributed to the wrong man.

Certain people, out for their own career advancement and status, should not be the personalities we choose as leaders. People, men and women, who continually talk about others, ask questions and have a clear other-serving purpose *should be*. That purpose should be wholly underscored by goals that have nothing to do with their own ego, yet everything to do with the companies' aspirations. These are the ethical characteristics we should be demanding in our leaders. These are the characteristics the world needs us to demonstrate ourselves.

The question now becomes what do you as a leader value? Aggressiveness, competitiveness, individuality, risk-taking? Relationship-focus, collaboration, being present not 'presence'? Do you even have to make a choice? Being selfless and focused on the other is probably the single most effective behavior in leadership.

Gandhi said: "A sign of a good leader is not how many followers you have but how many good leaders you create." In the days of social media and social pressure to create and have followers, many forget that this in itself proves little in isolation. Gandhi's quote is particularly poignant in an age when the narcissist is legitimized, and we assume people's popularity and ability as a leader through the number of followers they have. Even as the Stanford studies prove this is totally flawed and illogical, and Collins' work emphasizes this.

Ask yourself which of your leaders create more leaders and you've found your true leaders.

Promoting modesty

Lao Tzu said, "A leader is best when people barely know he exists, when his work is done, his aim fulfilled, they will say: we did it ourselves." This selfless humility is the very specific character trait Jim Collins uncovered in his research as being essential for the leaders who grew their companies to be the very best.[38] It is also a quality we've already cited that many women tend to display, and it's one that as a leader you should be looking out for and noticing in your employees if you're looking for leadership potential.

Yet as a culture we seem to put great weight on personality and powerful egos, and we are advising women to shout about their achievements without understanding that the social context will still influence whether that might still backfire for them, as well some know. We allow ourselves to be swept away by the illusion that authority and responsibility comes packaged in a large male ego, or mass-confidence. Yet it is large egos and over-confidence that are at odds with strong leadership.

So, rethinking our whole definition of leadership and addressing our often times illogical selection of leaders is key to addressing not just gender parity, but what underlies it. While human beings tend to select on charisma and confidence there's a greater chance these characteristics can lead to leaders asserting power and authority unethically and acting as oppressors over often more talented contributors. Selecting the best leaders is far less about gender and far more about being clear on the right skill set.

Assess and select for high emotional intelligence

By definition looking scientifically for the right skill set, doing it in a blinded fashion wherever possible, and avoiding the desire to find 'fit' and compatibility with the current tribe, will increase the number of diverse, inclusive, humble leaders. So too will assessing potential leaders on their level of emotional intelligence. Highly competent, emotionally and socially aware men and women. It also means we won't lose swathes of talented but disillusioned women, and talented but oppressed minorities. Until we do that Bertrand Russell will remain correct.

While many organizations may think they have hierarchical power over their people, legitimate power over people can only be earned through trust. When women don't feel valued that trust dies, and we see the result of this in the drop off of women at the senior leadership levels. When men with great ideas, who may be more introverted, quieter, less assertive, observe other less competent men taking the lead, they may become resentful and angry, and simply shut down.

Giving praise to others and holding blame at our own door is one of the most powerful ways to lead. Yet our ego wants recognition and dependent on the gender of the ego it wants recognition for different things. If men are held up to standards of being strong, assertive, winners successful in their careers with a heavy dose of high status for good measure, then their ego and self-esteem may feel it if they are not seen as these things in society's eyes. If women are expected to be nurturing, uninterested in ambition, supportive, then their ego and self-esteem may suffer if they are regarded as not demonstrating these qualities. And when our ego loses the recognition it needs then fear and shame leap in.

We know that success correlates negatively for women in terms of ambition, money and power. In other words, we see success as incongruent in these terms for women. We know that success correlates positively for men and aligns with aspirations for status, power and influence. But status, power and influence alone are not enough to run highly successful organizations. The ambition to be equitable supported by action may well be. The internalized forms of acceptability which the ego lives off to define itself feed our other behaviors and influence how we therefore behave.

The key lesson here is we can approach this at the individual level, dishing out well-meaning advice to women to display behaviors more similar to men, but we must keep top of mind the social context. We can tell men to be less dominating, assertive and status driven but we must keep top of mind the social context and the gendered expectations that they actually be these things.

So, while we remain in this quandary, how *do* we change the status quo?

Key Points

The Stanford annual student experiment demonstrates that nearly half the population choose less competent, confident men as leaders by default. This, even when other's competences are clearly demonstrated.

Research shows us that teams led by relevant experts perform the best.

The presence of gender pay-gaps, discrimination and harassment claims is usually a good indicator of a company that is being mismanaged.

We have to question the motives behind the ideas of the visionary leaders we may choose. Whether those motives in themselves are ethical. While they respectively talked of helping humanity by creating a revolutionary health diagnostic tool, or creating amazing communities to work in, it's well known that the core goals for both Holmes and Neumann had little to do with serving others. Elizabeth Holmes wanted to be a self-made billionaire; Neumann wanted to be the first trillionaire.

Companies are being increasingly expected to *prove* they have diversity, equality *and* inclusivity. Employee engagement numbers are a key indicator of the extent to which DE&I initiatives are actually working or failing.

Some women lack safety, not confidence, in the work environment, both physical and psychological.

The Dunning Kruger effect is pervasive to the extent that where we see over-arching confidence it may indicate the companies *least* able to achieve DE&I success.

Cultural cognition theory effects our ability to see facts that challenge our values and perceived place in society.

White male effect is a phenomenon that shows that white males are proportionally less able to properly assess risk than any other population demographic. Covid-19 and climate change provide examples of this. Inability to properly weigh risk is dangerous for everyone.

A fixed mindset that masculine qualities are essential in leadership is detrimental to making competent, balanced, decisions for the greater good.

We must be and choose other-serving, instead of self-serving, leaders.

Promoting modesty instead of confidence could solve multiple problems.

Training people on how to create safe, inclusive open places to communicate may be more effective than focusing on giving women confidence training.

Measuring emotional intelligence ensures we hire more competent people. Investment in developing people's emotional intelligence creates multiple business benefits.

Case studies

WeWork demonstrates that charismatic leaders don't necessarily run companies well. Investment companies focus all too often on individual leaders rather than the company's performance. Blitz-scaling also blinds people to this problem.

Theranos emphasizes that our bias for confidence may be even stronger than our bias for gender, and it is a misplaced one.

Self-reflective coaching questions and considerations

How might personal interests be clouding your judgement to properly assess the situation?

What uncomfortable feelings come up that might make you feel threatened or questioned?

How can you stay with this threatening feeling and explore your sense of self?

And reassess your values and beliefs?

What can you do to mitigate the effects of hiring based on charisma and confidence?

What might be possible for you and the people you serve if you considered further information, even when it at first appears threatening to you?

How ethical are the motives behind the vision?

How tied up in selflessness and serving others are the visionaries in your organization, and you yourself?

How many diverse views and facts have been reviewed to make a sensible assessment of risk?

Who are the people that appear to really care in your organization and what can you learn from them?

Consider using emotional intelligence assessments when hiring people.

Part 4

Actions

The Things We Can Do

9 If You Want Out-of-the-Box Thinking Then Don't Put Your People in Them

> It is politic to tell our own story for if we do not it will surely be told for us, and always a degree more disadvantageously than the truth warrants.
>
> Sara Coleridge, 19th Century, English author

Bias lumps people arbitrarily into groups. Those groups have perceived sets of skills, and propensities to do certain things certain ways. Through that patterning-process people get boxed. As we discussed box ticking can actually prime gender, that is the selection of certain boxes can prime our perception of ourselves, and the perception of those who view us. Depending on the prevailing stereotypes this might be good or bad.

Take the box female. There are many factors that hold women back specifically. These factors appear less likely to be experienced by males, far less recognized by them as issues. We say *appear* when actually it's very clear when coaching men and women that they more often experience similar challenges and psychological distress. These just manifest differently in the social context.

Female leadership talent development needs to be approached with new perspectives and with a different set of tools than it has been to this point. The predominance of advice has still been around fixing women's behaviors as a way to address some of the symptoms of bias for women. But rather than doing this, addressing the underlying issues instead, might mean that that advice on how they should fix themselves is not the best. From tackling our propensity to diminish ourselves, an apparent bent towards perfectionism, a preference for building rather than leveraging relationships, or a tendency to want to please others, these very positive traits are seen as useful, but only to a point.

They are seen as detrimental to getting women to the next levels in senior leadership. Is that true though? Or is it that a set of women, who've internalized sexism, are trying to fix themselves to deal with it, and help others do the same? Judging by the current trajectory, even from the better examples of companies who score well in gender parity, such as Ernst and Young, this may be the case.

Case study – The Ivy League women's startup advisor

Nicole advises women led startups who may need to seek venture capital investment. Affiliated with an Ivy League school she's advised hundreds of women on how they can increase their odds of success. She focusses on everything from shortening and strengthening their pitch and being more confident, to getting to know potential investors and seeking sponsors. All valid stuff, but we've been peddling this advice for years now. When we ask Nicole the question, what can men do to help the situation and support more successful women startups, it appears she literally cannot process this.

She responds, "well women need to be concise in their pitch. They need to be clear in their goals. They need to be selective in who they seek as an investor." They need, they need, they need. But the question was *what can men do to help?* We go in for a second attempt. Nicole is literally stumped. Her whole raison d'être is to help women. She has a tool kit for that. But she has not a clue about what men could do, no vocabulary, no words, no thought has gone into this potential option. This is internalized sexism. This is partly why we have women networks full of women. This is partly why we have women's groups trying to help women. This is why Warren Buffet asks, where are all the men, when he goes to awards ceremonies for women in business.

Might it be an option to point out to investors that women are a safe bet? Women run highly successful businesses. Women can build outstanding relationships. They are excellent in assessing risk. They are conscientious in their execution. They are amazing at looking after their customers. Are modest and humble, though this may appear as a lack of drive or lack of confidence. They are massively qualified. How can you as sensible investors *not* back them? How about go to men and say, why do you back confident men, when research shows you these are sometimes incompetent individuals? Why do you back people selling a promise when we have the proof that the business model doesn't work?

Fixing women rhetoric, internalized sexism

In our own interviews with women we asked what *men* needed to do to help women get into leadership roles. We made this frequent and fascinating observation. Did these women come up with a list of suggestions for men? No! They often did not. Indeed, they appeared to believe that men aren't interested in helping the cause of equality. Their cognitive dissonance demonstrated they just couldn't process this question, just as in the example above.

Many women have a fixed mindset that men are not interested in equality. For us it signaled just how far some women had internalized this as theirs and other women's problem to solve. This subsection of women would immediately start answering again in terms of what women needed to do. Incredible and not isolated to one or two individuals. It appears to be deep in the psyche of some women. These women held *women* solely accountable for fixing inequality, by suggesting *they* show up in a different way. And sadly, it showed a degree of sexism in their inability to consider that some men might want to and be able to help. Some men do actually believe equality is good for us all.

For them men appeared irrelevant to the equality discussion, which of course couldn't be further from the truth. Recall the idea we covered earlier by Pharr that sexism is internalized as something the person themselves need to solve. Remember it was the same belief many people have around bullying. Teach the victim to stand up for themselves. Research however shows that bullying is a group phenomenon dependent on the group endorsing the behaviors of the bully. Just as with the KiVa system the only way to solve it is to tackle it as a group, not to put the onus on the victim to do so alone.

This is the biggest problem with much of the advice for women. Women hear they need to change, and while some of the advice can be helpful for giving labels to things that might need addressing in *some* form, telling women to drop certain behaviors and adopt others is as erroneous as it is irresponsible, *without* understanding the psychological dimensions. The social context for *why* women may have adopted some of those behaviors in the first place must also be understood. It is also essential to keep refocusing everyone on things men can help with too, and what *they* may need to change.

While great leadership should not be gender specific many of the hurdles for women are, and certainly we can identify there are self-defeating behaviors we would all be better off not doing. But focusing on changing behaviors in isolation without the discussion around the possible repercussions in the social context for women who may change their behaviors, exactly because there is bias against women being leaders, is erroneous in the extreme. And understanding why some of the behaviors exist and how they can be valuable and *should also be promoted as desirable in men might be a better strategy*. Having witnessed many men coach women and vice versa we also see that without fully understanding masculine and feminine gender role norms, this coaching can *so* miss the mark.

Leadership is perceived as incongruent for women. This is essential for people to grasp in the social context. That means first we don't naturally choose women. Remember the Stanford study from chapter 8, and the think leader, think male workshop observations in chapter 7. We also know when asked who to choose for a risky business deal, most executives will select male over female. Most females will *also* select male over female.[1] But is this a matter of trust in men or of

7

queen bee syndrome showing up in an unequal setting? As studies have shown, women can be perceived less favorably in leadership roles, and the behaviors they perform necessary to leadership, especially agentic behaviors in more traditional command-and-control management settings, will be evaluated less favorably.[2] They will also be penalized for either being too nice or not nice enough.

Success is also seen as incongruent for women

We also need to recognize we see leadership only where we see success. But there is a double standard here too for men and women. Successful women, especially successful women in more male-dominated areas, are regarded as less socially appealing *if* they are successful. Not only that but they are quite literally punished for their success in the social context, whereas men will be rewarded. Take the study which evaluated the hypothetical vice presidents for an aircraft business, named Andrea and James.[3] When it was unclear how competent these two individuals were, they were assessed as being similarly likeable. We can confidently tick our belonging box. Yet when the vice presidents were described as 'stellar performers' Andrea was described in more derogating terms than James. Her uniqueness was not accepted.

The study also concluded that "being disliked can have career-affecting outcomes, both for overall evaluation and for recommendations concerning organizational reward allocation". In other words, unfair treatment, the number one reason for burnout, can show up very readily when women are successful, and it's our job as the leader to spot and mitigate it. Create more normality around women *being* successful, not the exception, by showcasing their successes frequently and we can. Make people aware of this very well-researched bias in human behavior and we get further still.

The choice

The issue of *choosing* behaviors is incredibly important psychologically for humans. Weighing up the cost and benefit of a specific strategy in a given social setting is essential. It makes the difference between being blindly steered into advice which may well backfire, or having the personal agency to make a properly informed decision based on what's actually going on. It's also important to weigh what's likely to happen in a given context. Much of the advice for women centers on behaviors they may need to adopt if they want to progress into leadership roles, and behaviors they may need to drop, with a complete lack of awareness of this point.

We discussed earlier how saying no to extra voluntary tasks might be a good strategy for not taking on too much non-promotable work. Yet remember this 'saying no' may also carry a social penalty. Both sides of the equation need to be weighed up. And that's the problem with much of the advice out there for women. While it might appear constructive, let's be clear choosing any behavior will carry a cost as well as a benefit, and that cost needs to be discussed. That's because the double bind exists, the 'damned if you do, damned if you don't' scenario for women. Being respected if you're strong, but not liked, makes for a pretty dismal work environment for women, who also want and need a sense of belonging.

Remember every human has a psychological need to belong. Being liked, but not respected if you are 'too nice', is a poor consolation prize if you feel a sense of community in your work team, but no real sense that your individual contribution is significant and respected. These binary biases are what women in leadership face while the role itself is seen as incongruent for women. That's why effective coaching in groups and with individuals can air this. It can neutralize the negatives of the stereotypes that exist.

Let's remind ourselves leadership is seen as congruent with being male, but it is seen as being incongruent with being female. So, advice to copy what works for men won't be the best, if given in isolation. Behaviors that might be deemed to bring more success at the group level might incur a cost at an individual psychological level and vice versa. The success of those behaviors in itself is gender dependent. And those behaviors will be interpreted differently depending on where other individuals sit within the Driftwood Inclusivity Framework. It will also be dependent on how conscious they themselves are of bias against women, specifically in leadership. Many well-meaning coaches, HR, managers and leaders need to understand this.

Higher competency threshold

The behaviors women often manifest are in direct reaction to how they've needed to adapt to try to navigate a world where the double bind, niceness penalty and a higher competency threshold rule supreme. Let's take an example to illustrate the point. Perfectionism can be seen as a very negative behavior because it can get in the way of finishing work to a sufficient level more quickly or might be regarded as a heavily time-demanding strategy that some women follow. But, if as a woman we know we are going to be judged more critically and held to a higher competency threshold, which research demonstrates happens to women, it might be sensible to cover our proverbial behind and do our absolute best work.

Rather than being a behavior that women apparently possess, it then becomes clear it's actually a behavior that might be showing up because of a discriminatory work setting, or as a reaction to past experiences. Recognizing this we might want to reconsider just telling women that 'done is good enough' as a strategy will work. It might just not work where bias abounds. Having a discussion around the benefits and costs of being more or less of a perfectionist will be far more valuable than simply saying to women 'don't be a perfectionist'.

Perceived perfectionism is a huge topic that tends to have a far greater hold over women's performance behaviors than men's, with implications for promotion. One female, in our research explained she had been put forward for a promotion and said, "I told my boss that I want to master the role I'm in first." Women frequently only believe they are right for a role when they are an expert. There is a deep psychological reason for this – the high competency threshold. Nothing to do with lack of confidence. If you have learnt over the span of your lifetime that your work will be more highly scrutinized, and that, if you fail, you will be penalized more harshly and for longer, it's not beyond the bounds of logic to adapt to ensuring these things don't happen.

Take the study done by Yale University that demonstrated that female leaders in high status roles were held to a higher accountability than their male counterparts.[4] Participants were asked to judge the merits of a police chief in a fictitious event where a public demonstration got out of hand and police officers were sent to the scene. In the scenario where the leader failed to dispatch enough police, which led to 25 people being injured, the ratings of the female dropped by 30%, as opposed to just 10% if the chief was known to be male. Not only that, but people wanted to *demote the female and not the male* because of this failure. The social penalty had greater negative implications for her than for him.

Compare this now to the story whereby there were no injuries. Now both male and female leaders were regarded as equally competent. The study also noted that where the male was in a leading role seen more stereotypically as a female leadership role, the leader of a women's college, he was also judged more harshly if he showed incompetence. So, we may also be able to conclude that both males and females are judged more critically if they fail in a leadership role not seen as congruent with their gender.

Since the study could only identify *one* leadership role as being both high status and primarily held by women, the leader of a women's college, it also explains why any other leadership role would automatically be seen as uncommon and therefore incongruent with being female. Women are open to far higher criticism in most leadership roles across tech, politics, finance, the judiciary, also *because* there aren't very many of them. Women as a novelty in senior leadership is therefore part of the problem. Make it normal to see women in successful leadership roles, equality in the numbers, and their perceived level of competence is likely to rise.

If we understand what's going on beneath the need to be

conscientious and thorough then, rather than changing the behavior, we can address the underlying cause of the behavior and then decide if it serves us well. Better yet we can strategize on ways to call out the propensity to hold women to a higher competency threshold. We check ourselves and our people when we criticize women if things don't always go well.

The corporate hype these days is all about allowing failure in order to learn and succeed. But do we allow women to do this as much as we do men? Change those behaviors in others and then 'when done is good enough' will be a good strategy to follow, but not before then. Why? Because 'done is good enough' won't necessarily be good enough in the social context if you're female.

It also wouldn't do any harm for everyone to aim for excellence, not just some women. A little more conscientiousness in an array of business decisions and processes are not bad aspirations for us all. They are something we need to demand far more of from some of our male leaders.

Leadership presence

Let's take another example, the parent (changed from 'mother' - you notice we're learning too) of all coaching engagements, - developing 'leadership presence'. The first thing to note about this mythical holy grail of what being a good leader is, is that it means entirely different things depending on who we speak with. Secondly, it's very much a superficial term that can run the danger of pursuing superficial results. Presence runs the risk of looking at the surface presentation of leaders, those "dazzling celebrity leaders" Collins identified. But remember successful leadership is much more about "inspiring standards rather than inspiring through charisma." Therefore, authenticity in the context of the individual is key.

Thirdly, we very much run the risk of believing 'leadership presence' means aspiring to all those masculine stereotypes that were earlier touched on in chapter 7. 'Leadership effectiveness', though

7

sounding rather humdrum no doubt, surely encapsulates far better the goal we ultimately want to achieve. Effectiveness. Not presence. We want results, not shiny packaging. We want competence. We don't necessarily need over-flowing confidence.

While we continue to give focus to *presence,* we perpetuate this idea that leadership is all about the ego. Leadership should *not* be about ego at all, nor status, nor power. It should be about creating a clear vision, fairness, positive influence, inspiring performance and results. Those results should be for the many not the few. Those results should be recognized as being achieved because of the many not the few.

Fair networking and hypocrisy around assertive women

Let's take another key interpersonal skill, relationship building. Relationship building is important, and the environment needs to be accommodating to it. Social events should be organized that appeal to both men and women so that there is an equal playing field for nurturing the chance to network. This is also relevant if you're more likely to be labelled political or conniving when you're viewed as leveraging relationships. Other leaders need to ensure they don't unfairly create more opportunities for men to network than women. Thought needs to be put into this.

Diminishing yourself is by nature what you do if you've learnt from an early age that pushing yourself forward is seen as unseemly, threatening or too domineering. Little girls learn early on it's not OK to be bossy, and little boys learn that it is OK. Context, social context, must always be kept in mind when dishing out advice to individuals. Context is everything and asking women for behavior changes without grasping the social context they find themselves in is tantamount to telling women to go put their head in the lion's mouth, when they've had it bitten off many times before.

It's not uncomfortable because it's not in women to be confident, strong or assertive. It's uncomfortable because confidence, strength

7

or assertiveness were very much inherent in them at one point. However, they more likely learnt from an early age these qualities weren't usually acceptable in females. Social context trumps individualism. That is why finding our tribe, a place where we'll fit is so important. We caveat, - without needing to be identical. And it's why so many people end up constantly looking if they feel on uncertain ground, notably women, who are more likely to search for new opportunities.

The remedy for women, therefore, is very often to find purpose, not to make major behavioral changes. The purpose almost creates the change, the adaptation. But that purpose needs to be one authentic to them, not to fit in the social order. The adaptation also needs to be an authentic one. When women find the right tribe they find fertile ground for their ideas. That's why working on this as an organization is so important. If you create the fertile ground, the open environment, then the innovation and contributions come forth, and women don't need to move on. You can retain them.

Create safety and believe in women

Women are also described as easily distracted because of their wide radar abilities – there's a perception that women tend to see more of what is going on contextually. Some women can have the tendency to appear thrown in situations where they need to appear laser focused. How much of this might have nothing to do with lack of focus, or women's so-called superiority in peripheral vision distracting them? As an aside, this perception itself appears to be more neurosexism. To this point there appear to be no sex differences in cognitive control and attentional focus.

Might apparent tendencies to lose focus have more to do with knowing, as a woman, that you are being judged based on your sex, a lack of psychological safety, or even both? Remember the suggestions of Cialdini for the math SAT test. Rather than focusing the students on thinking about how they'll tackle difficult problems, how about focusing them on situations in the past where they've solved things successfully. Setting women up for success, rather than assuming they might fail, because there are only a few of them who've 'made it' in leadership, would be a great strategy.

We as leaders and peers can choose to believe in women and help them remember their successes, rather than focusing on mitigating potential pitfalls when hiring them. In order to do that we need to be on equal footing, not feeling superior in the Elitist box. We also shouldn't create an illusion of leadership for them, the danger of the Tokenists. These women must have actual power and authority in the role they're in, and there must be a real succession plan for other women coming up the ranks. This is also why creating sponsorship organically, ensuring women, as well as men, are assigned a number of different sponsors invested in their development from a range of places within the organization, should be nurtured.

Women are also often cited as having more difficulty in speaking about their own achievements. Yet modesty is something cited as a clear Level 5 leadership trait (humility), and therefore an excellent leadership attribute. We can again link this back to the psychological context of the three issues women face. Double bind, higher competency threshold and niceness penalty.

The niceness penalty revolves around being seen to be nice but runs the risk that if you're too nice you won't be seen as competent. Women often try to demonstrate this by being agreeable and modest. But being modest is now regarded as being detrimental for women who want to get into leadership. People will not necessarily see their accomplishments, so women are advised to speak up more about their achievements to ensure promotion.

This advice might justifiably be described as conflicting, even erroneous, if we want to promote the best leaders, humble ones. We should therefore weigh carefully the effectiveness of this advice, *unless* it is given in the context of understanding the high competency threshold, niceness penalty and double bind. The presence of these factors creates a conflict. There's a need to choose what might be the most effective behavior in a given situation. In isolation, without the psychological understanding that the social context creates, the advice is tantamount to saying be more like men in the stereotypical sense of the phrase. And as we know there are penalties for doing that.

Key Performance Indicators are good for everyone

There's another crucial point here. Companies need to properly define and work on Key Performance Indicators (KPI's). These need to be clearly communicated. Check in and reassessment of these must occur on a very regular basis. Then the opportunity for discussion of results is created. Leaders really should be making themselves aware of what and who is contributing. Do this and women, in particular, wouldn't have to justify all the things they've worked on. Leaders should already know what they've done.

From the research we know that one of the frustrations with managers is that they often do not touch base with their team regularly enough. Alternatively, they might micro-manage which takes away an employee's own agency. Working on KPI's on a regular basis creates the opportunity to check in, discuss and give meaningful two-way feedback. This can be specifically valuable to women in more male-dominated work environments, as an example, where they've historically been reported as receiving less feedback, according to the research.

Effectively working on KPIs with *all* your employees can prevent the situation observed that men get frequent informal feedback from other male managers, whereas women are less likely to. It prevents the situation of lack of clarity in goals. According to Gallup more frequent one-on-one conversations increase employee engagement by a factor of three.[5] Continual performance management is cited by John Doerr as needing three things: conversations, feedback and recognition, CFR's. These lead to transparency, accountability, empowerment and teamwork.[6] Doerr was the venture capitalist who introduced the idea of OKR's into a startup in 1999, that had great ideas but no real business plan. That start-up was Google.

Continuous performance management can be an effective way of engaging women. Done well it can be particularly valuable in creating the conversations and check ins that lead to clarity in goals, transparency, and awareness of the results that need to be measured.

So-called habits, which may have potential for de-railing women, are amplified by the cultural conditioning that women should be 'nice', 'likeable' and 'nurturing'. Traditional coaching suggests women be more agentic, which we need to bear in mind people perceive as masculine. Fundamentally, behaviors that women are perceived as exhibiting, should not be presented as a set of negatives because they are all laudable qualities in the right setting.

This is one of the many important reasons strong male leaders need to pay attention to what's really going on and increase their awareness around how corporate culture may disserve women, and perceived 'feminine skills' in their organization. A focus on creating more 'taking care' behaviors in men would be equally beneficial. A great way to do this is to coach within a group setting both men and women. Coaching people and focusing on coaching 'the softer skills', would be another welcome new focus. Focusing on the power and strength of emotional intelligence, rather than focusing on leadership training, could be the most effective strategy of all.

Research has found that leaders with higher emotional intelligence have higher rates of engagement in their teams. Capgemini, in a 2019 study, found that 78% of executives believed emotional intelligence was a "must-have" skill.[7] It also cited that the demand for EI was likely to increase by 6 times over the coming 5 years. Self-awareness, awareness of others, authenticity, emotional reasoning, self-management and inspiring performance are all core emotional intelligence competencies.[8] They are all necessary if leaders are to create gender parity and inclusivity in their organizations.

Key Points

Why there are double standards for women in leadership and what they are.

Research shows women are penalized for longer and more harshly for mistakes than men.

They are held to a higher competency threshold than men.

They will be penalized if they are too nice or not nice enough.

The double bind means they will either be liked or respected if in leadership, but not often both.

Successful women are perceived as less likeable. Lower likeability may lead to inequality in reward systems.

Both males and females are judged more critically if they fail in a leadership role not seen as congruent with their gender.

Proactively creating diverse sponsorship avenues for women and minorities, as well as men, is critical.

KPI's and regular check-ins facilitate fair monitoring, goal setting and appraisals.

The issues for women highlight the stereotypes we have around leadership.

Focusing on emotional intelligence training, rather than leadership presence and confidence building, *for everyone*, can be hugely valuable.

Case study

Nicole the adviser to women startups. Internalized sexism means people don't look to men to help with the solutions for creating gender parity, but perpetuate the "what women need to do" rhetoric.

Self-reflective coaching questions and considerations

Where can you recognize that there is a double bind for women in your organization?

Think back to how mistakes made have been viewed, based on whether a man or woman has made them?

How much has your organization internalized sexism as something that needs to be fixed in women, rather than something to fix in the group?

Are you reaching out for coaches for your women only?

Consider that if you want gender equality in leadership you need to coach men and mixed gender groups on this topic.

How involved are men in your women's groups?

How do the men in your organization feel about having more women in leadership roles?

How are your senior leaders supporting your junior men and women?

Is there a double standard in terms of network access, types of social events offered, presumed rather than known interests?

Are you creating the same opportunities for networking, relationship building and sponsorship for both your men and women?

What can you do to create a diverse set of sponsors for each individual in your talent pool?

What can you do to create effective, frequently revised KPI's within your organization?

How can you create more regular opportunities for conversations, feedback and recognition within your organization?

How would you rate the level of emotional intelligence within your organization?

How might others rank your level of emotional intelligence?

Consider how you might create diverse sponsors for all of your employees, and a system of development and support. Think younger, older, gender, race, ability, seniority, difference.

10 Getting Men Involved and Pipeline Problems or Bad Plumbing?

> The castle of masculinity is not a mighty fortress. Gender is more fluid than our culture likes to admit.
> Arthur Holmberg, American author

Our research originally focused on assessing what men saw as the main issues around hiring and retaining women. What we had already identified in our initial research, Women in Leadership – Taking Charge to Take Care – Exposing the Real Blocks to Female Talent Retention, was that men generally cited 3 reasons for why women didn't get into senior leadership roles more frequently to create better gender parity in those senior leadership roles. The three causes cited were: 1) having families 2) lack of confidence 3) no pipeline of women.

Interviewing women on the issue we heard very different reasons, and the plethora of research in the public domain confirms that the perceived reasons often given by leaders are not the reasons why women don't progress. They go far, far deeper. For women we can capture these reasons into three main groupings: 1) psychological distress and conflict 2) unconscious and implicit bias 3) cultural and systematic pressures and barriers. It was clear from the initial research that there was a huge disconnect between what the males believed the problems to be and what they actually are.

We were therefore able to refute all three reasons we heard more often from men, while delving much deeper into the real reasons, and then target those in coaching male leaders. Yet fundamental to the success of this work was recognizing at every step of the way that men also have their own set of gender norm expectations to fulfill which also carry benefits and costs. Fulfilling these norms while contradictory in and of themselves, can also come into direct conflict with the types of behavior needed in the work on equality, and can also cause them psychological distress at an unconscious level.

Men and women

We created a program that takes small groups of senior executives from different countries and a variety of industries and run group and individual coaching around the gender dimensions to leadership. The global context allows individuals to share diverse stories, and from the outset a spirit of inclusivity, communication and respect is instilled to the group. It's regarded as novel and highly appreciated because it involves both men and women. The individuals initially do an executive leadership assessment and an emotional intelligence assessment to learn more about their leadership styles and behaviors in relation to each other.

Each individual also carries out an implicit bias test to understand possible unconscious bias, and these results are discussed within the group. The test itself is explained as not being in any way predictive of unconscious bias behaviors. It does nevertheless create a springboard for initial discussion around the possibility of bias and people's history and feelings around the subject. The group also studies research papers, articles and books and does reflective exercises. The purpose of the course is to better understand how broad gender dimensions in leadership are. Each participant is expected to work towards a practical outcome, a personal development goal, they can apply in the context of their own business.

Dealing with the basics

Tackling some of the background to the bias, we focus initially on the family issue, lack of confidence and lack of pipeline, cited as reasons why more women don't progress. Taking the family issue first it's explained to the group that we know, for example, that women often may not actually want to have families, [1] more often want to continue work even when they've started a family, and from some studies that they show up to be *even more* and at least *as* ambitious as men, *despite* having families. [2] We also know that confidence does not correlate to competence. [3] Work flexibility is also discussed and while it allows greater use of the female talent pool, flexibility is also appealing to men, especially younger generation workers. Work life balance is becoming even more important to males than females, again showing that work flexibility is not a women's issue but a human issue, and that cultural expectations of what it means to be male or female are also shifting over time. [4]

An obsession with presenteeism blinds many to the actual level of productivity of their people, and this can also show up in these discussions. Bias against women becomes an even greater problem generally and more specifically once they have families. The problem lies far more in not creating safe psychological spaces where women can talk about family, more than that they may necessarily have family challenges, though that may be a factor. What repeatedly showed up in the research interviews was that men cited this family commitment as an issue they saw in their female staff. Despite this 'issue' they were then unable to actually come up with concrete examples of these same women failing to perform at the level required.

The inability to highlight objective negatives presents as a further problem in the conversation around bias against mothers. The lack of objective data demonstrates that these men, and also some senior women, are unable to demonstrate that mothers are less productive. They realize it themselves, when we discuss it in group settings. Of course, there are exceptions on occasion. When we coach business leaders on this topic it can help them gain clarity around this area and learn about their potential bias. They realize they have a very limited understanding of their female employees lives and drives. They have a limiting perception around the abilities of these women to also take on additional responsibilities.

Through further conversation it can often become apparent that these leaders have often assumed that mothers don't want more responsibility, without the conversation having taken place to back that assumption. Further it gives at least some of the men the opportunity to discuss the cultural transition around masculine norms, what it means to be a father and the costs and benefits of being the main bread winner where that might still be applicable. It can air issues around missing out on family life, or work life balance. For some it gives them a platform to verbally assert the importance of sharing the care role in their family. These are enriching conversations for everyone.

Full pipeline, bad plumbing

Next comes a discussion around pipeline. With income parity being one of the essential ingredients linked to retaining female talent the World Economic Forum's 2020 Global Gender Gap report shows that the US ranks 53 out of 153 countries when it comes to gender pay and equality. No wonder its track record for women in senior leadership roles remains woefully low. In the Fortune 500 companies just 6.6% of CEOs are female. As participation rates of women in the general labor force are declining, with many mid-career women opting out of the labor force entirely, we should be asking why?

The share in senior leadership roles remains disproportionate which represents a real problem when we realize that more women than men actually graduate from higher education. The skills and intelligence are not lacking. Yet the corporate leaders we speak with often claim there is a pipeline problem. We use stories to undermine this perception. More valuable still, the dialogue among participants means they share their own stories too.

Take the story of Stephanie Lampkin who was told she wasn't 'technical' enough for a lead Analytical role at Google. On Makers Women, a feminist media brand, 'for newsMAKERS, historyMAKERS and troubleMAKERS' which exists to accelerate the women's movement she told her story. The first thing we loved about this story was how Stephanie begins it. "So, I always tell people my first image of a computer scientist was not a white guy in hoodie and flip flops. It was someone who looked like me." Stephanie is an African American woman. She became a full stack developer and explains, "APCS, Stanford, MIT, applied for a job at Google, Analytical Lead Role, and they told me I wasn't technical enough."

Retaining her CV for possible positions in sales or marketing she discovered at the time that, while Google had 55,000 employees, they had only 12 African American women in technical roles. She goes on to explain how this media story that it's a pipeline problem and that we can't find qualified women of color is nonsense. She decided to do something about it and designed her own app, starting her own company Blendor. As Founder and CEO, her mission is to help corporations to eliminate names, genders, and other labels that might lead to bias in the selection of candidates based on their CV. This leads to a fairer and more objective initial recruitment process.

What we know from the data is that we currently sit in a time when there are more qualified women than men available for most roles. Stephanie's story highlights this. When coached on this problem and shown the data around graduation numbers,[5] higher ambition and less interest in having a family, what often emerges is the realization that leaders are simply not properly tapping into the right markets, not selling their internal opportunities in the right ways, and not creating effective succession plans that involve suitably qualified women.

Leaders realize they have many biases in their recruiting and selection processes. They realize they do not necessarily have objective selection criteria to recruit and select fairly. They also recognize that taking steps to showcase female talent and source them from available talent pools in a more effective way, taking into account women's requirements early in the succession planning, is key to retaining more further up the career ladder. What is thought to be a pipeline issue turns out to be just bad plumbing.

Discussing neurosexism

There is also a general sense that perhaps gender disparity exists for immutable reasons in these group coaching discussions. Popular stories still center around these myths of sex differences, lack of confidence, ambition and actual leadership ability.[6] Much of the time the feedback the senior male leaders are getting from their DE&I Heads also centers on helping women increase their confidence, and that females need networks of other women and coaching in building confidence. This approach looks at things from one perspective, sometimes at too superficial a level. It does not address deeper issues and other perspectives. It looks at the issue on an individual level and not in the social and psychological context of what it means to be a certain gender.

Research data certainly helps leaders to open their eyes to the prospect that there might be more to the problem of not getting more females in senior roles than purely lack of confidence. Exposing the deeper psychological issues, which DE&I initiatives don't often touch on, importantly and fundamentally gives these leaders a far deeper understanding about the issues at hand. They finally have the right facts, not the easy throwaways.

The double bind, niceness penalty and high competency threshold

Understanding how pervasive the double bind can be, female leaders are either liked or respected but less often both, has a significant impact in helping leaders better understand how women present themselves in leadership roles. They learn about how incongruent leadership is perceived as being for females from a social and cultural perspective, and how it can ultimately undermine their well-being. They are far better informed to be able to identify when women might be perceived as either too nice or too tough. Leaders also learn how subjective observations could impact their own perceptions and judgements of these women in a positive way.

Once they understand the impact of the niceness penalty,[7] whereby a female leader might be socially penalized for being too nice or not nice enough, they are able to spot when they themselves, or others around them, are being biased or might be unduly criticizing women. They can read the situations and behavior in a whole new light. They realize how this has clouded and limited their view of women and negatively influenced their consideration of them as potential leadership material.

There is also a greater awareness that women are very quickly judged, often labelled with derogatory terms. This raised awareness helps leaders understand how unobjective and unfair this often is. Interestingly, in a review 6 months later, this particular point stays with everyone as they cite how they now regularly notice how women in positions of power or politics are negatively targeted. They quite literally see everything with a totally new perspective.

Going deeper into the research the leaders we coach can better relate to the finding in the research that women are often held to a higher competency threshold, using examples from the real world of politics and the media, as well as business case studies. This helps them understand the implicit bias that derails their own ability to see women as leaders, and their ability to accept any mistakes women may make as part of their growth. They realize that this capacity is often different for their male counterparts, and that the higher competency threshold is not an issue when determining men's competence, though it should be. Awareness of the higher competency threshold women are held to and men are not, runs the risk of unfairness in reviews of performance for these leaders.

Coaching as the foundation for change

Discussing strategies on how to address this in one-on-one coaching situations often brings to surface for male leaders, in particular, the deeper underlying issues around the potential minefield that promoting women actually can be. For example, male leaders become very aware that they may be the odd one out in trying to showcase a particular female for a leadership role. This can create a situation of breaking from the male rank and some masculine code in doing this, because they are not supporting a male candidate, also being considered for the leadership role. It is uncomfortable ground, not least because accusations around favoritism, sexism or even sexual misconduct can manifest for the male leader. Further evidence then that the more men understand about this bias, the less they need to be alone in stepping up and sponsoring women who might be good candidates for leadership roles within the organization.

An understanding of identity threat, that we culturally have notions about what men and women can and can't do that can actually create a self-fulfilling prophecy, brings home the message that men also get too easily pigeon-holed into being problem solvers and leaders by default. It highlights the bias that men are seen as less able to empathize. It emphasizes the cultural expectation that they are required to be assertive and confident to the detriment of displaying softer skills. Not limiting the conversation to just stereotypes that disadvantage women but also discussing male stereotypes helps these leaders identify where they were often limited by the constraints of what gender culturally requires us to be. It exposes the cultural expectations of what it means to be a male leader.

Perhaps most importantly of all the discussion involves and includes men. This creates a whole new opportunity for looking at which other leadership traits, more typically perceived as female in our culture, could be worth using more frequently for males. One example of this we frequently observe is being more actively interested in direct reports lives rather than just the business of the day. Another is checking in more frequently on how their work is going. Since we know from research that this can be a blind spot for many managers, which means they miss out on more meaningful relationships, where more trust can be built, this is seen as a very positive idea for them to work on. When they do, the quality of their interactions tends to improve, and the added business value is that extra check-ins create clearer communication and clarity around goals for employees.

In another example, male leaders are able to share with us situations where they have needed or have in fact shown some emotions, not anger, but tears, born through empathy. Yet these behaviors have been targeted as inappropriate by other males on the team. While being a demonstration of vulnerability, authentic and indeed empathetic, it is recognized that just such behaviors are also frowned upon as inappropriate for males. Openly discussing this and hearing others support of displays of emotion under certain circumstances can be powerful. When the group stresses this as being human and not something that should be present or lacking based on gender it can be very meaningful. It allows a conversation around the need to be vulnerable and how vulnerability is a critical characteristic in strong leaders.

Discussing gender norms and emotions

When we expect male leaders to have all the answers the problem of males asserting as default leaders is compounded. It is the antithesis to two of the crucial traits strong leaders need to have: vulnerability and humility. The vulnerability that comes from not always being right, not necessarily being the best in the room, and not having all the answers. The humility to recognize this and other's strengths simultaneously. The gender dimensions to leadership discussion ultimately enables everyone to discuss human elements and recognize when traits have been organized by gender, and how they rarely represent reality in deeper reflective discussions.

It's an emotional risk for everyone but through stereotyped expectations of how men should lead, it becomes even more difficult for some men to be vulnerable, admit failure, recognize they're wrong, ask questions. This is also noticeable in the group dynamic, as it may take more sessions for the males to become more open. However, open up they eventually do. The masculine veneers and stereotypes come off, and the human traits shine through. Coaching male leaders to find their own comfort level with their own style of leadership, including expressions of emotion, can be highly valuable.

It is also helpful in removing some resentment which some male leaders communicate as having when dealing with females. The feeling is often that they find it difficult to deal with women who might cry or show emotion, not knowing what to do with it. Some men often don't know how to react, possibly feeling even cornered by such behavior. By discussing their own emotions and the emotions of the group a greater understanding of how emotions can serve us positively in leadership is reached. An exploration of stereotypes helps many of these male leaders realize that they are as bigger dupes of gender bias as their female counterparts. In team dynamics this is particularly powerful, moving and indeed transformational.

Emotional intelligence assessments

The Emotional Intelligence (EI) assessment is particularly powerful in identifying behaviors that leaders assume they are better in than that they actually are. It helps leaders to see where there might be a disconnect between the level of importance they attach to certain behaviors and what the people who see them in action every day perceive. The emotions that arise in the gender dimensions in leadership discussion can be analyzed in terms of whether they stimulate positive or negative behaviors, measured within the assessment tool. Core competencies of self-awareness, awareness of others, authenticity, emotional reasoning, self-management and inspiring performance within the EI model help leaders drill down to specific behaviors that they may need to focus on improving. This can be valuable in identifying a goal and a key behavior to change.

By presenting information in a non-threatening and accusatory way men are more able to understand how unconscious both their own bias and behaviors may be. More positively they see how often it is unintended. Blame is more often removed. Men are able to open up to the information and report back that it is so much more valuable and relevant to them than they could ever have expected.

While some men are challenged in terms of their over-identification with some of the masculine gender norms, discussion of these norms enables them to recognize how threatened and how defensive they may feel in certain work settings. This leads to the group participants being able to identify similarities and differences between men and women in a positive way. More often than not people realize their behaviors can often be the same, but how they experience things can be different. These experiences happen both because of and despite gender. Through this they find a common language for good leadership that doesn't necessitate gendered stereotypes. This is where real break throughs are made and the polarization and backlash to any feminist movements, or female leadership drives, can be pre-empted.

Airing frustrations around confidence

The conversation around confidence and competence particularly piques the male leaders as they often cite stories of how they have witnessed situations where a male is selected who clearly does not have the competence for the role. Rather than approaching this from an accusatory standpoint of 'all men are incompetent', it is approached as a discussion of what is confidence and what is competence. A wider discussion around leadership competencies and different leadership styles for different periods in a company's life span is also facilitated. It highlights for many how unobjective leadership often is, why that's problematic, and why there's a need for greater scrutiny of the behaviors we should look for in corporate leaders.

From the research into leadership performance we know that confidence is poorly correlated to success, and that expertise, agreeableness to work with, and talent in the 'softer skills' are *crucial* to leadership performance. Again, the importance of EI is highlighted. The phenomenon for hiring based on confidence is exposed as a bias problem that many companies have. It facilitates having the conversation around why women are often cited as having less confidence. Rather than seeing perceived lack of confidence as a problem, it is actually a strength if it involves modesty. Perceived under-confidence might often be something else. Being reminded of the Dunning Kruger effect it can actually be seen as a sign of high competence. Lack of confidence might also be a sign of someone's discomfort in the psychological space.

A realization that coaching women on gaining more confidence and leadership presence may be an attempt at addressing a symptom rather than a cause of something more systemic often causes some ah ha moments within coaching groups. There's a greater realization that much of the coaching and well-meant advice given to women is actually at best unhelpful, and at worst irresponsible. Once the group understands the impact of the double bind, higher competency threshold and niceness penalty this becomes very clear to them. The flip side of the confidence discussion is that once male stereotypes are discussed everyone better understands why some men often may show confidence. It may be leading everyone down a blind alley. They may not be able to do the job. It *may* be a cover for insecurity and lack of ability.

Harassment and bullying

The discussion around workplace bullying and harassment with individuals is also a critical piece and requires careful handling. When the course lesson on neurosexism is discussed men have a greater openness and willingness to accepting how much objectivization of women there is in our culture and they recognize the existence of patriarchy still having a role to play in this.[8] While men hold most power positions and gain the highest economic returns patriarchy remains a reality and a problem. Women are still viewed as having a supportive role and inferiority in terms of leadership. A wider discussion that sexism and harassment are not just a women's issue but can affect everyone is discussed.

A discussion around #Me Too and #Time'sUp allows the male leaders to share their concerns around mentoring and sponsoring women and to create an action plan around how to do this with no repercussions or accusations of sexual misconduct or harassment, in

256

an open and public manner.[9] Input from women on what they believe can help and work is invaluable in this. What also often comes up is the frustration of men with other men who act in a dominating way. Being tarnished with the same misogynistic brush for all men is discussed. So too is the understanding that it is not just men who can be guilty of harassment. Once recognized, this conversation empowers both men and women to police against harassment and bullying behaviors from others.

Frustration with command-and-control styles of leadership is aired. Conflict around status, responsibility, fairness and work life balance are discussed. A discussion in the mixed group around "boy's club" activities and how they might exclude women and the peer pressure to follow certain assumed-masculine norms is also aired. It allows the men, for example, to confirm and assert that not all men are obsessing over sex, another gendered stereotype, or thinking of it the entire time they are dealing with women. This is again one of those myths of male behavior that it is helpful to air in the presence of women and which many women also don't understand. It can be very damaging for men who intend to do the right thing. The discussion is both necessary and needs to be sensitively handled.

Creating space for men to express their softer skills

We have been having many conversations around women's rights and opportunities for years, but we haven't around men. The world has been guilty of assuming all men are privileged and can do whatever they want. That is simply not true. Some men as much as some women suffer from the propensity of people to select some confident, decisive men, invariably white males, above other qualified males. Men are also straight jacketed by narrow stereotypes of what makes a good leader, and how men should behave to be deemed successful and socially acceptable. We see this discrimination most clearly against men of color most seriously. We also see this discrimination against men who are less likely to fall into those perceived 'masculine' categorizations of 'strong' leaders, and who are more likely to exercise some of the 'softer skills', or 'feminine skills.'[10]

We also see that it is difficult for some men to promote women in leadership for exactly the same reasons of bias that prevent more women being represented in positions of power and leadership. They will be penalized by other men and might risk the accusation of inappropriate behavior by both other men and other women. A discussion around this gives voice to the concerns male leaders face in sponsoring more vocally the promotion of women to more powerful senior roles. It highlights a really key point that men actually need to group together to support women for leadership positions.

He said, she said

Coaching women alone on the topic of women in leadership doesn't create solutions in companies but often silos. While women's networks have done much to empower women and allow them to mentor and share stories, they've done very little to engage men and ironically created exclusion. It's normal to see a women's leadership coach or women's leadership program but it is not common to see a men's leadership coach or men's network in the context of gender discussions. This is a crucial element that's missing in strategies around creating more inclusivity in leadership, and an explanation of why higher numbers of women in leadership have not gained much traction in the last decade. There is a massive disconnect between what men perceive the issues to be, and what the actual issues for women are.

Coaching in small groups and individually allows leaders to acknowledge this huge disconnect and knowledge gap, discuss it and reflect on it. The creation of a safe psychological place for them to voice their understanding with coaching support enables them to share their challenges, creates a clear sense of inclusion for everyone and a sense of accountability. Providing education on second-generation bias is essential learning and enables leaders to more clearly set goals around women leadership initiatives, as the issues are better understood at a deeper level.[11] The positivity and care taken in facilitating these sensitive discussions inspires a deep respect between the men and women and an openness to hearing the problems as each experiences them.

Personal development and individual coaching

Providing additional individual coaching cements the ideas already learnt and is key to creating behavior change goals and accountability structures. Facilitating these sessions to involve men, complementing the sessions with study, while also discussing the research together and talking about personal stories over a sustained period of time is a powerful and effective way for creating behavior-change. It builds groups of male champions who will promote women in senior leadership. It also critically develops everyone's emotional intelligence. Tying this together with business improvements and the executive's own leadership development and growth is key.

By doing these things male leaders gain a realization that they are central to the solution of gender parity in leadership roles, and that gender is not the problem, but rather subjective judgements of what makes a good leader are, leadership itself having been gendered to a degree in our culture. This gives them a better oversight of what objective talent measures are and helps them understand the increased importance of cultivating 'softer skills' or more 'feminine skills' in themselves and their male leaders and peers. This acknowledgement of 'softer skills' is crucial in simultaneously recognizing these skills' value. It also opens the door to fairly considering women for leadership roles who often demonstrate these skills. It also makes everyone more conscious of the risk of hiring that might lead to tokenism rather than equality. Understanding that assimilation, rather than proof of being in the same tribe, is more likely evidence of adaptation to a still discriminatory and non-inclusive work culture.

Figure 5
UNCONSCIOUS BIAS ISSUES
& SOLUTIONS

UNCONSCIOUS BIAS ISSUES	GROUP AND INDIVIDUAL TRAINING AND COACHING SOLUTIONS
Conflict with family	Exploring belief systems and limiting perceptions and assumptions around what women can do.
Lack of pipeline	Looking at resource avenues, understanding the research, exploring hiring and succession planning processes.
Work flexibility	Limiting self-perceptions often of those working longer/harder. Masculine stereotypes. Presenteeism vs actual results. Work life balance as important for everyone.
Default male leader	Stereotypical traits of males and females in leadership.
Gender differences and myths	How stereotypes limit both men and women.
Understanding the psychological issues for women on a deeper level	Double bind Niceness penalty Higher competency threshold
Confidence vs competence	Understanding how perception of confidence relates back to psychological issues facing women. Reflections on modesty and humility as important characteristics. What is confidence? Competence?
Fair measurements	Fair rewards, appropriate rewards, fair pay, objective measurable results.

7

Figure 6
WHAT MEN THINK,
WHAT WOMEN SAY

WHAT MEN THINK	WHAT WOMEN SAY
Family	Psychological conflict
Lack of confidence	Unconscious and implicit bias
No pipeline	Cultural and systematic pressures

Everyone better understands that confidence is not an indicator of competence, and that empathy, unbiased critical feedback and more personal engagement in actually leading are critical to demonstrating the 'softer skills' of leadership. Explaining that both males and females buy into gender bias in leadership helps many men reconcile that it is not a problem they alone can solve or should feel blame for. They have a massive part to play in helping, however. The business results and work culture will both benefit if they do this work.

It also awakens women into the realization that they are often complicit in sustaining some of the non-gender inclusive behaviors themselves and are often themselves biased towards males as leaders. It leads to them coming up with behavioral solutions that everyone can implement together and hold each other accountable to in the workplace. Leaders are then able to start to model more inclusive behaviors. The male leaders' sense of their own personal and professional growth gained through the program and through coaching makes them feel they have a competitive edge. They undoubtedly do. While most male progressive leaders do not think of themselves as having gender bias, are not actively engaging in this discussion and are unlikely to immerse themselves in gender bias training and coaching, these male executives realize that this is an investment of time well spent.

Key Points

When men realize how gender equality is as relevant to them as to women, they want to be involved in these conversations.

When women understand that bias and stereotyping also effects men, they understand the need to have men in these conversations.

Group and individual coaching are very effective in gender equality work.

They create benefits far beyond helping women get into leadership roles.

Emotional intelligence training is the corner stone to this work.

It uncovers some deeply held limiting beliefs that most people have.

People highly value these conversations. They create enriching learning, sharing experiences for everyone.

They lead to a shared sense of belonging.

They lead to an understanding of uniqueness beyond gender.

Relationships and self-esteem grow through these conversations.

Individuals feel accountability to change certain behaviors and commit to certain actions.

Discussion of how to sponsor and mentor between men and women, without repercussions, is valuable.

Men realize that grouping together to support women for leadership positions is a powerful strategy.

Gender dimensions in leadership is recognized as a critical topic in leadership development.

Self-reflective coaching questions and considerations

What benefits would you personally want to gain from a Gender Dimensions in Leadership program?

What goals would you want to reach in committing to this type of work?

What prevents you from engaging men as an essential component in this conversation?

What can you do to turn that around?

What individual benefits would come from coaching men and women around diversity, inclusivity and emotional intelligence?

How might this benefit your business?

How might this be valuable when dealing with customers and other stakeholders?

Who might benefit from these inclusive conversations between men and women about gender and leadership in your organization?

How might you weave this into a broader leadership program for your people?

How might you use the research to help promote equality in your organization?

How might coaching improve your employee's engagement?

How could you tailor this type of approach into your own organization?

Consider the power of having everyone in the room when it comes to DE&I work.

11 Coaching Better Behaviors

Inclusion is within Everyone's Ability – Indiana Disability Awareness Month

As believers in the idea that the little things make a big difference this chapter explores some of the behaviors that can have a significant impact on how inclusive you as a leader or as an organization might really be being. We know from recent studies that most people don't even know what inclusive behaviors are, so it is imperative we identify, measure and monitor these.[1]

To do this we introduce the HONOUR model for leaders. It is a useful tool to use in becoming masterful at inclusion. Being masterfully inclusive means that we create *both* a sense of belonging *and* a sense of individual value through recognizing uniqueness in all our people. The acronym HONOUR stands for Humble, Objective, Nurturing, Open, Unique and Reverent and is depicted in Figure 7. Modelling these core values by utilizing certain behaviors creates inclusive, fairer work environments. Modelling HONOUR enables people to feel positive, involved and engaged. It also leads to the higher likelihood that they too will model these positive behaviors. There are certain key behaviors that achieve the goals of the HONOUR model.

Modelling humility

We begin with the trait of humility. When we exercise humility, we acknowledge that we have self-worth, while at the same time not tying that self-esteem to any perceived social status. We recognize that we don't know everything, and we can always learn things from other people. We are no more and no less than anyone else. Behaviors that demonstrate we believe we are on equal footing, value others, don't have all the answers, don't need to be in the spotlight, simultaneously demonstrate humility.

There are some maladaptive behaviors that can derail demonstrating humility. Key ones are interrupting others, not listening deeply and dominating the conversation. Another key one is the need to always be seen as right, or the one who solved the problem. In gender dimensions in leadership we need to pay specific attention to these. These less than helpful behaviors are often activated by limiting beliefs around how we *should* show up as men and women.

For example, limiting beliefs like needing to be the hero, an unwillingness to show vulnerability, or a need to be in control may show up in all people. However, masculine gender norms of 'need for status', 'winning', 'self-reliance', or 'emotional control', may make some men particularly susceptible to these limiting beliefs. Demonstrating humility then becomes a challenge. By reframing how demonstrating humility might help men reach these goals, we can effectively navigate and disarm the limiting belief.

We know from research, for example, that men do *not* tend to be aware that they interrupt. We also know from the research that men quite literally do not hear when women speak up and that is why women so often experience the phenomenon of bropriating, where a man in the group recites the idea she has just presented and everyone else in the room also appears to be hearing it for the first time.

Did she just imagine it? Imagine the sensation when your idea is taken and presented by someone else and gets everyone's praise and approval. It is unbelievably demoralizing. Women must deal with the conflicting information they were not heard, they were heard but ignored, they were heard but not influential enough, and / or that they are not respected. There is something inherently wrong and unjust in having something like this happen. Yet it happens all the time.

If we understand that interrupting is at best rude and at worst a form of bullying and asserting dominance, we might check our behavior and that of others doing it more readily. When we interrupt, we think we can second guess someone, get the idea out quicker, or that their idea although as yet unuttered, is simply going to be rubbish. The effect of the behavior, although we may not intend it, is that we send the message we are more important, and they don't count.

In the social context, where it's more likely that the group will default to the male or louder members, this also has the added effect that quieter, more introverted members will diminish themselves when speaking, or not speak at all. For those of us more like that we send the message we don't have anything important to say or we are not confident in what we do have to say. This presentation may have far less to do with the content of what's said or the way it's said, and far more to do with the social context and environment into which it is being delivered.

It's why advising women to lean in doesn't address this underlying issue and is often misplaced. Leaders have to be astute to this subtle but essential point, and as we've already seen on the discussion about confidence and competence, we know that assuming that women lack confidence is deeply flawed but is a widespread belief. Instead of expecting women to lean in, as leaders we need to pull them in. We also need to acknowledge them, when they have joined, as equal partners.

Self not social worth

Equal footing for all parties is essential to preventing the situation where men are the apparent default leader. People need to feel valued, respected and that their opinions and ideas will be heard. This is why meritocracies and heavily hierarchical organizations so often fail in being able to include and thus ultimately retain their employees. Hierarchy and meritocracy, by definition, create visible boundaries and divisions which go beyond being merely structural. Individual leaders would do well to practice the concept of happy high status which Viv Groskop refers to in her book for helping women find their voice.[2]

Happy high status is the concept that the most powerful and influential people are the ones who are quite comfortable blending in with others, doing menial as well as more privileged tasks. With this humility we don't get all uppity about it if we are placed in situations where our status is somehow overlooked. Our self-esteem is high because our self-worth is tied in with who we are as humans, and not with any gender norms. It's definitely not about what we've achieved, what title we have, or what we happen to own. Nor is it about what rights we might perceive we have or don't have based on our gender. Having humility, we don't have a perceived superiority over any other person. In layman's terms we "keep it real", and we treat *all people as equals*.

We might call people with happy high status humble leaders. While we remember that the desire for status has the potential to derail us in this important requirement to radiate humility, a display of our desire to be on equal footing and not superior, can win us many allies. Yet equal footing might be challenging both for men and women, who have cultural ideas around who's supposed to be superior in what, or who's supposed to be in charge.

We observe this more often when coaching women. Women tend to be less likely to want to approach people in higher status positions. Or they place too much emphasis on the perceived expertise of someone. Some men can tend to lack the awareness that they need to encourage more junior people or females to actively contribute. Men often present as the lecturing expert, without realizing the extent of knowledge that others, especially other women around them, might also have. They might default into problem-solving mode, both feeling the need to move things forward, *and* the need to be seen as the individual doing that.

Don't interrupt

Using interrupting as an example, men are proven to interrupt women more often than they do other men, and what is more interesting still is that the more women present, the higher the chance of being interrupted by a man is. It is very likely that violating a masculine gender norm, - for a man being seen as weak by not being in charge, - might partly be the reason for this.

Coaching on communication, on what one intends and what one's actual impact *is*, can be very helpful. It should also be noted that women are far less likely to interrupt which should be a nod to the positive presence of having humility and concern for relationships. However, allowing oneself to be interrupted, and having bystanders also allow this behavior within the group, is also harmful for everyone.

Everyone needs to know what to do in this situation and do it. In the face of an interrupter point out the behavior and allow the original person speaking to finish what they were saying. As leader, think of ways to share out meeting time fairly between participants. In this way you value each person's time and their contribution. Another benefit of this is that it focusses us on the reason for the meeting and forces us to think critically about who needs to be there.

Leaders need to be highly vigilant to their own propensity to interrupt. We know from research on CEOs' behaviors that they are 3 times more likely to interrupt and far less likely to be challenged by anyone when doing so.[3] If we want to be a good leader this is an essential behavior to work on, because we need to allow people to challenge us. We need to send the message that it is safe and OK for our smart people to speak up. We need to send the message that everyone should feel safe to offer their ideas and opinions.

In her book, Time to Think, Nancy Kline talks about the need for leaders to create spaces where people can think. This revolves around allowing each and every member of a team their time to the floor.[4] In this way no one should have to proactively 'lean in' because the leader pulls them in and gets their valuable input. This has as much relevance to everyone around the table, and while also allowing women a chance to speak up, it encourages anyone who's feeling disengaged and unheard, often minority groups. Introverts might be another example here of a group that can be encouraged to contribute.

It requires the creation of a safe place to speak and voice opinion, without the fear of being shouted down. Done well it provides the very real opportunity to share and understand each other's perspectives and gives meaning and value to each personality in the room. Valuable insights invariably come from this very deliberate approach to hearing individual contributions. And using this approach prevents certain people from monopolizing the floor and pushing their ideas, before others are heard with different perspectives. This pre-empts the risk of the confidence above competence paradigm, and any damage that over-dominant individuals might cause.

Kline has this to say about interrupting. "To be interrupted is not good. To get lucky and not be interrupted is better. But to *know* you are not going to be interrupted - that is categorically different. That is bliss. ...The fact that the person can relax in the knowledge that you are not going to take over, talk, interrupt, maneuver or manipulate is one of the key reasons they can think so well around you." And allowing people to think and express ideas around us should be on the critical list of every sharp leader's behaviors. Remember, respect creates trust which leads to engagement and facilitates creativity.

However old habits die hard and women are often aware that they might get interrupted or that they need to get their answers out quickly. So do more men than we think. As leaders it's important we take a step back and create the space for our people to think smartly around us.

When we talk about diminishing as a behavior, we observe women sometimes display it, not just in reference to the physical act of making themselves small, making space for others, not taking the head seat at the table, as examples. Diminishing can also manifest in how much, or how long a woman might speak for. But this behavior, that might mean speaking quickly, less often, and not always in the most effective way, comes from how much psychological safety is created in the space to express. It is less likely to be from the lack of ideas an individual might have, or per se, a lack of confidence. This is why Kline's statement is so incredibly valuable. People don't need to diminish themselves or be fearful around humble leaders.

Listen

Understanding the subtlety of this psychological effect on behavior is far more helpful than simply telling women to lean in and speak up. Having everyone in the room watchful for this phenomenon and actively conscious of creating an open, safe place to communicate is also hugely helpful. It is in everyone's interest to stay alert to this behavior of interrupting, and good leaders will not allow it to happen and certainly will not do it themselves. If you want to be an effective humble leader, speak a lot less and let *everyone* contribute. Even more importantly, once they do talk, let them finish. Remember there's another word we can make from the word listen. It's called silent.

By listening attentively, we also demonstrate a deeper tolerance for other people, their ideas and perspectives. So, listening allows us to tick all the other boxes in the HONOUR model. Facilitating listening to everyone means we are more likely to be Objective, as we collect different perspectives. We also Nurture our people by providing them both the support to express themselves, and by valuing them when they do. We create Open cultures, by showing our own willingness to hear differing sides and by creating safe-psychological space for people. This leads to them being willing to be more open and authentic themselves.

By doing this we make room for the U, the Unique individual. As an aside, this book has adhered to the US spelling of words. The word HONOUR provides therefore a great metaphor in itself for demonstrating the importance of uniqueness. In British English we add U to the word to spell it. By adding the U we make space for the unique, the individual, for difference, for other-ness. Exactly what we need to do to create a deeper sense of inclusivity. We make people feel unique and significant because we value their input. We Revere them. Being Reverent literally means feeling and showing deep respect for another.

Creating space for everyone's voice and listening deeply and objectively is a core behavior of masterfully inclusive leaders. Recently it has been observed that the act of "supervisor listening may be an underrated aspect that fosters creativity." [5] It was observed that, when paired with *good listeners*, participants were less anxious, more self-aware and had a higher degree of clarity. While being prepared to listen to others will help leaders gain insights, there's another benefit. When we listen to people actively, we foster psychological safety that allows *them* to be more creative, exactly what Kline propounds and what studies now begin to show. In a meta-analysis of studies into the effects of listening and creativity, researchers concluded that listening can *influence creativity positively* by creating a safety sphere.

Figure 7
TRAITS OF AN
INCLUSIVE LEADER

Humble
Observant
Nurturing
Open
Unique
Reverent

Case study – Harvard Executive Development Program

It's 2017 and global business leaders, men and women, are attending a Harvard Executive Development Program in Boston. They are given a group exercise. For five minutes one of the executives must talk about a particular problem they are having within their organization. All the other participants are instructed simply to listen. After the five minutes is up the other participants must make suggestions and respond to the problem described. The original business leader is not allowed to react or say anything in response.

This is a great exercise in practicing honing listening skills. Invariably someone in the group usually fails to be quiet while the executive describes their dilemma. And usually the individual fails just to listen to the suggestions the rest of the group provide, without challenging or interrupting them. For the more observant and objective viewer however, this interaction can often highlight the gender dimensions in leadership. Watch closely in your meetings.

Simon spends his 5 minutes offloading his worries, but not just to everyone. No. He invariably describes them to the perceived caring, female listeners in the group, and it would appear specifically Stephanie. In that 5 minutes he really appears to take her presence seriously and clearly values it. Perhaps he feels she empathizes better with him?

But wait. Now it's time for the five minutes of suggested approaches to solving Simon's business dilemma. Everyone is offering valuable insights, in particular Stephanie, because Simon appeared to engage in communicating most of his problem to her. But Simon's switched his attention and now appears to be only open to hearing the other men in the group. He's looking to them to help solve his problem. Not Stephanie.

Logically both the men and the women are equally able to empathize with the business problem. They are all successful business executives. Logically both the men and the women are very likely to have valuable insights and suggestions to solve it. To repeat they're all successful business executives! But, that's not what happens here. Instead we see a clear example of gender bias in communication. Bias in *what we communicate and to whom*. The problems are downloaded to the perceived empathetic ear and care giver, Stephanie in this case. The solutions to the problems are expected and welcomed from the other men, and crucially *not* from Stephanie.

When these behaviors are pointed out people are very often unaware of them, more so if their emotional intelligence is less developed. But the recipients more often *are* aware of them. That's why measuring how others perceive us can be extremely valuable in understanding how we *actually* show up and impact other people's feelings. Emotional intelligence assessments become invaluable in this.

The other males very likely realize that Simon is not actually comfortable being vulnerable with them. Perhaps he also doesn't perceive them as being so empathetic to his problem, so he directs his attention to Stephanie. Because of their own conditioning with masculine gender norms, they understand this and even accept this. But we do a huge disservice to men by assuming they are not well placed to be vulnerable themselves, to accept vulnerability in others and to recognize their strong ability to also empathize. Remember the studies done in empathy that demonstrate there are *no* differences between the sexes in ability to emphasize.

And the impact here is huge. Empathy is downgraded as less important. Men apparently don't need to have it or demonstrate it. Their job is to find the solutions. The impact on Stephanie is very negative. Because Stephanie will have experienced variations of this behavior many times before it makes it pernicious. First, she's perceived as the empathetic witness and she's invested in helping solve the problem by first listening deeply. But when Simon switches eye contact and attention from her to the other men she's sent the message her job here is done.

The power play of 'taking charge' and 'taking care' behaviors

Do not underestimate the impact of this. Stephanie went from feeling very much involved, to being disregarded in the blink of an eye. Simon has failed to demonstrate that he values her ability to solve the business problem for him, as a unique individual. His behavior has reduced her to the token female, representing stereotypical abilities of her sex, but not to be taken seriously as a business leader.

But let's remember the context *is* business leadership. This program is for business leaders trying to help each other solve business problems. Stephanie is a business leader. Simon's failure to involve Stephanie in the solution means she feels neither that she belongs, nor that she is valued as a unique individual, separate from her sex. The stereotypical advantages of her sex meant she gained a place at the table, a novelty among a sea of male faces. But the willingness to accept her contribution evaporated, and her individual worth was not supported in this business leadership context.

We need to recognize that listening can create power, status and dominance differentials. In the gender dimensions to leadership discussion we need to keep top of mind the social behavior norms that *may* expect women to listen and support, and men to talk and make the decisions. Behaving counter to these 'norms' might just get us some valuable new perspectives and foster a culture of retention.

If Simon had demonstrated more inclusive behavior, he'd have downloaded his problems to the whole group, *and* he'd have accepted solutions from the whole group. Simple behaviors to demonstrate this might be making eye contact with different people. Leaders certainly need to be careful not to direct most of their attention to either one gender, or only some of the people. By doing so we send the signal we're actually a really poor leader. In contrast, if we acknowledge people individually and repeatedly, it's extremely powerful.

Deep listening requires more than simply being silent. And as we know being silent to listen is already a stretch-behavior for many leaders. It's one we very often hone-in on when working on behavior change to increase engagement and inspire performance from employees. Had Simon been Stephanie's manager he'd have inspired her to leave. And hopefully everyone would understand at this point that her departure would have *nothing* to do with confidence, babies or lack of competence.

Nurture the individual

The best antidote to this problem is to get to know your people as individuals. Actively initiating this relationship-nurturance, the N for Nurture in the HONOUR model, means meaningfully engaging with everyone in the team. It requires us to make the effort to understand the lives and drives of our people. Nurturing then guarantees that we see them as unique individuals and that *they feel seen as such*. In the gender dimensions to leadership discussion we cannot prioritize one sex over the other.

While we're on this important topic of listening, we need to recognize that one-sided conversations in themselves create binaries, the superior versus inferior, the power versus the subordinate roles. In the gender dimensions to leadership conversation it's often the male versus the female. Having balance in these communications is incredibly important if you want to create a sense of equality and inclusivity in the room.

Limiting beliefs

Classic limiting beliefs that tend to show up more often for women can be 'conflict is bad', 'I need to be liked', or 'everything has to be perfect'. The feminine norms of 'being nice in relationships' make avoidance of conflict and the need to please particularly powerful limiting beliefs. We've already discussed the social penalties of not being perceived as likeable for women, which will lead directly to exclusion. These penalties then impact a willingness to show up authentically, challenge, or speak up.

As we've discussed earlier the limiting belief that everything needs to be perfect invariably comes because women are penalized more if they make mistakes. So being aware of these and encouraging women to speak up, demonstrating that it is safe to do so, is a particularly powerful behavior. One that Simon failed miserably in demonstrating, but one that we can excel in if we're proactive in encouraging women's input.

Boxes and bubbles

We know from research that CEOs tend to talk more than anyone else. That means as a CEO or executive leader we need to get out of our leadership bubble.[6] Executive director of the MIT Leadership

7   277

Center at the Sloan School of Management, Hal Gregersen, describes this bubble as occurring when we acquire more power as leaders. Gregersen observed that subordinates are less willing to challenge leaders with a lot of power and prefer to give good news rather than bad. He interviewed 200 senior business executives and noticed that the ones whose companies were most innovative were the ones who strove to escape this bubble. "When you're in a box in an office, you've got to invent a way out of the box," according to Jeff Bezos, the founder of Amazon, and one of the leaders Gregersen interviewed.

It has been observed that as leaders acquire greater degrees of power and status people around them might be less willing to question them or give them feedback. As we acquire more power as leaders, we can also run the risk of having an inflated self-view. This is also compounded by the male female hierarchy that's implicit in our culture. As leaders we might also be less open to feedback. This is why hiring diverse people who are willing to treat us as an equal, despite gender, and challenge us, is important for leaders. And it's why we must treat them as equals too. It's why it's essential we understand whether how we identify with being a man or woman might bring any sense of inferiority or superiority. 'Yes' men and women are not likely to help the organization grow but sustain status quo. We need to act beyond prescriptive gendered behaviors.

Studies have found that as people gain more power and status their propensity to have empathy, and ability to be fair and collaborate can dwindle.[7] In one particular study it was found that the existence of power reduced the person holding the power's motivation to affiliate with the lower status group, extending to the leader having less empathy towards them. It seems it really is true,"Power tends to corrupt; absolute power corrupts absolutely." [8] We know for example, that the more power the more likely people are to be selfish and abuse that power. We need to keep this in mind as leaders, because the ability to affiliate with everyone is an essential component in demonstrating inclusive behaviors.

This potential for power to corrupt us is compounded by the hubris syndrome, which David Owen, a British parliamentarian and neuroscientist, wrote about.[9] He observed it as a disorder created by having power and massive success over a sustained period of time. This led to those who had it ignoring those in lower status positions. He specifically noted that one of the behaviors of these leaders was their impulsivity to "make swift decisions – sometimes based on little evidence" regarded as "of particular importance - arguably necessary - in a leader." Hubris syndrome may well have similar roots to the white male effect.

It's making impulsive decisions about others that senior executives need to be particularly wary of doing though. The need instead for empathy and the ability to put oneself in others' shoes is very necessary in modelling inclusive behaviors. It requires the ability to remain humble. It also requires a degree of gender agility. To not be overwhelmed by responsibilities requiring us to disconnect from other human beings as somehow inferior. To not be too overly invested in whatever gender norms prescribe we *ought* to be like.

Approaching situations with a beginner's mind and being open is of far greater benefit than asserting our dominant position. This again highlights the second O in HONOUR, Open. As the Dalai Lama puts it, "When you talk you are only repeating what you already know. But if you listen you may learn something new." Prompting others to speak and share by asking questions is the most powerful strategy of all for leaders. We need to have the humility to realize we may not know so much, and we may learn a lot by asking and listening. Being open enables this.

False assumptions

One of the greatest pieces of advice we ever heard was on a sales training course decades ago. If you're ever going to be really successful in sales one of the first things you need to understand is that you should never make assumptions about the people in front of you. It was sound advice, that carries very nicely over to the work of inclusivity. Never assume anything about anyone. Why?

Because to ASSUME makes an ASS out of U and ME!

Being Observant and Open are the antidote to many limiting beliefs around false assumptions. In the gender dimensions in leadership discussion these are widespread. Here are just a few examples. Prophesying about the future, we might assume our women are going off to have babies, or that they somehow will become incapable of doing their jobs once they do have babies. We simultaneously assume men will always be there, remaining ambitious and committed to the company. As we go on to expose in chapter 12, however, what men and women want looks very different to these assumptions in the research.

The classic sucker's choice of either / or thinking are the limiting beliefs we spent much of the first part of the book on. It's the myths around how men and women supposedly *are*. The binaries that persist that limit so much of us as humans, because others put us in boxes that they think we belong in, or because of the ones we close ourselves in. Prescriptive gender norms influence these beliefs powerfully, and often unconsciously. Our supposed 'innateness' and identity will influence the extent of these limiting beliefs' maladaptive effects.

The absolute judgement that someone 'is' something is another limiting belief. In the gender dimensions in leadership discussion this absolute judgement 'is' means you either conform to gender norms or you do not. And let's remember for women this creates a double bind, because conforming to being feminine is not congruent with stereotypes of leadership. This is because of another limiting belief, that we judge that leadership 'is' masculine.

Being Observant and Open to more information, different information and wider experiences, rather than absolutes, are the antidote to many of these false assumptions. By being Observant and Open we recognize our ignorance on certain topics, our blind spots, our bias and most powerfully our cognitive dissonance. Really exceptional leaders, people who personally and psychologically develop the most, are those who challenge their own values and beliefs. In the gender dimensions to leadership discussion we challenge our beliefs around gender, *and* around leadership.

Coaching using active inquiry

Coaching cultures for a long time have been propounded as creating positive, productive spaces. But the traditional interpretation of coaching where a superior, more experienced individual relates their knowledge and skills to a subordinate is not the type of coaching we mean. Mentoring often runs the danger of only telling. While there is a degree of 'telling' and 'teaching' necessary in mentoring or coaching, there is also a need for asking and enabling the mentee to self-manage and self-solve.

True coaching environments promote the crucial behavior that we ask questions to help another find *their* answers. That requires asking great, open questions. We don't ask leading questions that might have an agenda thus. As Charles Handy put it, "Necessity may be the mother of invention, but curiosity is the mother of discovery."[10] Leaders exercising this type of coaching behavior foster highly inclusive cultures, and highly innovative ones. But the skill doesn't stop at asking the question. It requires the ability to listen deeply to the answer. The skill of being able to actively inquire can be extremely difficult for leaders, more often used to telling or to a command-and-control style. But it is incredibly powerful if mastered.

Peter Drucker said, "The leader of the past knew how to tell. The leader of the future will know how to ask." Ideologies of patriarchy and business cultures built with a strong hierarchy and multiple layers of leadership do tend to have the command-and-control default behaviors we touched on earlier. Indeed, it's exactly this knowing 'how to tell' that has encapsulated the traditional view of coaching. And the traditional view of management.

And the traditional view of power structures in certain gender role dynamics.

Knowing how to ask however creates the situation where employees' basic psychological needs of "competence, relatedness and autonomy" are met.[11]Asking simultaneously invites and involves. It tells employees your input is valuable because you are unique. It tells employees you belong here with us because of and despite your uniqueness.

Recalling the study showing that the people with the most psychological well-being had a sense of agency and competence, draws on this theory of self-determination. We need to recognize that self-determination is as essential for women as for men. Agency is not gendered, but in our society it is. While we *tell* or micro-manage our employees, we don't enable this agency. We're more likely to dominate and suppress it. And we do it especially to women.

Feedback situations

Coaching can be particularly crucial in feedback situations where we know, for example, that women get lower quality feedback and less often. In turn some men can tend to become defensive when given feedback. These gendered reactions can be attributed back to the masculine and feminine gender norms, and how strongly some men and women may be adhering to them or be conflicted because of them. Downloading judgements may reinforce an expectation to conform to some gender norm.

By asking questions those leaders who effectively coach in a feedback situation in a curious and interested manner create safety, trust and self-autonomy in their employees. Gender norms are not relevant. Coaching can facilitate very meaningful interactions. Effective coaching utilizes the behaviors necessary to create a sense of feeling included, seen and respected. Humility is not telling but asking. Humility is not having the answers but wanting to understand what the other's ideas, and importantly feelings, are. This simultaneously demonstrates being open, welcoming others' uniqueness and our respect for them. It's also a nurturing behavior which can make the other person feel valued and supported.

From lip service to action

We finally come to Reverent in the HONOUR model. Feeling and showing respect for another. This is an intensely proactive word. We have to do it. It won't happen automatically. And by feeling it, really internalizing the sensation that this other person matters, we can build incredible, meaningful connections.

Exceptional leaders make those around them feel great, empowered and included. They inspire performance. This isn't sycophantism, or manipulation. Being Reverent to someone is saying you are worthwhile. You are equal with me. You are significant. You are exceptional. You are unique.

Being reverent is being other-focused. It's not just showing respect, letting bygones be bygones, allowing to live and let live, tolerance. It's actually putting people on a pedestal as unique, amazing, and belonging, no matter who they are.

This *is* the HONOUR model.

When you proactively and consistently feel and show respect to others, they will walk through fire for you.

When you don't do to others what you would not want them to do to you - like judge, criticize, diminish or make assumptions, - bridges instead of walls are built.

And we can move mountains together.

But we can actually only revere others when we revere ourselves. And this we can only do when we strive to self-actualize. When we are *more than just gender norm constructs*.

Key Points

Effective leadership communication is key to preventing people feeling they don't belong or aren't seen as unique.

Successful communication is about not interrupting, asking questions and listening deeply.

In inclusivity work the leader's self-worth is invaluable, their social worth not so much.

Equal footing, not power plays, are essential.

Leaders may lack empathy because they have more power. This creates a blind spot that leaders need to be aware of. It can diminish perspective taking, critical in modelling inclusive behaviors.

Empathy is noticing someone else's feelings *and* trying to understand why they might feel like that.

Disconnection from others may lead to lack of information. People may not share the bad news with leaders. Leaders may have an inflated self-view.

Leaders need to seek out information from diverse areas of the business, and from different people.

Every person will have a different perspective. Viewpoints are essential for getting new information.

Coaching skills are incredibly valuable for leaders to develop.

Limiting beliefs and false assumptions are discussed. Why 'to assume' makes and an 'ass out of u and me.'

The HONOUR model is a tool that can be used to model inclusive behaviors.

When we show Reverence towards people, we move from lip service to action.

Case study

Harvard Executive Development Program Simon and Stephanie, gender role behavior, tiny behaviors have a massive impact.

Self-reflective coaching questions and considerations

What would someone else do in my role as leader?

How can I be more empathetic?

How can I show more interest in the people in my organization who I wouldn't normally come into contact with?

What can I do to make people feel safer and listened to?

What might I be wrong about?

What if the answer is the opposite of what I think it is?

Who are all the people who made today possible for me?

How can I learn from all the people I have around me?

What am I demonstrating that allows people to share problems with me?

What am I doing that allows us to solve this problem together?

What am I doing that shows people I don't have all the answers and am not complacent?

Identify one behavior which you and your colleagues can implement immediately to prevent gender bias in yourselves and in your organization.

Practice coming up with different possibilities to the situation you see before you. Get comfortable being uncomfortable – learn to stay with the feeling.

Listening – Listen means Silent

What can I do to ensure I talk less and listen more?

What can I do to ensure everyone feels included?

What can I ask rather than tell?

The HONOUR model

How can I 'honour' the people I work with?

How can I demonstrate Humility?

How can I become more Objective?

How can I Nurture the people around me?

How can I become more Open to other's ideas, or their help?

How can I understand people's Unique contribution and sense of self?

How can I Revere people?

12   When Less Is More

The psychic entropy peculiar to the human condition involves seeing more to do than one can actually accomplish and feeling able to accomplish more than what conditions allow.
Mihaly Csikszentmihalyi, Hungarian American psychologist

For women judges in the Netherlands the lack of women in senior leadership roles is something of an anomaly. 62% of judges are women and it seems that there are certain critical factors that create this situation.[1] Elif Isitman wrote an excellent account of the issues at play here in a report she wrote for The Financial Times (Het Financieele Dagblad) in the Netherlands in 2018. In a role noted for its need for fairness and equity women seem well suited.

After an initial letter selection, candidates are tested in an open system and assessed on their analytical and logical thinking. Despite what the stereotypes say women do very well on this test and many go through to the next stage of selection where they are assessed on their firmness and social commitment. What the results show are that more women than men make it through this process.

Contrast this with the 19 law firms in the country who all notably signed up to the Charter for Top Talent in 2008, which had the express goal of getting at least 30% of the partner roles assigned to women. A decade later, according to the Nederlandse Orde van Advocaten (The Netherlands bar for legal professionals), 44% of women are lawyers, so gender is almost equal in 2017, yet of the 19 law firms only 3 could boast having reached the threshold of over 30% of their *partners* being female.

We should remember that judges don't need to make a profit or be particularly ego centric. They need instead to be fair and logical, showing clarity and a commitment to the communities they serve. It should also be noted that there have been no clear gender differences found between how men and women sentence. It's certainly interesting that as soon as the need for profits re-emerge women are apparently not in those top positions. While the average judge earns 137,000 euros, a partner in a law firm can earn many times more that amount. Isitman reported Evelie de Greene, judge and President of the Noord Holland Court as saying: "The sector isn't arrogant. We're not so fond of showing off. That does not fit with a judge."

It's a clue that there's still an over-emphasis of dominance and the need to win that still pervades the corporate world culture. This ego-centric style is *not* the style of leadership that creates great companies according to Collins' research. Judges don't need to make a profit or be arrogant. They simply need to be equitable, fair and make decisions based on the facts. Might some of those traits tie in with being better leaders, especially when we're talking about really making something of inclusivity? Shouldn't corporations also be run based on equity, fairness and factual objective decisions? Remember the Gallup survey that cited the number one reason that led to burnout, which costs businesses millions, was unfair treatment.

Flexibility

Women in the most senior roles show up less in profit driven establishments and it should be noted also in the very highest ranks of the judiciary. While judges are well-represented none of the top courts in the Netherlands have female presidents. Is this about women avoiding competitive situations, men failing to share power or something else still? One of the biggest differences between judges and lawyers is that of the workday and flexibility.

Since 1989 it has been possible to be a judge part time in the Netherlands and there are as many men as women who work as part time judges, dispelling the claim that this is something only women want or need, in the judiciary at least. Finding ways to make the job as flexible as possible can be more effective for retaining women than creating policies or stipulating quotas that might be less effectual in isolation. Running quotas might also run the risk of compromising the quality of the candidate, if done for the sake of the exercise. Flexibility baked into the role, rather than as a possibility, depending on the candidate's circumstances, might also retain men who are motivated by things other than status, purely financial reward or the need or expectation to work all hours.

Retaining talent despite lifestyle changes

There's also another fundamental point to be made about what sets the judges' system apart. It's normal to become a judge in your thirties and once you become one, you're a judge for life. That takes away pressure to perform another function, say becoming President of a court, within a certain time frame. It means the potential conflict between starting a family and chasing for a promotion don't become an issue. And it forces us to ask what makes the judiciary any different from any other career trajectory? If women and men are both seen as equally competent for a high-profile role, whether they're 30 or 70, why is it that in roles in the corporate world there appears to be a distinct link between age and promote-ability? Between a career break and ability to pick up where one left off on returning to work?

Could this be another excuse to keep economic power in the hands of the few, with an apparent propensity to over-emphasize primacy of a work as proof of commitment to the job as a senior corporate leader? And then because primacy of work is seen as a masculine norm, might we exclude women because of the binary nature of our thinking? Not only that, but by reducing the contenders, we reduce the competition, thereby making it easier to win these roles for competitive types. Competitive types may lack other key characteristics that are essential in leadership. Specifically, we think here of the Elitists in the framework, high on unconscious bias and low on inclusive behaviors.

The implicit career freeze that becoming a judge creates ensures that talent is retained despite external personal factors. Presidents of courts can become so for 10 years and they can apply for this at any point during their career as a judge, which means the age limits and associated time pressure on reaching a specific high point of a career don't exist. Let's recognize too that implicit ageism, and associated gender biases so closely associated with ageism, are coming into play and can also be mitigated with such an approach. Imagine if such systems were also woven better into corporate hierarchies such that talent could be retained and capitalized on.

Once a judge finishes being a President of a court after 10 years, they can simply return to judge-status again without all the hierarchical drivers of more and better. These pressures simply don't have a place. In the corporate world ageism conspires very often against women and men, after gender discrimination has already begun to derail many, especially women. This ageism should prompt us to ask questions. How many older talented women with exactly the fairness and social commitment that corporations would benefit from, are lost from the workplace? How many older males with a great deal of experience, circumspection, and less ambition, might benefit corporate culture as a whole, but are being passed over?

One study showed that while managers and over 50's rated themselves low on management potential, over 50's, not surprisingly, scored higher on knowledge, skills and customer understanding than younger workers. As the study pointed out, older workers are frequently overlooked, despite the fact they have essential knowledge to fill the leadership skills gap.[2] What an irony and a lost opportunity.

While the emphasis is often on the unfairness for women, we must recognize that this ageism comes equally into play for many males. The tenure of the average CEO can often be short lived, and we frequently coach males who feel they've no place to go once they've reached the pinnacle, CEO status, of their career. Returning to the conformity to masculine gender role norms list, many of these men deal with psychological distress around no longer having the status they once had, or the same primacy of work that gave them identity.

Likewise, the highly competent women who apparently fell into the maternal ditch, if indeed they ever managed to get over the maternal wall are often over-looked for simply trying to re-enter the job market. They are often deemed as not being current, or not having recently 'contributed' if they happened to take extended time off for family. If more corporate leaders demonstrated more judge-like characteristics they might better address the facts, objective performance criteria, and spot the best talent for the job, rather than creating the inequity of more of the same.

Overwhelm is a huge problem

It is also necessary to question the overriding assumption here that if you are in a senior leadership position it somehow equates to needing to give more of your life to your work or suggests that this might be a necessary pre-requisite. The counter argument to this is that those who can balance commitments harmoniously within their life between work, play, family, and hobbies are more likely to be effective as people and as leaders.

Time management and overwhelm show up as some of the most prevalent issues executive leaders seek to discuss in coaching and creating cultural change in many environments is urgently needed. Promoting quality and excellence above unrelenting dedication and workaholism, leaders can better thrive themselves, and better serve their people. Plummeting productivity and engagement at all-time lows, with even more worrying statistics of disengagement – remember people who are actively sabotaging their organizations at all-time highs, - is simply a result of the de-humanizing condition of working today, and the unhealthy working cultures that plague many organizations.

While the World Economic Forum is exploring which types of jobs could embrace a shorter working week, progressive corporations should think about how they can introduce a shorter working week for *all* their workers. Plenty of research exists showing that people can focus better, be just as productive, often with increased levels of quality and creativity, and are thus much more loyal and therefore engaged if companies give them flexibility. Happy and rested people are far more productive than jaded and overwhelmed ones. And if this flexibility is offered to all workers, instead of just those with families, then new leaks for inequality and the related resentments they create don't get sprung.

Lessons from this kind of experiment regarding the shorter work week were recently learnt in Microsoft when the Japanese office closed every Friday in August. The Work-Life Choice Challenge Summer 2019 project led to a productivity rise of 40%. With the explicit orders by the CEO to "Work a short time, rest well and learn a lot", the result was that 92% of its 2,300 employees said they liked the shorter week. The company also saved in terms of electricity use which was 23% lower and paper printed reduced by a staggering 59% demonstrating that other savings could also be made. It seems that people rose to the challenge of being able to produce the same results with 20% less time. Rest really does make us more productive.

It is also helpful to reflect on the effects that the Covid-19 pandemic has had on people's view of remote working. Pre-pandemic many companies seemed to carry the attitude that this was not conducive to producing effective work, and workers wouldn't want it. However, Gallup reported that three out of five workers would prefer to continue working from home after the pandemic.[3] Now it's been forced upon many it seems some organizations have learnt that this was possible after all. With large companies like Twitter telling their workers they can work from home "forever" and Facebook's Mark Zuckerberg predicting that 50% of workers will be working remotely within 5 to 10 years.

Google, a company that notoriously didn't allow remote work, also made the statement that workers not needing to work onsite could extend working from home until the end of the year. It's ironic that these technology companies themselves didn't seem to understand the value that technology could facilitate in terms of remote work until forced to do so. It also shows just how difficult it appears for organizations to change even when everything was in place for them to do so. It seems even the ability to do affective work was stereotypically associated with being in the office space. Remember stereotypes have no logic.

Valuing availability above competency, males are often expected to be available for longer hours, and women are often assumed to be busy with family once they've started one, and are therefore assumed to be unavailable. In our second study conducted around the disconnect between what men and women thought were the issues that led to fewer females in senior leadership roles, demands of senior jobs and the implicit requirement to dedicate many hours above the normal working week were seen as a factor that might get in the way for women especially. In the United States, the Fair Labor Standards Act (FLSA) doesn't prescribe any legal guidelines that dictate whether or not a worker is a full-time employee. The determination of what constitutes full-time employment depends on the company's policy and practice of defining full-time employees, unless other country laws define this differently. For most countries the average working week is 38-40 hours.

We have to question does the ability to work longer hours make the work better? As we are finally beginning to grasp, amidst an epidemic of burn out, and unmanageable workloads which often necessitate longer working hours, these are key reasons employees are overwhelmed.[4] While the unnatural expectations and pressures that seem to promote workaholism prevail, men and women are both suffering. The assumption is that women want life balance more than men, yet the research suggests men are in search of it *even more* than women. A study done by A Great Place to Work, which polled more than 3 million employees in the US alone found that men were likely to cite work life balance as an important factor in their choice of employer 2.8 times more than women at 2.6 times.[5]

Main bread winner or tear and share

Another important point to note is that men are far more likely to suffer stress around their ability to hold onto a job, again showing that they are still expected to be the main career pursuer and bread winner. This stress around being the financial bread winner is also linked to the earning capacity of wives in heterosexual couples. For example, we know that where men were the sole bread winner in households, they experience some stress, whereas where the female partner in the household earnt 40% of the household income, the males were the least stressed. Psychological distress in men reached its highest level when men were solely dependent on their wives' income.[6]

This last fact demonstrates again how distress is created in men through gender norm deviance, that is where the situation departs from the gender norm expectation that males generally should earn more than their wives. If you don't believe this fact Pew Research Center recently found that 76% of people believed men faced a lot of pressure to support their family financially. It's not far from the truth to conclude that generally men are uncomfortable earning less than women, or not earning at all, and yet 48% of men surveyed by Pew said they would like to be stay-at-home-fathers.[7] Let's just repeat that: 48% of men said they would like to be stay-at-home fathers.

Here we see the conflict of expected gender norms with individual desires. We see how they play into the discussions around the gender pay gap. Studies have shown that having women in managerial roles does not of itself lead to more equality in pay, although in one study it was found to have a positive influence on the wages of the lower qualified within organizations. This particular study used a sample of 5,022 workers in 94 large workplaces in Germany.[8] Germany still has a high gender pay gap. It is also observed that policies in Germany have traditionally tended to sustain the traditional male bread winner/female-home-maker-family situation. This continues to institutionalize women as secondary earners and men as main providers.

The same study also showed that having a same sex supervisor paid off for men, but not women. In other words, the pay gap remained consistent specifically at higher levels within the organization. The researchers found "evidence that male supervisors use their power to promote their in-group". We'd argue this is evidence that men are under psychological pressure with respect to the societal expectations about who earns what. This last fact is emphasized in the Pew Research by the fact that, in couples where the women earned more than their husbands at the *start* of the relationship, the husbands did *not* suffer psychological distress. This should again give us significant pause for thought. Stereotypes of what gender norms should be, that the male *should* earn more than his wife, are also at odds with having a healthy psyche. And they are getting in the way of true progress in organizations where some women do make it into managerial positions.

The German study further suggested that there are limits to women as change agents, further finding that the biggest discrepancies in earnings were found when females managed other females. This has been highlighted in other work that females themselves are biased towards males and are more likely to promote them than females.[9] It emphasizes the very real impact that implicit bias has on the choice of leaders we make. It underlines again that the queen bee syndrome may well be instrumental in sustaining gender inequality. We must understand that gender norms too easily straight jacket our attributes as individuals. And without discussion within leadership circles about all these nuanced risks we are unlikely to see change. The German study concluded that "Integrating women into managerial and supervisory roles does not automatically reduce gender inequalities; its impacts are contingent on organizational context."

We also suggest it might well be worthwhile doing research into the psychological distress that women who have earned a significant amount, but who are then impacted by the bias that is the maternal wall and ditch, may also have. We'd suggest, just as men suffer if they have been the main bread winner in the family, and no longer are, women too experience this distress. We believe this is a key additional stressor for a lot of women who were in highly successful executive roles, but then chose to leave to have a family.

Not only do these women no longer have the status they once had, they no longer make the economic contribution they did, and they are simultaneously assumed by society to be incapable of having achieved such agency, economic independence and status in the first place. That last point has consequences. Were a system like the one for judges being able to become presidents at any point in their lifetime built explicitly into hiring, or rather re-hiring practices for women who were formerly in executive roles, this issue would also be addressed.

Stepping out of gender roles

Rather than caving to the group that suggests that men should 'man up' or that women should be more of a 'real woman' in a given social context, we need to recognize there's a serious human issue here. Societal expectations of conformity to gender norms are detrimental to many individuals, men and women. Shouldn't people as individuals decide how much they themselves want to identify with their given gender? Shouldn't we in the social context allow them the freedom to step out of those gendered expectations if they so choose to? And let's remember while there's been greater opportunity to assume male roles for women the same has not been true for men. This is culturally significant.

In the Netherlands it might be more normal to see a man at the school gates collecting his kids, but when we interviewed senior executives in the US, they reflected on how uncommon it was to see men doing this. But with masculine norms changing over time, work-life balance a more pressing issue for men, and familial participation by men being recognized as leading to higher psychological well-being not just for fathers, but also for their children, re-assessment of these gendered roles is critical.[10]

Corporations potentially ensure this by creating paid leave that is specifically reserved for fathers, and that if taken, has proven to lead to more equitable care of the children at home years later. It's also led to greater well-being for both mothers and fathers, better psychological and behavioral development of the children themselves, and more equity in the sharing of household tasks. This share in care then ultimately creates more freedom for women within the work context. However, what we still see is that men are far less likely to take this paternal leave if it is voluntary. They are very conscious that they might jeopardize future promotion should they do so.

Our own research highlighted the prevalent idea among many that women find it much harder to combine child-rearing and working. Yet we know from other research that childless women are also not progressing beyond the third or fourth promotion. While all the leaders identified recognized there was a huge problem in not retaining female talent higher up the pipeline, there was a general lack of clear knowledge about what the issues really were that have been confirmed in other research. In a Lean In and McKinsey Women in the Workplace Report[11] only 2% of women planned to leave work to have a family, numbers so low one has to question what else is going on apart from nature, baby-bearing and family considerations.

So why are women not progressing? Our research showed that the male rational mostly centered around baby-bearing and family pressures as the central problem, with women displaying a lack of confidence and lack of willingness to go for the lead role as reason two. The women meanwhile provided a plethora of reasons for why they were not able to progress. While family issues undoubtedly played a role, there was a strong feeling that roles were not open to women. More often, rather than lacking confidence per se, there was a general frustration that they would have to fight very hard to make the next role a success. Twenty years into their careers many of these women were jaded and fed up.

Psychological burn out for women

One can draw many conclusions from this, but many led to the conclusion that the double bind and high competency threshold are core sticking points. The high competency threshold leads to a sense of 'psychological burnout' over time for many women. In our research we have discovered that women remain frustrated and unable to uncover exactly what the next hoop is that they may need to jump through to be heard, recognized, valued. These issues of psychological burnout should not be underestimated, nor ignored by senior leaders.

Looking at the 5 reasons for burn out that Gallup cites, we can see how the double bind might play into many of them. Remember bias is at the top, followed by unmanageable workloads and lack of clarity on the role. We know from other research that women are far more likely to suffer from burnout than men, and we can directly correlate this to the differing conditions for men and women within the workplace.[12]

Could it be that the other reasons cited for burn out over and above bias might have a greater impact on women when we consider the cultural and societal expectations that are placed on women – being nice, not saying no, putting relationships before self? These all contribute to women's lack of clarity over their role, setting boundaries and taking account of what others expect of them. And while it's partly their responsibility to find that clarity for themselves and to set boundaries, it's the leader's job to spot these invisible but ever-present pressures. It's the leader's job to ensure unbiased expectations in the work setting.

Not just a wall, but a ditch

Very many women returning to work find a ditch past the maternal wall. Seen as having been out of the talent pool for too long, and therefore undeserving of the places that their hardworking colleagues have earned by sticking around through the years, they are placed in more junior roles with less responsibility, and less pay. The so-called motherhood penalty is well researched and observed at this point. Parental status effects women in negative ways, but may improve conditions for men. This again reflects the cultural norm that men be the main breadwinner for their family and women the family-focused carer.[13]

Pay discrepancies are the most obvious example of this discrimination but not the only one. At the same time those women who stay in work while rearing a young family, sometimes working part-time, many still remaining working full-time, are frequently passed over. They are judged unable to commit in the way the role will demand.

One male we interviewed said, "It weighs heavy on me that my grandchildren are in day care from 8.30 until 6." While he gave socio-economic reasons as key stressors in requiring women to continue working while bringing up small children, he recognized that they were not getting into leadership roles as easily, and put it down to them having to run the household and a career simultaneously. His impression was that companies were very slow to adapt to allowing sabbaticals, flexible work and mid-career breaks.

It might well be that through the expectations set on women some are quicker to reflect on the likely strain that trying to combine a leadership role and family life might inflict on them. Meanwhile the expectation from society on men is still that they are simply expected to be the bread winners. We also know women still do more household tasks and care giving tasks at home.[14] These conflicting expectations of intense, prolonged work, while trying to have a life outside of work, are creating impossible odds for success in either, and an additional barrier to taking on leadership roles perceived as requiring more dedication. But if family is really the issue, why is it that 15% of mothers surveyed were more interested in being a top executive than women without children?[15]

Let's remind ourselves of the case of Medini Bardhi at WeWork, demoted after each of her pregnancies. The key word here is *demoted*. Why would she somehow be now unable to fulfil a role that she had been apparently earlier competent to fulfil? Too easily, it seems, women are often edged out of positions they were in while men, often without the experience, are then given these roles. There is no logic in the idea that a woman is no longer capable of doing a job she had proven capable of doing, simply because she was absent for some time. But let's remember stereotypes have no logic.

Juxtapose this against a situation where another employee, male or female, has not actually yet done the role but apparently shows 'potential', and so earns the right to that role, and the irrationality is complete. It's the same knee jerk emotion that means males often get promotions years earlier than women. It's the same irrational logic that might prevent a woman, say in her early fifties poised to take on a senior leadership role, but not being given the chance. Remembering that ageism is just another form of bias and discrimination.

Everyone can care, and luckily many do

Women are at risk of being disempowered in some way all the time, while patriarchy exists, since let's be reminded, patriarchy dictates that men are ultimately in charge. We talked earlier about the boxes that shape identities in women and men so powerfully, and the negative impact it can have on how women specifically are perceived in the working world. Full time job? Then you're not home with the kids. Home with the kids? Then you're not a very strong woman, or intelligent. Young woman venturing into the world? - must be looking for a husband, threat, threat. Time and again women's worth, where heterosexuality is still viewed as the norm in society, is attained through their positioning to men.

This is problematic for everyone, not least all those who don't define themselves through a traditional heterosexual framework, but frankly for everyone who doesn't define themselves solely on their relationship to others, let alone men specifically. Part of the problem in this discussion is that so much of the conversation has centered around families that it has often excluded other people who don't follow the model of heterosexual relationship as the norm or have children. That is also why crucially benefits, - whether they be part-time work, flex work, job share, sabbaticals, career breaks, - should be offered to everyone.

7

Taking the paternal maternal leave discussion as an example. An even more effective way to reduce bias, stigma and ambiguity is to simply offer caregiver benefits to all employees, rather than naming them as maternal or paternal. There are more reasons than just children that can interfere with a person's ability to work. Elder parents, sick spouses or other relations also require care, and the so-called sandwich generation's increasing responsibilities add to this need to monitor the social trends that influence the pressures on employees.[16] It has been observed that in the US for example, nearly half of those aged between 40 and 59 are supporting both aging parents, younger children and/or grown children (18 years or older) who are struggling to achieve their own financial independence.

While the additional stress of this adds an emotional and financial burden, the care giver benefit would certainly help to alleviate some of this burden on employees, and at the same time take away the perceived inequality that can sometimes be seen when benefits are available for mothers and no one else. Of course, this latter issue is less of an issue in America, one of only two countries in the world where paid leave for new mothers is not guaranteed, with the associated result that one in four mothers are back at work within 10 days of giving birth. Not just seen as something quite barbaric by other developed countries with more sophisticated social welfare systems, health systems and corporate parental leave packages, there may be other consequences for this situation.

The right to create life
and the right to earn to pay for it and thrive

The United States is the only developed country with a *rising maternal mortality rate*, which actually surpasses every other *developing* (that's right, developing) country in the world. Not only that but there are significant health disparities for Black women[17] and Alaskan American women, both three to four times more likely than white women to die from pregnancy complications and/or childbirth.[18] While many might think this not relevant to the corporate world quite the opposite is true. Raise the social determinants of health, by raising incomes to be in line with others and access to health insurance, and this number would reduce significantly. How? By preventing racism, sexism and pay inequality.

Taking the Black women's experience as an example, the chronic stress of not just poverty but racism has been shown to have deleterious effects on health outcomes for Black women.[19] And crucially for those assuming that it's not the corporate world's responsibility to address the social inequities beyond their doors, whose is it then if Black women are paid just 63 cent on every dollar white, non-Hispanic men make? Take it a step further. The median wage for a Black woman in the US was $36,227 per year, *$21,698 less* than for a non-white Hispanic man.[20] These inequities in pay, which we know are well researched across the corporate world, and hidden in many corporations who avoid any transparency over their pay scales for just this reason, have a serious knock-on effect for those with reduced economic power and reduced access to care.

Problems related to pregnancy and maternal mortality rates in Black women span all incomes and education levels which mean this is an issue for all Black women.[21] And having inequalities in health care and economic access are not just a Black woman's issue but a human issue. If you are employing Black women then, as the National Partnership reflects in its conclusions, "we need systemic change that... makes the places Black women live and work healthier, fairer and more responsive to their needs. Only when we do that will Black women be able to achieve their optimal health and well-being throughout their lifespan, including if they chose to become parents."

Let's remind ourselves: when there is gender equality, economies and societies thrive. Having a rising maternal mortality rate *higher* than all other developing countries certainly exposes gaping holes in the so-called superiority of Western capitalism. And there is certainly nothing exceptional about that.

Access to paid leave is crucial to everyone but even more so to those groups who have lower health outcomes and are less likely to get paid leave to care for themselves or family members. These same people are undoubtedly some of the most talented among us. We cannot afford to lose these talented people because of embedded structural and illogical biases, racism and sexism. Choosing to have a family should NEVER preclude anyone from the equal right to economic access and opportunity.

The challenge is set.

Sit with your team and state the following: "We are going to create a diverse, inclusive, engaged work force within three months. What are all the things we are going to do to make that happen?"

It's time for action.

Key Points

The meaning of status for men and women is important to discuss.

Older workers are frequently overlooked yet have just the skills we need to fill the leadership gap.

Overwhelm, presenteeism and pressure to work long hours do not lead to more productive workplaces.

Experiments with shorter working hours lead to more productivity.

There's a clear conflict of gender role norms with individual desires.

Women appear more ambitious than men, and men want work life balance more than women, according to the latest research.

Bias in terms of *who should earn what* is fueled by gender role norms and creates gender role strain.

Surely who earns what and who does what should *not* be determined by gender, but by ability and personal desire.

Burn out in the workplace is much higher for women. Unfair treatment is likely to be the main cause.

Having care leave for everyone prevents inequality.

48% of men in the US want to stay full-time at home.

Creating 'creative' succession plans which tackle the very costly loss of talent inspire engagement. That saves a lot of money for businesses.

Case study

Judges in the Netherlands. It's possible to be a judge part time. There are almost equal numbers of men and women judges.

Judges are appointed for life which creates a career freeze, meaning they can apply for a position as the President of a Court as a high point of their career, at any time in their lifetime.

Self-reflective coaching questions and considerations

How can you build more flexibility into people's roles to accommodate people's own agency and personal life choices?

What can you do to help people feel able to share aspects of their personal lives and fully express themselves?

What can you do to better understand people's loves, lives and drives?

What can you do to create more work life balance personally?

How might you share that with others and role model the importance of taking down time?

What ideas could you implement that might create ways to retain people who leave the organization for a period of time due to changes in their personal life.

What policies do you have for welcoming older people/mothers/people who may have been unemployed/ people with disabilities/minority groups into the work force?

What more things could you be doing?

What levels of overwork and overwhelm are there in the organization at the current time?

How overwhelmed and overburdened do you feel yourself?

What can you do to alleviate this?

Who can you ask to help you?

What are you doing to support and check that your people are not over-burdened?

What creative and novel ideas do you have around reducing the number of hours people work, while maintaining levels of productivity?

How might you be able to re-define leadership roles such that more people can have the opportunity to lead and sponsor others?

What are you doing to ensure that your remote workers feel valued and seen?

Take actions. Lip service is completely insufficient.

Sit with your team and state the following: We have to create a diverse, inclusive, engaged work force within three months. What are all the things we are going to do to make that happen?

Conclusion

13 NIMBY, Nationalism, Namaste

If they don't give you a seat at the table, bring a folding chair.
Shirley Chisholm, first woman to run for a presidential nomination,
and first African American woman to do so

We've been applying Shirley Chisholm's rhetorical advice to women for years now. We need to start applying it to men in the gender parity discussion. If you as a male leader have reached this point the takeaway should be this. Men need to 'lean in' to this conversation about gender parity. It is absolutely in our interests to do so. Leaders may need to step aside and let different leaders in. These other leaders ought to represent what's missing from the world demographic in senior corporate roles, - women and other marginalized groups. Homogeneity stifles innovation and change, and misses market opportunities.

In the early 90's there was a great drive towards getting environmental issues on the corporate agenda. In the UK the Environmental Protection Act 1990 was ratified. Most organizations were beginning to look into creating their own environmental policies for the first time. NIMBY became a buzz acronym of the time. It stood for Not In My Back Yard. It referred to the idea that people tended to shirk their responsibilities in terms of environmental responsibility. These same people did not want the problems environmental pollution delivered on their doorstep. NIMBY's message contained the same seeds as the belief system in the current wave of nationalism. The kern of its message was we do not want those problems here, and if it's not here it's not our problem. Responsibility for equality appears to be shirked in a similar way.

Embrace what's in your backyard

NIMBY's ideological framework is not dissimilar to nationalism in that it states we had no problems until you people showed up, missing the whole point that 'you' people might inextricably be linked to 'us', whether they bring problems with them or not. In a global economy nationalism is an ideology that has irrelevance fraying its seams. It's a great irony that many of the countries that have this drive towards nationalism themselves have overturned people's, nations, cultures and claimed them as their own. The seeds of dominance and 'our normal and our ways', assimilation being the normal and the way, abound. Our ignorance of our own interdependence is a damning failing of what should mark us out as an otherwise intelligent species. We're still evolving.

Planetary health, a new discipline that focuses on the increasingly visible connections among the well-being of humans, other living things and entire ecosystems, is something we ought now to embrace. The ancients already understood this. Many indigenous people and tribes around the world, living in harmony with the natural world, respected the boundaries with the natural environment, and the need for diversity and biodiverse ecosystems. The loss of this indigenous knowledge, language and ancient wisdom about the natural world, is a loss for us all. Most of it was dismantled and destroyed by colonizers. Homogenists, who don't know what they don't know, and Elitists who want to dominate and not let others in, may act in a similar way in the corporate space.

We are undeniably and utterly interdependent and pretending otherwise as individual, leader or organization is a fallacy. Despite the joy of the Brexiteers none of us are islands anymore, neither are our countries, surrounded by sea or landlocked. Nor are our corporations. These are inextricably linked through trade, our thirst for progress and knowledge, and through our humanity to every other human on this earth. Events in recent times have proven again our dependency upon each other for better or worse. As leaders, just as the countries and corporations we represent, we can ill-afford to act like islands.

The Covid-19 pandemic has exposed massive social injustices. The extent of its devastation within a given country has exposed those leaders who didn't act swiftly enough to lock down or impose, hard, unpopular but necessary measures. The white male effect was widely pervasive, with some male leaders claiming Covid-19 would not be a problem. These same leaders were unable to unite people, and instead divided them. The pandemic has exposed the massive discrepancies between the haves and the have nots. It's exposed the health and social fragility of people already vulnerable because of injustice and prejudice.

Stereotyping and bias are diluted 'nicer' terms for what's ultimately this injustice, prejudice and discrimination. Stereotypes and bias can have massive damaging consequences, and they lead to unsafe, non-thriving societies, in a multitude of ways. The pandemic very probably inflamed prejudices that confronted white people with the indiscriminate murder of Black people by some white policemen.[1] This brutality is not isolated to these groups though. Just another wakeup call, in a series of wakeup calls, that leaders, by definition, shouldn't need waking up to. Masters at inclusion make sure they don't have blind spots and turn blind eyes. They make it their business to know what's happening with *all* the people they are responsible for. They take the responsibility to ensure everyone is thriving.

Thinking back to Maslow's triangle and our inverted equality triangle we need to recognize that addressing bias and stereotyping at the most basic levels for all humans is essential to preventing these massive discrepancies in how people are seen and treated. It also prevents any unpleasant consequences that follow when there *are* massive discrepancies. For everyone. The sooner we accept that fact the better we'll be able to cooperate and collaborate for the challenges ahead. Corporate leaders can have a massive influence in society, for better or worse, in this endeavor.

Be loud and proud about inclusivity

Aristotle wrote, "Man is by nature a social animal…anyone who either cannot lead the common life or is so self-sufficient as not to need to, and therefore does not partake of society, is either a beast or a god." Leaders can ill afford to act like either. We live in a global society and corporations create their own global societies and cultures. As leaders we need to have the capacity to deal with the human implications of a corporate global society in an inclusive, interculturally and gender articulate way. The ideal is to create these, not just as great places to work, but as thriving societies in themselves. As Brené Brown says, "Daring leaders who live into their values are never silent about hard things".[2] To be a good leader we need to show massive proactivity in DE&I work. Now. And we need to be loud and proactive. Now.

Having people who undeniably care for others through their relationships will be essential to this. Having people unequivocally effective in taking charge, stepping up and taking tough decisions with compassion, humility and humanity will also be essential to this. Being man, woman or gender identified in some other way will be *irrelevant* to this. Creating gender parity throughout the organization starts at the bottom. It means getting fundamentally equality in pay, opportunity for everyone and care giving structures that everyone needs, not just mothers, in place. Leaders possessing the right awareness, skills and emotional intelligence will mean everything in differentiating the great corporations, businesses and leaders of the future, from the solely profit seekers.

Business has a profound job to play on the stage of the world. It needs strong ambassadors who possess taking charge and taking care qualities. If men can step up to the challenge, they'll remain in prime leadership positions, continuing to make a positive impact. If women and minorities can step up and be *pulled* in, not *just* be told to lean in, they'll take a rightful share in those leadership positions. That share will lead to better decisions that lead to better business for everyone. The middle way will be for everyone to take their share of the responsibility and that means that men in positions of power need to critically assess what that power means and how they are using it. As Buffet said, "Resistance among the powerful is natural when change clashes with their self-interest." The white male effect and socially organized denial are very real phenomenon that leaders, all of us, must reconcile. The health of ourselves, our businesses and our planet depend upon it.

Leaders sold on the masculine stereotype will struggle to let women in, and their businesses will struggle too. Leaders who want the best bottom line for their companies and are motivated for that reason to take active steps to get more women in their leadership positions, may fare a little better. But it's the leaders who unequivocally recognize and act to correct the unfairness and disparity that currently exists who'll soar. These leaders are already able to exercise leadership skill far beyond the limits of command-and-control behaviors. These leaders are unthreatened by the skills and talents of smart women and people of difference around them. People, men, women, and everyone who identifies in some other way with gender, who are able to unify rather than separate, are the leaders we need. It's for us all to hire the *most competent*, regardless of gender, not the loudest or most confident. We must select emotionally intelligent leaders. We must select people who are *masters at inclusion*.

Having read this book you've learnt that we can clearly correlate a lack of more senior female leaders to unconscious, explicit and implicit bias.[3] We can equally correlate a lack of competent male and female leaders to bias around what traits are perceived to be needed in good leaders. It is therefore beholden on companies to help their leaders understand bias. It's crucial to understand the psychological impact that gender identity and the social context have on our behaviors.

Since most leaders are men it is logical to create coaching and training programs specifically geared toward men on how to recognize bias, and not just programs for women. It's imperative to get beyond conversations and to take action. In the true spirit of inclusivity this should be done together.

We must constantly strive to remember that focusing on 'fixing' women and blaming men will fail everyone. It exacerbates internalized sexism, and it creates gender role strain. Being in denial around institutional and social issues across gender will lead to poor outcomes. Closing our eyes and ears to the Pandora's box of intersectional issues will similarly fail. It's become very necessary to deepen our knowledge around the reasons for insisting on giving the types of advice we currently give to women. The current conversation and drive to get more women into senior leadership roles is dominated by women and women networks. It should be an inclusive conversation with as many men involved.

Social, psychological and emotional intelligence are needed,
and we need to measure them

Most of the literature is written by women, read by women. Men are rarely engaged in the conversation, often feeling blamed for it, being blamed for it, or powerless to change it. Sometimes this is accompanied by a belief that women don't want or shouldn't be in leadership roles. Often there's a disconnect between the important work DE&I groups do and an understanding that the CEO and senior leaders make or break the take up of any diversity and inclusivity initiatives. Like any other change this needs to be led from and modelled at the top.

Male boards, CEOs and senior leaders need to be socially, psychologically and emotionally aware of how common bias is. How destructive it can be. How much it's costing in terms of lack of retention. Bias reduces visibility to talent, feeding the 'war on talent' mentality. It leads to poor leadership choices. It reduces revenues and profits. It makes many companies less appealing to global markets and customers. Being targeted in the approach to coaching men and women to navigate bias in the workplace is a profoundly helpful tool, some say ground-breaking. This helps male leaders struggling with the problem of promoting good leaders, irrespective of gender. It also leads to promoting more women and more minorities by default, not by quota.

Focusing on talent and skills, rather than gender and perceptions of presence or lack of confidence, will directly lead to gender parity.[4] An understanding of gender bias in leadership and bias towards stereotypes of leadership is essential in identifying the right talent and skills. The subject has been approached from the lens of the male for too long in terms of masculine ideals of leadership. The subject has been approached for too long in terms of women being the only ones who suffer. And the focus on a white heterosexual narrative in a white hierarchy needs to end now. There are far too many incredibly talented, intelligent, other-serving people from all walks of life being passed over.

Stereotypes do continue to break down for the most successful, adaptable and enlightened humans. Be assured women and minority groups *are* rising. Whether told to or whether held down, women and minorities are coming up. Men, who can recognize that growth attained by monopolizing power in a global economy will no longer be tolerated by emotionally intelligent leaders, will rise with them. If emotionally intelligent people don't find welcoming corporate cultures, they'll build their own. Self-actualizing people who can operate beyond ego and the constructs of what it means to be male or female will be the ones with the edge. Are we ready to take them on, understand the biases that still prevail and treat them as full and equal partners as a business imperative?

Characteristics, determined as more masculine in our culture, show up in both men and women. It is culture predominantly that has dictated a de-lineation of leadership traits into two more gender specific sets of behaviors. What we can be clear on is that what defines a great leader, based on the empirical work of Collins, defies these stereotyped norms of leadership in our culture. Elimination of judgements and biases is the best way to create inclusion. Gender remains an issue because, whether we like it or not, there are significant biases. These biases serve no one. The presence of more masculine traits in isolation do not create good leaders, but quite the opposite. They create psychologically unhealthy humans.

Though there were a couple of exceptions, most of the males we have interviewed believe most of the reason for gender inequality in leadership centres around childbearing, and conflicts with family as the major stumbling blocks for women progressing. Women believe it centres far more on their unwillingness to keep continually having to perform at a greater level than their male peers, while simultaneously being criticized for it *and* not rewarded. They know they are often being held to a higher competency threshold and likely receiving less pay. The double bind is a very real phenomenon for women. The double bind, which no one can even name unless it is explained, is insidious in our culture at all levels. While 95% of the advice in the mainstream targets women about how they should change and assimilate to fit what is largely a patriarchal system in the corporate world, we are unlikely to see a change.

If we keep in mind the findings from Jim Collins this need not be the case, and we can re-address what advice we give to women about how they need to show up in the workplace to have the greatest impact. We can also give greater consideration to helping more men demonstrate the 'softer skills' that they need to show. 'Humility' and 'Will' according to Collins are essential for the best leaders, regardless of gender. It is ultimately a blend of this spectrum of traits loosely falling within 'taking care' *and* 'taking charge' groupings that will make the most successful leaders.

We call it emotional intelligence.

It will also shine more of the spotlight on some of those traits that are somehow regarded as less important in our culture. We see this finally with the current fascination with EI. 'Softer' traits are now regarded as essential leadership skills.[5] As one female senior sales performer for a software company responded in one of our interviews, "You have to be tough to survive and break away from command-and control-leadership, not using fear as a motivator. It's hard to put a stake in the ground with different behavior in male-dominated cultures." But it is absolutely essential for all leaders, irrespective of their gender identity, who want to lead successfully.

Coaching is essential to create behavior change

While men are leading in the majority yet are showing their own lack of awareness 'the goldfish bowl effect' means they are not gainfully equipped to help until they understand their own leadership strengths and weaknesses better. Behaviors that actually reinforce stereotyping for a specific gender need to be addressed in coaching. Education on its own is not enough to change these behaviors.[6]

Fundamentally the stereotyped ideas that present around what is perceived as holding women back is telling. Skill in challenging this biased perception will set the great leaders apart from the rest. In Collins' words the leader who "demonstrates an unwavering resolve to do whatever must be done to produce the best long-term results, no matter how difficult," will be the one that succeeds. It has become imperative for leaders to demonstrate inclusion in a vocal, proactive, uncompromising manner. It's possible.

Get more women into senior leadership positions as a strategic imperative. Get more minority representation into leadership positions as a strategic imperative. People, corporations and societies can thrive if we have more diverse and equitable leadership. "Humanity, at least as represented by the world's governments, reveal instead a preference to ignore the risk until forced to react – even when foresight's price-tag is small. It is an abdication of responsibility and a betrayal of the future."[7]

This was the Editor-in-Chief of the Economist referencing the Covid–19 pandemic. Actually, a foreseeable event, many political leaders nevertheless claimed to have been blind-sided by the pandemic. The analogy applies very well to corporate leaders, many of whom continue to pay lip service to diversity and equality issues.

To not take massive strides now is an abdication of responsibility and a betrayal of the future. It's NIMBY all over again.

The power, influence and wealth that males exercise in an organization and their genuine willingness to share this will determine which male leaders succeed and which fail as attention and momentum to this topic grows and grows. How can leadership roles be shared to create gender parity? Organizations who state a *clear purpose* demonstrating social responsibility towards their employees in terms of family breaks, career plans and flex-working have a competitive advantage over those that do not. Significantly mental health and well-being will become increasingly relevant as a measure of how well companies are working in an inclusive way.

We've seen that conformity and non-conformity to gender roles can stimulate maladaptive behaviors and psychological distress for men, women and people who identify in another way with gender in the workplace. Well-intentioned proactive male leaders are essential for realizing gender equality.[8] They do need, however, to be educated on the psychological issues for men and women behind why equality is actually hard to achieve. The 'fixing women' dialogue that perpetuates in most organizations must be challenged. The culture that men need to 'man up' and take the lead in all things that implicitly and explicitly pervades must also be challenged. Selecting competent leaders using objective measurements is absolutely essential if we are to prevent hiring more incompetence who's packaging appeals to our primitive minds.

Leaders need to be vigilant to the fact that quotas for women could be futile if they do not simultaneously emphasize the focus on skill and talent. We need to go further than balancing the numbers. We need to go further than getting senior leadership roles for a few white women. Immediate diverse representation in leadership needs to happen now. Remaining alert to token assimilation is necessary. Gender parity is a human issue, not a women's issue. Patriarchy is a human issue not a men's issue. Racism is a human issue not a minority person's issue. Leadership needs to wholly embrace these realities.

Social demand for equity is huge

The talent pool wants to work for equitable companies, buys into them. Companies need to follow their example. As a Glassdoor survey in 2019 found when it surveyed 5,000 people in the US, UK, Germany and France, 77% of people found that culture was highly relevant in considering applying for a job, with 79% finding that the mission and purpose of the company were essential considerations.[9] It also found that for 56% of the respondents culture was more important than salary.

According to Rosling, and as importantly the data, the world really is improving. We have better rates of literacy, a reduction in poverty relative to population, big improvements on women's and children's rights and a reduction in wars. But we need all hands-on-deck to deal with the challenges of an ageing population, climate change, a pandemic, sustainability and the sensible distribution of wealth, food and other resources. The sense of scarcity that drives our fears, and our resolve to not question our biases can derail this mission. Fear is our default state of being when we possess a mind still wired for negativity bias. Sexism, racism, ageism and all the other phobic driven 'isms' feed from a scarcity and fear mindset.

We need to get positive about tackling the hard stuff. We need to remember there's Hope in Pandora's box.

Now is the time to step up every one of us, each to play their own essential role in service to each other, our pursuit of happiness, and fairness. Now is the time to step up, challenge our fears, our biases, our definitions of leadership. The World Economic Forum[10] points out, "policy-makers and other stakeholders can fast-forward this process and should take stronger actions in the years to come. There is a strong imperative to do so, in terms of justice and greater social equality as well as the economic returns of a broader base of diverse human capital."

But it won't work as a project for HR as an unsupported silo. Nor as a small initiative working on the side lines of the corporate business.

It requires HR to think strategically about the whole business, and to be regarded as an equal and necessary partner at the senior decision-making level. It requires the strategic intervention of leaders from every part of the organization. It requires a budget and actual authority. Holding each other accountable for the way we treat people. Recognizing talent objectively is a business prerogative. If done successfully, engagement and profit will take care of themselves.

The problem with identity

A final note on identity. We've spent an entire book writing about considering people and creating safe places for them and their identities. We urge leaders to recognize how making assumptions about someone's identity can lead to bias and discrimination. Identity is ego. And ego is where our suffering comes from. Clinging to the idea of being the best leader, the best nurturer, the most competitive, the most feminine, the greatest CEO, the most Woke, the highest earner, the most victimized, the poorest paid, belonging to the best country, the most exceptional – such labels fall short in capturing our true humanity. All humans need exactly the same things. To feel unique, to feel they belong, and to ultimately self-actualize.

While we deal with discrimination, we need to deal with those things that trigger discrimination. Those are the labels, the boxes and the stereotypes. We've been in the first four sections of Maslow's hierarchy. We've made room for everyone's identities, the psychological challenges, the conscious and unconscious biases, the stereotypes, the pain, the passed over talent. We've become aware of how differing intersections impact these identities, and how they can trigger bias and discrimination. Understanding this in greater detail is essential for leaders. We understand that when we organize people by gender it can create binaries. But we must recognize what connects us all.

"We all know the truth: more connects us than separates us. But in times of crisis the wise build bridges, while the foolish build barriers. We must find a way to look after one another as if we were one single tribe." [11] This quote is from King T'Challa, Black Panther, the eponymous hero of the 2018 Marvel American Superheroes film. He makes a speech to the United Nations at the end of the film. Initially believing in the need for each country to look after its own interests, he fights with his cousin, Erik Killmonger, to protect his country Wakanda's resources. After a bloody fight in which his cousin dies, King T'Challa realizes the need for globalization and that sharing technology for the betterment of all is the only way to live peaceably together. [12]

King T'Challa was right. We must recognize what connects us all. To do this we need to self-actualize and detach from all those identifiers. We must see each other's humanity. There is a path to true freedom, to the self-actualization, joy, growth, equality, that is our birth right, and we depict it in the outer ring of Figure 8. It's the message encapsulated in the meaning of the word Namaste.

I honor that place in you in which the entire universe dwells

I honor the place in you, which is of love, of truth,
of light and of peace,

When you are in that place in you and I am in that place in me,

We are One

Namaste

It's why we should use the HONOUR model.

When we are enough

In the Book of Joy two of the greatest spiritual leaders of our time, the Dalai Lama and Desmond Tutu, discuss what joy is. How do we as people achieve happiness? What stands in our way? When the Dalai Lama meets Desmond Tutu, he asks "Who is Desmond Tutu?" [13] It's a rhetorical question designed for us to think about the essence of the human being. Not the superficial identifiers that are color, gender, or social situation. He doesn't look at him as Black, as a man, as a spiritual leader who led an oppressed people, Black people, through an abhorrent regime called apartheid in South Africa. He looks at him as a soul with a lack of identification or need for identifiers. He wants us to consider him in terms of his human essence, not as ego.

As leaders this is what we need to do for ourselves and those we are *privileged* to lead. We need to regard ourselves and them as enough.[14] People who feel enough don't need to see themselves as exceptional, the greatest or the best because those ideas are illusions. Since no two people are alike, we can never be anything other than unique. Comparisons, by definition, are futile. When we see ourselves as enough, we free ourselves from the need for more. We open ourselves up to seeing others in the same way. We no longer play the see saw of who's up and who's down. No need for superiority, nor inferiority. We are on equal footing. No need to diminish another, or to inflate ourselves. No more discrimination. We are open to recognize others' pain. We are open to see the talent people have. We are willing to share.

We are willing to lean in, lean out, step in, and sometimes necessarily, to step down.

The Western pursuit of success and achievement magnetically pulls us to overwork, overvalue status and power, and if not our own, then that of others. We give our time to tasks rather than interactions with loved ones. We live in a world of to-do lists and action addiction, unable to focus for at least half of our waking day. We are blinded to appreciating those closest to us. And our definition of happiness? Pleasure-seeking and the next goal to attain on the hedonic treadmill.[15] We straight-jacket ourselves and others in terms that narrowly define us all, limiting us in convenient little boxes with those labels we earlier mentioned: breadwinner, caregiver, single parent, divorcee, economist, homeowner, free spirit, winner, loser, academic or cake-baker.

Figure 8
INTERSECTION MODEL
AND HUMAN NEEDS

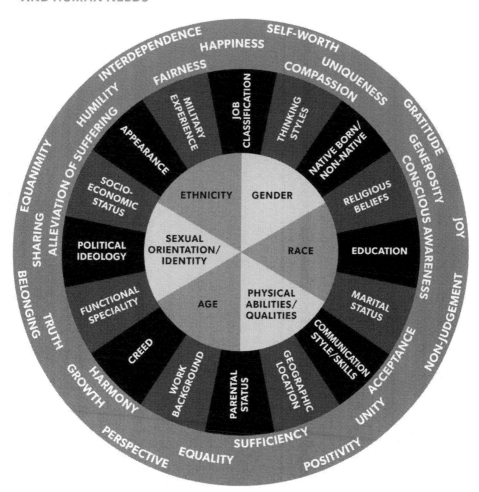

Finally get rid of the boxes

There are a lot of labels available. Paul Graham famously wrote in a blog, "Most people reading this will already be fairly tolerant. But there is a step beyond thinking of yourself as x but tolerating y: not even to consider yourself an x. The more labels you have for yourself, the dumber they make you." It's a cruder version of the Dalai Lama's message. There's more to us all than boxes and labels. There are deeper human needs that we absolutely all share. These are our true bridge to each other. They mean anyone of us can serve and anyone of us can lead in a given moment.

Boxes are what hoarders have, filling every corner of the home. They belie treasures, memories, possessed and hidden, secrets, inaccessible, un-enjoyed, untapped. A world of delight and growth, or a dark place of mess and confusion. Either way, unopened, you cannot tap into their riches, their knowledge, the possibilities.

People are unique and individual and though we all come with baggage and boxes it's worth opening and exploring them to air them out. It's worth seeing what we really need and what we can get rid of. If we open them, open up our people, ourselves, we can value what's in them for the contribution they can bring, and the inherent value that they have. We can make ourselves a beautiful and safe place to live, work, and thrive.

It's in the spirit of this book that we recognize all humans as having tremendous potential, capacities for creativity, compassion and leadership - treasures that we ought all to consider as worthy of finding, regardless of gender. Treasures that we really have to insist on finding in our people before we appoint them as our leaders. It is in this vain that we ask you to embrace all those you are surrounded by, see past theirs and your own labels, gender definitions, stereotypes. Instead look to the potentiality, and all the things that can connect us as humans. As leaders we must nurture ourselves and those around us.

As Joshua Fields Millburn pointed out when he said, "Love people, use things. The opposite never works."[16] It would be a good credo for many a corporate leader to adopt. People are a unique spectrum of talent and possibility. They aren't just boxes after all.

ACKNOWLEDGEMENTS

Thank you to all the senior leaders who helped in the research behind this book, as well as to some powerful mentors who added different perspectives at different times. To the large numbers of men who were willing to contribute to this discussion and who are committed to understanding and changing the status quo in corporate leadership. As the endorsements demonstrate, this is a topic that very many people *do care* about; that many male leaders *do care* about; that many leaders across race, culture and country *do care* about. People who want to take charge to take care, to cure and care simultaneously. I am grateful to have had so many open discussions with people from around the world. Thank you especially to Greg Hewitt, CEO of DHL Express, US, and David Golden, Alan and Ruth Harris Chair of Excellence, College of Business & Technology, East Tennessee State University. Both of you have shown the essential elements of good leadership: courage, openness, curiosity and humility. I admire you both for encouraging and supporting the need for equality, and for your support of women as leaders. Greg and David, your compassion and integrity are appreciated by the many lives you have positively touched in your work and projects. Thank you for your help and support.

Specifically, I want to thank Professor Cordelia Fine, from Melbourne University, Australia, who read and edited this work. Cordelia, thank you for sharing your prodigious intellect and valuable time. Thank you for the constructive critique on the neuroscience and psychology content in this book, and your comments on the research and its relevance. At one point you claimed leadership is not your expertise. I beg to differ! You personify courageous, modest, expert leadership. You have challenged and exposed poorly constructed studies, often from prestigious academic institutions, and created a global awareness around its damaging by-product, neurosexism. Your dedication to the intellectual debate and desire to find the truth are inspirational. Thank you too, to Professor Dr Angela Maas, First Chair in Cardiology for Women at Radboud University, Nijmegen, The Netherlands and Dutch Women's Council Representative to the United Nations. Your valuable contribution and generosity in giving your time are deeply appreciated. Cordelia and Angela, I hope you both realize how much your dedication and commitment to the work you do are valued, and just how powerful they are in the wider context of gender equality for us all.

Two years ago, at a Women's Leadership summit, I saw Magdalena Mook, President of the International Coach Federation, talk about the systemic and structural causes of sexism. Magda, thank you for your encouraging words and support for this work, and for working towards ensuring that the ICF continues to increase diversity, inclusion, belonging and justice for all. Coaching is an essential tool in uncovering and dismantling systemic sexism, racism and inequalities that fail us all. Andrew Neitlich, Founder of the Center for Executive Coaching in Florida, thank you for your down-to-earth, action-orientated, smart approach to both business and coaching. Your self-deprecation, personifying humble leadership, has created a following of bright, professional, ethical coaches. Thanks for the mojo, support and encouragement. Magdalena and Andrew, thank you for your uncompromising commitment to professionalizing and advancing the field of coaching.

Debs, John, Marije, Claus, Elizabeth, Dennis and Moira, thank you. Your willingness to experiment with the very first global cohort of senior executives for the GPS to Gender Dimensions in Leadership online coaching course, demonstrated how committed you are to the importance of this topic. We showed together just how relevant it is to men and women, and how helpful it can be. It was a great example of how far we can come when we work together, on equal footing, and make the effort to learn and understand each other's perspectives, and others' besides.

Thank you, Magali Aimée Toussaint. Sharing a need to belong and a need to be seen as unique, our very human connection immediately neutralizes any and all 'isms'. We need to distil it and sell it in bottles! It certainly transcends boxes. You are a wonderful example of how people working in the DE&I space *should* show up. Non-judgemental, kind, loving and wise.

Finally, Willem Jan, Gerben and William. Thank you for all the debates, discussions and support. This research journey convinced me of just how important gender parity is for our psychological health, safety and for thriving communities. Gender parity is as essential for boys and men, as it is for girls and women, and for everyone who identifies beyond binaries. Seeing how much it all touched you and made you think, inspired me every day. Thank you for all the contemplation, cuddles and care. I love you three to the moon and back a 'gazibillion' times.

ABOUT THE AUTHOR

S E Drijfhout, is a British-born Dutch national, and a law graduate from University College, Durham, in the United Kingdom. Drijfhout has more than 25 years' experience in the corporate world, and has worked as a business analyst, consultant, and sales representative for Northumbrian Water, Price Waterhouse Coopers, and Johnson & Johnson respectively. She subsequently worked in a variety of US software development companies in senior international business development roles and has been a top sales performer throughout her sales career. An International Coach Federation accredited executive coach, diversity and inclusivity leadership coach, women's leadership coach and sales leadership coach, she's also an accredited practitioner in the Profile XT and the Genos Emotional Intelligence assessments. Drijfhout splits work time between business consulting, specializing in sales excellence, inclusivity, high performance and talent retention, research, writing, speaking and executive coaching. She runs the GPS to Gender Dimensions in Leadership online coaching course for executives. For more information visit www.progenyleadership.com.

ENDNOTES

Introduction

[1] Hyde, J. S. (2005). The Gender Similarities Hypothesis. *American Psychologist*, Vol. 60, No. 6

[2] Zell, E., Krizan, Z. & Teeter, S. R. (2015) Evaluating gender similarities and differences using metasynthesis, *American Psychologist*, Vol. 70(1), 10-20

[3] Peter Salovey and John D Mayer coined the term 'Emotional Intelligence' in 1990

[4] Capgemini Research Institute, Emotional Intelligence – the essential skillset for the age of AI, 2019

[5] Genos International's core emotional intelligence competencies. Genos International is recognized as a world leader in emotional intelligence programs. https://www.genosinternational.com/genos/

[6] Sandberg, S. (2013) *Lean In: Women, work and the will to lead*, (First Edition) New York: Alfred A.

[7] Pharr, S., (1988) *Homophobia as a Weapon of Sexism*, Inverness, CA: Chardon Press

[8] Fetch, B., Poliner, J., (*Un)Skirting the Issues: A Guide for the Well-Intentioned Man in Today's Work Place*, Lioncrest Publishing, 2017

[9] Marcus Noland, Tyler Moran, Barbara Kotschwar Is gender Diversity Profitable, Evidence from a Global Survey, February 2016

[10] The Economist 2018, The old-girls' network, Ten years on from Norway's quota for women on corporate boards

1   No Honeymoon Without Engagement

[1] Boston consulting Group, 2018 How Diverse Leadership Teams Boost Innovation

[2] Harvard Study of Adult Development, the longest longitudinal study that began studying sophomore Harvard graduates in 1938 and followed them through their lives, subsequently expanding

[3] Matthew Lieberman, Social: Why are brains are wired to connect, 2013

[4] Employee Engagement on the rise in the US, *Gallup*, Jim Harter, August 2018

5 The Conference Board, white paper, DNA of Engagement: How Organizations Can Foster Employee Ownership of Engagement, 2017

6 The Predictive Index Annual Employee Engagement Report, 2019

7 Gallup, Engagement white paper, 2019

8 Payne, Keith, (2017) The Broken Ladder: How Inequality Affects the Way We Think, Live and Die, New York: Viking

9 The Business Case for More Diversity, Dieter Holger, Wall Street Journal, October 23rd 2019

10 Warren Buffet is bullish…on women, Fortune, May 2013, essay by Warren Buffet

11 Women in Senior Leadership, Taking charge to take care – exposing the real blocks to female talent retention, A Report by Progeny Leadership, 2018

12 Crenshaw Kimberlé, () "Demarginalizing the Intersection of Race and Sex: A Black Feminist Critique of Antidiscrimination Doctrine, Feminist. Theory and Antiracist Politics", University of Chicago Legal Forum: Vol.1989: Iss. 1, Article 8

13 Judge Harris Wangelin in his ruling against the plaintiffs in DeGraffenreid v. General Motors, "The prospect of the creation of new classes of protected minorities, governed only by the mathematical principles of permutation and combination, clearly raises the prospect of opening the hackneyed Pandora's box."

14 Coaston, Jane, The Intersectionality Wars, The Highlight by Vox, May 28, 2019

15 Hesiod, Works and Days, 6th Century BC, contains the myth that when Prometheus stole fire from Zeus, Zeus took vengeance by sending Pandora to his brother Epimetheus, and with her a jar which she opened to release all sorts of ills on the world, closing the jar again before Hope could join them.

16 https://www.thecut.com/2017/01/psychologys-racism-measuring-tool-isnt-up-to-the-job.html

2 The Business Case, Status Quo, Assimilation

[1] Resolution 70/1 United Nations General Assembly goals set in 2015 for 2030

[2] World Economic Forum Global Gender Pay Gap report 2016

[3] Marmott, M, Bell, R. Fair Society, Healthy Lives, *Public Health,* Volume 126, Supplement 1 pp. S4-S10, 2012. https://doi.org/10.1016/j.puhe.2012.05.014

[4] Marcus Noland, Tyler Moran, and Barbara Kotschwar, McKinsey's Delivering Through diversity study, January 2018 Is Gender Diversity Profitable? Evidence from a Global Survey, Working Paper 16-3, February 2016

[5] Doerr, Patsy The business case for gender parity, Thomas Reuters, March 2018

[6] Marcus Noland, Tyler Moran, and Barbara Kotschwar, Is Gender Diversity Profitable? Evidence from a Global Survey, Working Paper 16-3, February 2016

[7] World Economic Forum, Global Gender Gap Report, 2020

[8] Thomas Reuter and Acritas, Transforming Women's Leadership in the Law, 2019

[9] Steele, C.M., Spencer, S.J., & Aronson, J. (2002) Contending with Group Image: The psychology of stereotype and social identitiy threat. In M. P. Zanna (Ed.), *Advances in*

experimental social psychology, Vol. 34 (p.379-440). Academic Press.

[10] Understanding the Backlash Against Feminism, November 2019, Linda Napikoski, *ThoughtCo.com*

[11] Adams, Barbara B., (2018), Women, Minorities and other Extraordinary People: The New Path for Workforce Diversity, Greenleaf Book Press

[12] Women in Senior Leadership, Taking Charge to Take Care – Exposing the Real Blocks to Female Talent Retention, *Progeny Leadership*, 2019

[13] Derks, Belle, Van Laar, Colette and Ellemers, Naomi, The queen bee phenomenon: Why women leaders distance themselves from junior women, *The Leadership Quarterly*, 2016

[14] Derks, Belle, Ellemers, Naomi, van Laar, Colette, Raghoe, Gauwrie, Extending the queen bee effect: How Hindustani workers cope with the disadvantage by distancing the self from the group, *Journal of Social Issues*, Vol.71, No.3, 2015, pp.476-496

[15] The underrepresentation of women in science: differential commitment or the queen bee syndrome? Naomi Ellemers, Henriette van de Heuvel, Dick de Gilder, Anne Maas, Alessandra Bonvini, *British Journal of Social Psychology*, 2004

[16] Catalyst, Report: Inclusive leadership: the view from six countries, May 2014

[17] Slepian, Michael L., Jacoby-Senghor, Drew S., Identity Threats in Everyday Life: Distinguishing Belonging From Inclusion, Social Psychological and Personality Science, August 2020, https://doi.org/10.1177/1948550619895008

[18] Unemployed men who take traditionally female jobs make more money, The Fast company - Jill Yavorsky, Janet Dill, January 2020

[19] Payscale, The State of the Gender Pay Gap, 2019

[20] Payscale, Racial Wage Gap for Men, Jackson Gruver, May 2019

3   What you don't see will hurt you as a leader – The Blind Spot

[1] Collins, James C. Good to Great: Why Some Companies Make the Leap…and Others Don't, New York: Harper Business, 2001

[2] Pharr, S., (1988) Homophobia as a Weapon of Sexism, Inverness, CA: Chardon Press

[3] Dobbin, Frank and Kalev, Alexandra Why Sexual harassment Programs Backfire, Harvard Business Review, May-June Issue 2020

[4] I had to submit to being exoticized by white women. If I did not, I was punished, The Guardian, 27 February 2019, extracted from Safe: On Black British Men Reclaiming Space, Orion, 2019, an anthology of writing by 20 Black British men, edited by Derek Owusu

[5] Berdahl, Jennifer L. Moore, Celia, (2006) Workplace Harassment: Double Jeopardy for Minority Women, Journal of Psychology, Vol. 91, No. 2, 426-436

[6] Trade Union Congress, Sexual Harassment of LGBT people in the Workplace, April 2019

[7] McGinn, Daniel If something feels off, you need to speak up, Harvard Business Review,

May-June Issue 2020

[8] Dobbin, Frank and Kalev, Alexandra Why Sexual harassment Programs Backfire, Harvard Business Review, May-June Issue 2020

[9] https://www.kivaprogram.net

[10] Huitsing, G., & Veenstra, R. (2012). Het KiVa-antipestprogramma: de cruciale rol van de groep. (The KiVa anti-bullying programme: the crucial role of the group.) In: Goosens, F., Vermande, M., & Van der Meulen, M. (Eds.), Pesten op School (pp.152-159). Amsterdam: Boom.

[11] Kruger, Justin, Dunning, David, Unskilled and Unaware of It: How Recognizing Difficulties in Recognizing One's Own Incompetence Lead to Inflated Self-Assessments, Journal of Personality and Social Psychology (1999), American Psychological Association, Inc. 1999, Vol. 77, No. 6. 1121-1134

[12] David Schneider, The Psychology of Stereotyping (New York: Guilford Press, 2005)

[13] Viv Groskop, (2019) How to Own the Room – Women and the Art of Brilliant Speaking, Transworld Publishers Ltd

[14] Bourke, Juliet, Espedido, Andrea, Why Inclusive Leaders are Good for Organizations and How to Become One, March 2019, Harvard Business Review

4   Patriarchy, Paradox and Pain - The Blind Eye

[1] Plato, The Republic, Book V, (5th Century BCE), The role of women in the ideal state, Rep: 451c – 457b

[2] Hyde, J. S. (2005). The Gender Similarities Hypothesis. *American Psychologist*, Vol. 60, No. 6

[3] Zell, E., Krizan, Z. & Teeter, S. R. (2015) Evaluating gender similarities and differences using metasynthesis, *American Psychologist*, Vol. 70(1), 10-20

[4] Steele, C.M., Spencer, S.J., & Aronson, J. (2002) Contending with Group Image: The psychology of stereotype and social identitiy threat. In M.P.Zanna(Ed.), *Advances in experimental social psychology*, Vol. 34 (p.379-440). Academic Press.

[5] Laurie B. Mintz and James M. O'Neil, Gender roles, sex and the process of psychotherapy: Many questions and few answers, *Journal of Counselling and Development*, March 1990

[6] Levant, Ronald F. and Pollack, William, S., (1995) *The New Psychology of Men*, NEW York, NY: Basic Books

[7] Richmond K, Levant R. Clinical application of the gender role strain paradigm: group treatment for adolescent boys, *Journal of Clinical Psychology*. 2003;59(11):1237-1245. doi:10.1002/jclp.10214

[8] Kane, Emily, Racial and Ethnic Variation in Gender-Related Attitudes, *Annual Review of Sociology*, Vol. 26, 419-439, Nov. 2003. DOI: 10.1146/annurev.soc.26.1.419

[9] Fortune 500 Companies 2019: Who made the list, Fortune

[10] #MeToo was a social media movement that encouraged victims of sexual harassment and abuse, mostly women, but not always, to speak out so the extent of the problem

could be seen. It followed the exposure of sexual abuse allegations against Harvey Weinstein, but the 'Me Too' phrase was initially used in this context on social media in 2006, on Myspace by Tarana Burke, a victim and survivor of sexual harassment and subsequently an activist on the topic of ensuring women's stories of abuse were taken seriously and they were not silenced

[11] #TimesUp was a movement founded by Hollywood celebrities on January 1st 2018 in response to the former allegations against Harvey Weinstein, to give voice and legal aid to victims of sexual harassment, and had the specific goal to support women, men, people of color, and the LGBT community who have less access to media platforms and funds to speak up about harassment

[12] Levant, Ronald F. and Pollack, William, S., (1995) The New Psychology of Men, NEW York, NY: Basic Books

[13] Pleck, Joseph H., (1981), The Myth of Masculinity, Cambridge, Mass.: MIT Press

[14] Gender and Psychological Well-Being, M.Pilar Matud, Marisela Lopéz-Curbelo,Demelza Fortes, 20 September 2019

[15] Ryff's Psychological Well-being Scale (measures the respondent's ability to resist pressures and remain independent, as well as their self-regulating capabilities) and the BEM Sex Role Inventory were used in this research.

[16] Pleck, Joseph H., (1981), The Myth of Masculinity, Cambridge, Mass.: MIT Press

[17] Levant, Ronald F. and Pollack, William, S., (1995) The New Psychology of Men, NEW York, NY: Basic Books

[18] Clinical Application of the Gender Role Strain Paradigm: Group Treatment for Adolescent Boys, Ronald F. Levant 2003

[19] Failure is not an option for Black Women: Effects of organizational performance on leaders with single versus dual-subordinate identities, Ashleigh Shelby Rosette, Robert W. Livingstone, Journal of Experimental Social Psychology, Vol 48, issue 5, Pages 1162-1167, September 2012

[20] Hard Won and Easily Lost: The Fragile Status of Leaders in Gender-Stereotype-Incongruent Occupations, Victoria L., Brescoll, Erica Dawson, Eric Luis Uhlmann, Psychological Science, 2010, Volume: 21 issue, 11, page(s) 1640-1642

[21] Wendy Ashley, The Angry Black Woman: The Impact of Pejorative Stereotypes on Psychotherapy with Black Women, Social Work in Public Health Journal, Vol.29 (1), 27:34, 2014,

[22] Crenshaw Kimberlé, () "Demarginalizing the Intersection of Race and Sex: A Black Feminist Critique of Antidiscrimination Doctrine, Feminist. Theory and Antiracist Politics", University of Chicago Legal Forum: Vol.1989: Issue 1, Article 8. Available at: http://chicagounbound.uchicago.edu/uclf/vol1989/iss1/8

[23] How Masculinity Contests Undermine Organizations and what to do about it, Jennifer L Berdahl, Peter Glick and Marianne Cooper, Harvard Business Review, November 2019

[24] Smiler, A. P., Challenging Casanova: Beyond the Stereotype of the Promiscuous Young Male, Wiley, 2013

[25] Johnston, Elizabeth, The Original Nasty woman. For centuries Medusa has been used

to criticize powerful women. So, it's no surprise that the mythological Gorgon has re-emerged this election cycle, (2016) *The Atlantic*

[26] *https://www.workingmother.com/best-companies-ernst-young-llp*

[27] Post #MeToo Ernst and Young Grapples with Diverging Views of its culture its NPR radio, November 7, 2019 in which a controversial women's training program at Ernst and Young is discussed

[28] Training Programs and Reporting Systems Won't End Sexual Harassment, Hiring more Women Will, Alexander Professor Frank Dobbins and *Harvard Business Review*, Nov 2017

[29] Dobbins, Frank, Kalev, Alexandra, Why Sexual Harassment Programs Backfire, *Harvard Business Review* May/June Issue 2020

[30] Sexual Harassment at Work in the Era of #MeToo, *Pew Research Center*, 2018

[31] Ibid., Why Sexual Harassment Programs Backfire, *Harvard Business Review* May/June Issue 2020

[32] Twenge, J. (1997) Changes in masculine and feminine traits over time: A meta-analysis. *Sex Roles*, 36 (5-6), 305-325

[33] Roger Horrocks (1994) Masculinity in Crisis, *Self & Society, An International Journal for Humanistic Psychology*, Volume 22:4, 25-29

[34] Ban Bossy is a campaign launched by LeanIn.org which criticizes the use of the word bossy for describing assertive girls and women, and which can be perceived as problematic in their attempts to fulfil leadership roles

[35] Barrie Thorne, Zella Luria, (1986), Sexuality and Gender in Children's Daily Worlds, Society of the Study of Social Problems, Oxford University Press, Vol. 33, No. 3 (Feb 1986), pp.176-190

[36] Holmberg, Arthur, (2012) David Mahmet and American Macho, *Cambridge University Press*

[37] Miron, O, Yu K, Wilf-Miron R., Kohan, IS, Suicide Rates Among Adolescents and Young Adults in the United States, 2000-2017, JAMA 2019; 321(23):2362-2364

[38] Kposowa AJ, Aly Ezzat D, Breault K. New Findings On Gender: The Effects Of Employment Status On Suicide. *Int J Womens Health*. 2019;11:569-575 https://doi.org/10.2147/IJWH.S216504

[39] Van Hal G. (2015). The true cost of the economic crisis on psychological well-being: a review. *Psychology research and behavior management*, *8*, 17–25. https://doi.org/10.2147/PRBM.S44732

[40] Zhang J, Jiang C, Jia S, Wieczorek WF. An Overview of Suicide Research in China. Archives of Suicide Research : Official Journal of the International Academy for Suicide Research. 2002 ;6(2):167-184. DOI: 10.1080/13811110208951174.

[41] Centers for Disease Control and Prevention (2016) Sexual Identity, Sex and Sexual Contacts, and Health-Risk Behaviors Among Students in Grades 9-12: Youth Risk Behavior Surveillance. Atlanta, GA: U.S. Department of Health and Human Services

[42] https://www.thetrevorproject.org/survey-2020/?section=Diversity-of-Gender-Identity-Sexual-Orientation

[43] Joiner, T. Why People Die by Suicide, *Harvard University Press*, 2007

7

[44] Schumacher, Helene, Why more men than women die by suicide, *BBC Future*, March 2019
https://www.bbc.com/future/article/20190313-why-more-men-kill-themselves-than-women

[45] Johnson, K., Kaskey, M., Rand, K., Tucker, R., Vohr, B.R., Gender Difference in Adult-Infant Communication in the First Months of Life, *Pediatrics*, 134 (6), November 2014

[46] Ana Aznar, Harriet R. Tenenbaum, Gender and age differences in parent–child emotion talk, *British Journal of Developmental Psychology*, (2015) Vol. 33, 148-155

[47] Modern Parenthood: Roles of Moms and Dads Converge as they Balance Work and Family, *Pew Research Center*, March 2013

[48] Patterson, Kerry, eds, (2010) Crucial Conversations: Tools for Talking when the Stakes are High, New York: McGraw-Hill, We use this term in our course to explain how we frequently make binary, black and white, either or choices that fail to gives us the options when most problems we face are varying shades of grey, with spectrums of issues, perspectives and alternatives. While we still gravitate to the 'men are like this', 'women are like that' dialogue and the associated 'suitability' for given roles, such as leadership in the gender discussion, we perpetually limit our options. This is the sucker's choice we need to move away from as leaders.

5   Myths, Martyrs and Monsters – The Blind Alley

[1] Pharr, S., (1988) Homophobia as a Weapon of Sexism, Inverness, *CA: Chardon Press*

[2] Cialdini, R.B. (2007), Influence: The Psychology of Persuasion, New York: Harper Collins, 2007

[3] Catalyst Report 2005, Women 'Take Care', Men 'Take Charge', Stereotyping of U.S. Business Leaders Exposed

[4] Fine, Cordelia, Delusions of Gender: the Real Science behind Sex Differences, London: Icon 2010

[5] Understanding the role of the self in prime-to-behavior effects: The active-self account, Wheeler, DeMarree and Petty, 2007, Stanford University

[6] Catalyst Report, 2005, Women 'Take Care', Men 'Take Charge', Stereotyping of U.S. Business Leaders Exposed this report also cited problem solving as a key leadership behavior also attributed as a stereotypical male trait that women are perceived as being poor in

[7] Self-stereotyping in the context of multiple social identities, Sinclair, Hardin, Lowery, 2006

[8] Goldin, Claudia, and Cecilia Rousse. 2000. "Orchestrating Impartiality: The Impact of "Blind" Auditions on Female Musicians." American Economic Review, 90 (4): 715-741

[9] Gender Correlated Systematics in HST Proposal Selection, Space Telescope Science Institute, Baltimore, I. Neill Reid, publications of the Astronomical Society of the

Pacific, 126:923-934, 2014 October

[10] Gender differences and bias in open Source: pull request acceptance of women versus men, Terrell et al. (2017). Peer J Computer science, DOI 10.7717/peerj-cs.111

[11] Science Faculties Subtle Gender biases, Yale University study, Corinne A. Moss-Racusin, John F. Dovidio, Victoria L. Brescoll, Mark J. Graham, Jo Handelsman, published in Proceedings of the National academy of Sciences, October 2012, 109 (41) 16474-16479

[12] J.K. Rowling wrote the Harry Potter series, the best-selling book series in history according to the Guinness World Records, 2012

[13] Gray, J. (1992), Men are from Mars, women are from Venus – a practical guide for improving communication and getting what you want in your relationships, *New York: HarperCollins*

[14] Brizendine, L, (2006), The Female Brain, *New York: Morgan Road Books*

[15] Simon Baron-Cohen, (2003), The Essential Difference: the truth about the male and female brain, *Basic Books*

[16] Gina Rippon, (2019), The Gendered Brain: The new neuroscience that shatters the myth of the female brain, Random House

[17] Farrel, B. and Farrel, P. (2001) Men are like waffles – women are like spaghetti; Understanding and delighting in your differences. Eugene, OR: Harvest House

[18] Fine, Cordelia, (2018) Testosterone Rex: Unpacking the Myths of our Gendered Minds, *Icon Books*

[19] James Damore wrote a 10-page memo to Google offering his opinion at the time on the push to get more women and minorities into tech, arguing that it was reverse discrimination against men. Citing various scientific papers, he argued that it was biological differences which were the reason there were not more women in tech. Ultimately his poorly chosen words argued for inequality based on biology, and for this reason he was fired.

[20] Daphna Joel and Luba Vikhanski, Gender Mosaic, 2019

[21] Joel, D. et al. (2015) Sex beyond the genitalia: The human brain mosaic, Proceedings of the National Academy of Sciences, USA 112(50):15468-73

[22] Sex differences in empathy and related capacities, Eisenberg and Lennon, Arizona State University, 1983

[23] Graham and Ickes 1997, When women's intuition isn't greater than men's

[24] Ickes, Gesn and Graham, 2000, Gender differences in Empathic Accuracy: differential ability or differential motivation?

[25] Ickes, 2003, Everyday mind reading: Understanding what other people think and feel

[26] Kristi Klein and Sara Hodges, 2001, Gender Differences, Motivation and Empathy Accuracy: when it pays to understand.

[27] https://www.aei.org/carpe-diem/2016-sat-test-results-confirm-pattern-thats-persisted-for-45-years-high-school-boys-are-better-at-math-than-girls/

[28] Rosling, Hans, Contributors, Rosling, Ola, Ronnlund Rosling, Anna, (2018) Factfulness: 10 reasons we're wrong about the world and why things are better than you think, New York: Flatiron Books

7

[29] https://reports.collegeboard.org/archive/sat-suite-program-results/2016/class-of-2016-results

[30] https://www.brookings.edu/research/race-gaps-in-sat-scores-highlight-inequality-and-hinder-upward-mobility/

[31] Cialdini, Robert, Pre-Suasion, (2016), *Penguin Random House* pp.128-131

[32] Inzlicht, Michael and Ben-Zeev, Avi, Do High-Achieving Female Students Under-Perform in Private? The Implications of Threatening Environments on Intellectual Processing, *Journal of Educational Psychology*, Vol. 95 (4):796-805, 2003, December 2003

[33] McCormick, Jasmine and Morris, Wendy, L., The Effects of Stereotype-Threat and Power on Women's and Men's Outcomes in Face-to-Face and E-mail Negotiations PSI CHI, *Journal of Psychological Research, The International Honor Society in Psychology*, Vol. 20, no. 3, ISSN 2164-8204, 2015

[34] Miyaki, A. et al 2010, Reducing the Gender Achievement Gap in College Science: A Classroom study of values affirmation. Science, 330 1234-1237. Doi:10.1126/science.1195996.

[35] Rydell, Robert, McConnell, Allen, Beilock, Sian, Multiple Social Identities and Stereotype Threat: Imbalance, Accessibility and Working Memory, *Journal of Personality and Social Psychology*, Vol. 96 (5) 949-66, June 2009

[36] Taylor, V. J., & Walton, G. M. (2011). Stereotype Threat Undermines Academic Learning. *Personality and Social Psychology Bulletin*, 37(8), 1055–1067

[37] https://en.wikipedia.org/wiki/Replication_crisis. The replication crisis (or replicability crisis or reproducibility crisis) is, as of 2020, an ongoing methodological crisis in which it has been found that many scientific studies are difficult or impossible to replicate or reproduce. The replication crisis affects the social sciences and medicine most severely.[1][2] The crisis has long-standing roots; the phrase was coined in the early 2010s[3] as part of a growing awareness of the problem

[38] Ceci, S. J., Ginther, D. K., Kahn, S., & Williams, W. M. (2014). Women in Academic Science: A Changing Landscape. *Psychological Science in the Public Interest*, 15(3), 75–141

[39] Lindberg, S. M., Hyde, J. S., Petersen, J. L., & Linn, M. C. (2010). New trends in gender and mathematics performance: A meta-analysis. *Psychological Bulletin, 136*(6), 1123–1135

[40] Walton, Gregory, M., Cohen, Geoffrey, L., Stereotype Lift, *Journal of Experimental Social Psychology*, 39 (2003), 456-467, September 2001

[41] O'Dea, R.E., Lagisz, M., Jennions, M.D. *et al.* Gender differences in individual variation in academic grades fail to fit expected patterns for STEM. *Nat Commun* **9**, 3777 (2018). https://doi.org/10.1038/s41467-018-06292-0

[42] Fine, Cordelia, Joel, Daphna, Rippon, Gina, Eight things you need to know about Sex, Gender, Brains, Behavior: A Guide for Academics, Journalists, Parents, Gender Diversity Advocates, Social Justice Warriors, Tweeters, Facebookers, and Everyone Else, *The Scholar and Feminist Online*, Issue 15.2, 2019. This paper provides an

excellent summary for further reading on this essential topic.

http://sfonline.barnard.edu/neurogenderings/eight-things-you-need-to-know-about-sex-gender-brains-and-behavior-a-guide-for-academics-journalists-parents-gender-diversity-advocates-social-justice-warriors-tweeters-facebookers-and-ever/

[43] Gina Rippon, The Gendered Brain: The new neuroscience that shatters the myth of the female brain, The Bodley Head, 2019

[44] Center for Disease Control and Prevention, 2020
https://www.cdc.gov/heartdisease/women.htm

[45] Hart Voor Vrouwen, Professor Dr Angela Mass, 2019, A Woman's Heart (English translation) September, 2020

[46] Gender Equality, Norms and Health 5, Gender Equality and Gender norms: framing the opportunities for health, *The Lancet*, May 2019

[47] http://www.genderedinnovations.com/

6 Uniqueness and Belonging, Needs and Norms, Self-identity and Shame

[1] Maslow, A. H. (1954). *Motivation and personality*. New York: Harper and Row

[2] Gender and Psychological Well-Being, M.Pilar Matud, Marisela Lopéz-Curbelo,Demelza Fortes, 20 September 2019

[3] Diener, E., Tay, L., Needs and Subjective Well-being, *Journal of Personality and Social Psychology*, 2011

[4] Shawn Achor, Andrew Reece, Gabriela Rosen Kellerman, Alexi Robichauz, 9 out of 10 people are willing to earn less money to do more meaningful work, *Harvard Business Review*, November 2018

[5] Brené Brown, Men, Women and Worthiness: The experience of shame and the power of being enough, Audio Book published by Sounds True, 2012. Brown's TED talk on The Power of Vulnerability in 2012 is one of the top 5 most viewed TED talks with over 40 million views.

[6] Babcock, Linda P., Recalde, Maria, Lise Vesterlund, Why Women volunteer for tasks that don't lead to promotions, *Harvard Business Review,* June 2018

[7] Christensen, Clayton, M. How will you measure your life? The Clayton M. Christensen Reader, (2015), *Harvard Business Review Press*

[8] Ibid., pp.196

[9] Heilman, M. E., & Chen, J. J. (2005). Same Behavior, Different Consequences: Reactions to Men's and Women's Altruistic Citizenship Behavior. *Journal of Applied Psychology, 90*(3), 431–441

[10] Roger Horrocks, Masculinity in Crisis, Palgrave MacMillan, UK, 1994

[11] Roger Horrocks (1994) Masculinity in Crisis, *Self & Society, An International Journal for Humanistic Psychology*, Volume 22:4, 25-29

[12] Mahalik, James R., Burns, Shaun M., and Syzdek, Matthew, Masculinity and perceived normative health behaviors as predictors of men's health behaviors, *Social Science &*

Medicine, Vol. 64, Issue 11, June 2007, pp.2201-2209

[13] Mahalik, J.R., Morray, E.B., Coonerty-Femiano, A. *et al.* Development of the Conformity to Feminine Norms Inventory. *Sex Roles* 52, 417–435 (2005)

[14] Ibid.

[15] Gilligan, Carol, (1982) In a Different Voice, Psychological Theory and Women's Development, *Harvard University Press*

[16] Cialdini, R.B., Trost, M.R., 1998, Social Influence: Social norms, conformity and compliance. In *The Handbook of Social Psychology*, ed. D.T. Gilbert, S.T. Fiske, G. Lindzey, 2:151-92. Boston: McGraw-Hill. 4th ed.

[17] Nathan DeWall, C., MacDonald, Geoff, Webster, Gregory D., Masten, Carrie L., Baumeister, Roy F., Powell, Caitlin, Combs, David, Schurtz, David R., Stillman, Tyler F., Tice, Dianne M., Eisenberger, Naomi I., *Association for Psychological Science*, Acetaminophen Reduces Social. Pain: Behavioral and Neural Evidence, Volume: 21, issue 7: page(s): 931-937

[18] Cherlin, Andrew J., (2014) Labor's Love Lost: The Rise and Fall of The Working-Class Family in America, *Russell Sage Foundation*

[19] Dill, J. S., Price-Glynn, K., & Rakovski, C. (2016). Does the "Glass Escalator" Compensate for the Devaluation of Care Work Occupations? The Careers of Men in Low- and Middle-Skill Health Care Jobs. *Gender & Society*, 30(2), 334–360. https://doi.org/10.1177/0891243215624656

[20] U.S. Bureau of Labor Statistics, Projections of Occupational Employment 2014-24, December 2015, https://www.bls.gov/careeroutlook/2015/article/projections-occupation.htm

[21] Claire Cain Miller, Pink Collar Work Why Men Don't Want the Jobs Done Mostly by Women, *New York Times, The Upshot*, 4 January 2017

[22] David Schneider, *The Psychology of Stereotyping* (New York: Guilford Press, 2005)

7 Our flawed definition of Leadership - why taking charge to take care could be the middle way

[1] Collins, James C. Good to Great: Why Some Companies Make the Leap...and Others Don't, New York: Harper Business, 2001

[2] Catalyst Report, 2005, Women 'Take Care', Men 'Take Charge', Stereotyping of U.S. Business Leaders Exposed

[3] Tina Kiefer, Professor of organizational behavior, University of Warwick, UK. Professor Kiefer fell upon the exercise accidentally while leading a workshop full of executives who did not speak much English. When asked to draw a leader most people will automatically draw a white male. Since then it has been adopted by organizational psychologists across the world.

[4] **Think** manager—**think male, think** follower—**think** female: Gender bias in implicit followership theories. S Braun, S Stegmann - Journal of Applied 2017 -

Wiley Online Library Schein (1973, 1975) showed that the mental picture of a typical **leader** includes more masculine attributes and is more strongly associated with the **male** gender stereotype. She concisely phrased this effect **think** manager— **think male** ...

5 Eagly, Alice, H., Carli, Linda, L., Through the Labyrinth, *Harvard Business Review Press*, 2007

6 Martinsen Oyvind and Lars Glaso (2013): Personality for Leadership, Norwegian Business School study of 2,900 managers showed women were more effective

7 Boston Consulting Group's Decoding Global Talent Survey which was conducted in collaboration with The Network and included 203,756 respondents from 189 countries, of which over 141,000 were women

8 Lean In and McKinsey and Company, Women in the Workplace Report 2018

9 Maccoby, Michael (2012), Narcissistic Leaders: who succeeds and who fails, *Crown Publishing Group*

10 Catalyst Report 2007, The Double-Bind Dilemma for Women in Leadership: Damned if You Do, Doomed If You Don't

11 A Great Place to Work, Job Satisfaction in Senior Leadership, 2017

12 Pleck, Joseph H., (1981), The Myth of Masculinity, Cambridge, Mass.: MIT Press

13 James, D. and Clarke, S, 1993, Women, Men and Interruptions: A critical review in D. Tannen (Ed) Gender and conversational interaction, pp.231-280, New York, NY: Oxford University Press

14 Men in Senior Leadership: Why we need more men's leadership coaches – the missing link in creating more gender parity in leadership roles, Progeny Leadership, 2019

15 McKinsey, Changing companies' minds about women, Joanna Barsh, Lareina Yee, 2011

16 McKinsey Global Institute (MGI) Report, The Power of Parity: How advancing women's equality can add $12 trillion to global growth

17 Ernst & Young, Women, Fast Forward, https://www.ey.com/en_gl/women-fast-forward

18 Peterson Institute Working Paper Is Gender Diversity Profitable? Evidence from a Global Survey, Marcus Noland, Tyler Moran, Barbara Kotschwar. N.B. this paper does not specify board level, just females in leadership in the company at 30%

19 Governor Jerry Brown, California signed a bill in 2018 stating, "given all the special privileges that corporations have enjoyed for so long, it's high time corporate boards include the people who constitute more than half the 'person' of America

20 Employee burn out Part 1, Gallup, July 2018

8   Confidence does not equal competence

1 Cliffe, Sarah, Leadership Qualities vs. Competence: Which Matters More? *Harvard Business Review*, 2015, refers to the Stanford University annual student team building exercise

[2] When does power disparity help or hurt group performance? Taracki, Murat, Greer, Lindred L., Groenen, Patrick J.F. Journal of Applied Psychology, Vol 101 (3), Mar 2016, 415-429

[3] Chamorro-Premuzic, Tomas, (2019) Why do so many incompetent men become leaders? (and how to fix it), Harvard Business Review Press. Also watch his TEDx talk University of Nevada, March 2019

[4] WeWork – The IPO that shouldn't, Nori Gerardo Lietz, Senior Lecturer of Business Administration, Harvard Business School, September 2019

[5] The New Yorker, Adam Neumann and the Art of Failing Up, WeWork's chief risk-taker found a kindred spirit with an open check book: Softbank's Masayoshi Son. Now he's walking away from the wreckage with more than $1 billion, by Amy Chozick, 2 November 2019

[6] Neumann's often unconventional behavior of walking sometimes in bare feet around the office, skateboarding through the cubicles, instigating tequila-fueled parties, and much more

[7] Pitchbook, Do female founders get better results? 2018 2.2% of all US VC funds goes to businesses with female founders. They get funding less than 2% of the time, as opposed to all- male founded businesses which get funded 35% of the time in the first round. One wonders how often in the first 12 minutes!

[8] Blitzscaling, fast massive company scaling, is a term created by Reid Hoffman, co-founder of Linked In

[9] The Wall Street Journal, How Adam Neumann's Over-the-Top Style Built WeWork. This is not the way everybody behaves, 18 September 2019, by Eliot Brown

[10] Los Angeles Times, News Analysis: Gender bias turned out to be a wonderful indicator of WeWork's incompetence, by Sarah Green Carmichael, Bloomberg, 5 November 2019

[11] WeWorkers Coalition sent a letter to the WeWorkers Management Team, 8 November 2019

[12] WeWorks Adam Neumann once said he had a 'beautiful relationship' with Softbank's Masa Son; now he calls out 'abuse of power' in lawsuit filing, CNBC report, Deidre Bosa 5th May 2020
https://www.cnbc.com/2020/05/05/weworks-adam-neumann-calls-out-softbank-abuse-of-power-in-lawsuit.html

[13] #DeleteUber: how social media turned on Uber, Elena Cresci, The Guardian, 30 January 2017

[14] Internal Data shows Uber's reputation hasn't changed much since #DeleteUber, Faiz, Siddiqui, The Washington Post, August 2019

[15] Carreyrou, John, (2018), Bad Blood: Secrets and Lies in a Silicon Valley Startup, *Alfred A. Knopf*

[16] Gallup, Employee Burnout Part 1, the 5 Main Causes, 2018

[17] Gender, Work and Health, Margaret M. Quinn, Peter M. Smith, Annals of Work Exposures and Health, 2018, Vol. 62, No. 4, 389-392

[18] Russell, Bertrand, The Triumph of Stupidity, 10 May 1933

[19] Kruger, Justin, Dunning, David, Unskilled and Unaware of It: How Recognizing Difficulties in Recognizing One's Own Incompetence Lead to Inflated Self-Assessments, *Journal of Personality and Social Psychology* (1999), American Psychological Association, Inc. 1999, Vol. 77, No. 6. 1121-1134

[20] Joel, Daphna and Fine, Cordelia, Can we finally stop talking about male and female brains, *New York Times,* Opinion, December 3 2018

[21] Norgaard, Kari Marie, Living in Denial: Climate change, Emotions and Everyday Life (MIT) The MIT Press 2019, DOI: 10.7551/**mitpress**/ 9780262015448.001.0001

[22] Norgaard, Kari Marie, Living in Denial: Climate change, Emotions and Everyday Life (MIT) The MIT Press 2019, DOI: 10.7551/**mitpress**/ 9780262015448.001.0001

[23] Kahan, Dan, M., Misconceptions, Misinformation and the Logic of Identity-Protective Cognition, 2017, working paper, no.164, The Cultural Cognition Project

[24] http://www.culturalcognition.net

[25] James, Flynn, Slovic, Paul, Mertz, C.K., Gender, Race and Perception of Environmental Health Risks, *Risk Analysis: An International Journal*, Vol. 14, Issue 6, pp 1101-1108, December 1994, https://doi.org/10.1111/j.1539-6924.1994.tb00082.x

[26] McCright, Aaron M., Dunlap, Riley E., Cool Dudes: The Denial of Climate change Among Conservative White Males in the United States, *Global Environmental Change*, 21 (4) 1163-1172, October 2011, DOI: 10.1016/j.gloenvcha.2011.06.003

[27] Intergovernmental Panel on Climate Change (IPCC), Fifth assessment Report (AR5), 2014.
https://www.ipcc.ch/site/assets/uploads/2018/02/AR5_SYR_FINAL_SPM.pdf

[28] https://www.scientificamerican.com/article/destroyed-habitat-creates-the-perfect-conditions-for-coronavirus-to-emerge/

[29] Socrates was reported as saying that "I know that I know nothing", paradoxically demonstrating, as a highly knowledgeable individual, how fundamentally wise he was.

[30] Vidal John, Ensia, 2020, Destroyed habitat creates the perfect conditions for coronavirus to emerge, Covid-19 may just be just the beginning of mass pandemics

[31] https://www.fox5ny.com/news/us-has-4-of-the-worlds-population-but-more-than-25-of-global-coronavirus-cases

[32] https://www.brookings.edu/research/covid-outcomes-update-health-and-employment-impacts-in-the-us-compared-to-other-countries/?preview_id=1050791

[33] Dweck, Carol S.. (2008) Mindset :the new psychology of success *New York : Ballantine Books*

[34] Ben Hardy, PhD (2020) Personality Isn't Permanent – Break free from self-limiting beliefs and re-write your story, *Penguin Random House, UK*

[35] Soraya Chemaly, The White Male Effect is Real and Dangerous to Us All, January 2017, Medium.com, https://medium.com/the-establishment/the-white-male-effect-is-real-and-dangerous-to-us-all-95ffacc0fb4c

[36] Bill Gates, https://www.gatesnotes.com/Energy/Climate-and-COVID-19?WT.mc_id=20200807100000_COVID19-and-Climate_BG-

7

LI_&WT.tsrc=BGLI

[37] W. L. Sheldon, 1897 April, Ethical Addresses, Series 4, Number 4, What To Believe: An Ethical Creed by W. L. Sheldon (Lecturer of the Ethical Society of St. Louis), Start Page 57, Quote, Page 61, S. Burns Weston, Philadelphia, Pennsylvania. This quote is often mistakenly attributed to Ernest Hemmingway. https://books.google.nl/books?id=PkYxAQAAMAAJ&q=%22nobility+is%22&red ir_esc=y#v=snippet&

[38] Collins, James C. Good to Great: Why Some Companies Make the Leap…and Others Don't, New York: Harper Business, 2001

9 If You Want Out-of-the-Box Thinking Then Don't Put Your People in Them

[1] Bevelander, Dianne and Page, Michael John, Ms. Trust: Gender Networks and Trust – Implications for Management and Education, *Academy of Management Learning and Education*, Vol. 10, No. 4, 2012, https://doi.org/10.5465/amle.2009.0138

[2] Role Congruity Theory of Prejudice Toward Female Leaders, Alice H. Eagly, Steven J. Karau, Psychological Review 109(3):573-98, August 2002

[3] Penalties for Success: Reactions to Women who Succeed at Male Gender-Typed Tasks, Heilman, M.E., Wallen, A.S., Fuchs, D., & Tamkins, M. M. (2004) Journal of Applied Psychology, 89(3), 416-427

[4] Hard Won and Easily Lost: The Fragile Status of Leaders in Gender-Stereotype-Incongruent Occupations, Victoria L., Brescoll, Erica Dawson, Eric Luis Uhlmann, *Psychological Science*, 2010, Volume: 21 issue, 11, page(s) 1640-1642

[5] Mann, Annamarie and Darby, Ryan, Should Managers Focus on Performance or Engagement? *Gallup Business Journal*, 2014

[6] Doerr, John, Measure What Matters – OKRs the Simple Idea That Drives 10X Growth, John Doerr, *Penguin Random House*, UK 2018

[7] Capgemini Research Institute, Emotional Intelligence – the essential skillset for the age of AI, 2019

[8] Genos International's core emotional intelligence competencies. Genos International is recognized as a world leader in emotional intelligence programs. https://www.genosinternational.com/genos/

10 Getting Men Involved and Pipeline Problems or Bad Plumbing?

[1] Lean In and McKinsey and Company, Women in the Workplace Report 2018

[2] Boston Consulting Group's Decoding Global Talent Survey which was conducted in collaboration with The Network and included 203,756 respondents from 189 countries, of which over 141,000 were women

[3] Kruger, Justin, Dunning, David, Unskilled and unaware of it: How Difficulties in recognizing one's own incompetence lead to inflated self-assessments, Journal of Personality and Social Psychology, Vol 77 (6) Dec, 1999

[4] A Great Place to Work, Report 2018

[5] US Census Bureau Educational Attainment in the US, 2018 shows higher numbers of graduates and master holders were female than male

[6] Catherine Tinsley and Robin Ely *Harvard Business Review* 2018, What most people get wrong about men and women

[7] Bowles, H. R., Babcock, L., Lai, L. Social incentives for gender differences in the propensity to initiate negotiations: Sometimes it does hurt to ask, *Organizational Behavior and Human Decision Processes*, 103 (2007) 84-103

[8] Fine C. (2010). Delusions of Gender: How our Minds, Society and Neurosexism Create Difference. Cordelia Fine defined this term to draw attention to problematic practices in neuroscience which might be contributing to the sustaining of stereotypes and belief in hard wiring

[9] A Wall street Rule for the MeToo era – avoid women at all cost, Bloomberg, 2018

[10] John Gerzema, BAV Consulting, WPP Group Plc, Harvard Business Review, 2012

[11] Second-generation gender bias refers to practices that may appear neutral or non-sexist, in that they apply to everyone, but which discriminate against women because they reflect the values of the men who created or developed the setting, usually a workplace. It is contrasted with first-generation bias, which is deliberate, usually involving intentional exclusion.

11   Coaching Better Behaviors

[1] Harvard Business Review, Why Inclusive Leaders are Good for Organizations and How to Become One, Juliet Bourke, Andrea Espedido, March 2019

[2] Viv Groskop, (2019) How to Own the Room – Women and the Art of Brilliant Speaking, Transworld Publishers Ltd

[3] Dacher Keltner, Don't let power corrupt you, October 2016, *Harvard Business Review*

[4] Kline, Nancy, (1999), Time To Think - Listening to Ignite the Human Mind, Hachette, UK

[5] Castro, D. R., Lloyd, K. J., Anseel, F., Kluger, A. N., & Turjeman-Levi, Y. (in press). Mere-Listening Effect on Creativity and the Mediating Role of Psychological Safety. *Psychology of Aesthetics, Creativity and the Arts*

[6] Gregersen, Hal, bursting the CEO Bubble, *Harvard Business Review*, March-April 2017

[7] Van Kleef, Gerben A., Oveis, Christopher, van der Lowe, LuoKogan, Aleksandr, Goetz, Jennifer, Keltner, Dacher, Power, Distress and Compassion: Turning a Blind Eye to the Suffering of Others, *Psychological Science*, 2008; 19 (12): 1315-1322

[8] Sir John Acton, 1934-1902, an English historian, politician, writer who made the famous quote in a Letter to Bishop Mandell Creighton, 1887, Transcript of published in historical essays and studies, edited by J. N. Figgis and R. V. Laurence (*London:*

MacMillan, 1907)

[9] Owen, David, Hubris Syndrome: An Acquired Personality Disorder? A study of US Presidents and UK Prime Ministers Over the Last 100 Years, *Brain - A Journal of Neurology*, Volume 132, Issue 5, pp. 1396-1406, May 2009. https://doi.org/10.1093/brain/awp008

[10] Charles Handy, English social philosopher

[11] Van Quaquebeke, Niels, Felps, Will, Respectful Inquiry: A motivational account of leading through asking open questions and listening, *The Academy of Management Review*, Vol. 43 (1), July 2016

12 When Less Is More

[1] Vrouw Justitia heeft geen quota nodig, (Women judges don't need a quota) Het Financieele Dagblad, Elif Isitman, December 2018

[2] The Institute of Leadership Management, UK, Ageism at work is widening the leadership skills gap, survey December 2014 of 1400 respondents

[3] US Workers Discovering Affinity for Remote Work, Megan Brenan, *Gallup*, April 3 2020

[4] Gallup, Employee Burnout Part 1, the 5 Main Causes, 2018

[5] A Great Place To Work, 2017 Report

[6] Spousal Relative Income and Male Psychological Distress, Joanna Syrda, University of Bath, School of Management, first published online October 2019

[7] Americans see different expectations for men and women, Kim Parker, Juliana Menasce, Renee Stepler, Horowitz, Pew Research Center, December 2017

[8] Abendroth, Anja-Kristin, Melzer, Silvia, Kalev, A., Tomaskovic-Devey, Donald, Women at Work: women's access to power and the gender Earnings Gap, *Industrial and Labor Relations Review*, September 2016

[9] Maume, David J. 2011, Meet the new boss…same as the old boss? Female supervisors and subordinate career prospects. *Social Science Research* 40: 411-23

[10] Father Involvement and child well-being, Wilson, Katherine, Prior, Margaret, Journal of Paediatrics and child health, Vol 47(7): 405-7, July 2011,

[11] Lean In and McKinsey and Company, Women in the Workplace Report 2018

[12] Gender, work and health, Margaret M Quinn, Peter M Smith, Annals of Work Exposures and Health, volume 62, Issue 4, May 2018, pages 389-392

[13] Correl, S. J., Benard, S., Paik, I., Getting a Job: Is there a Motherhood Penalty? 2007, *American Journal of Sociology*, 112:5, 1297-1339

[14] World Economic Forum, Women Spend Twice as Much time on Housework as Men, Leah Ruppenar, Senior Lecturer in Sociology, University of Melbourne, 2016

[15] Lean In McKinsey key finding in Women in the Workplace Report, 2017

[16] Pew Research Center, Kim Parker and Eileen Patten, The Sandwich Generation, Rising Financial Burdens for Middle-Aged Americans, January 2013

[17] Levels of Maternal Care, The American College of Obstetricians and Gynecologists,

Volume 134, Number 2, August 2019
https://www.acog.org/-/media/project/acog/acogorg/clinical/files/obstetric-care-
consensus/articles/2019/08/levels-of-maternal-care.pdf

[18] American Indian and Alaska Native Women's Maternal Health: Addressing the Crisis,
National Partnership for Women and families, Fact. Sheet, October 2019

[19] Black Women's Maternal Health: A Multi-faceted approach to addressing persistent
and dire health disparities, 2018, https://www.nationalpartnership.org/our-
work/resources/health-care/maternity/black-womens-maternal-health-issue-
brief.pdf

[20] National Partnership for Women & families (2017, September). Quantifying America's
Gender Wage Gap by Race. Retrieved 4th April 2018, from http://www.national
partnership.org/research-library/workplace-fairness/fair-pay/quantifying-americas-
gender-wage-gap.pdf

[21] Black Mamas Matter Alliance & Center for reproductive rights. (2016). Research
Overview of Maternal mortality and morbidity in the United States, Retrieved 2
April 2018, from
https://www.reproductiverights.org/sites/crr.civicactions.net/files/documents/U
SPA_MH_TO_ResearchBrief_Final_5.16.pdf

13 NIMBY, Nationalism, Namaste

[1] 25th May 2020 George Floyd, a Black African American was murdered by a white
police officer, during an arrest in Minneapolis, United states. Three other police
officers stood by, preventing other bystanders from intervening. The filmed actions
triggered global protests against police brutality, racism and lack of accountability.

[2] Brené Brown, Dare to Lead, Brave Work, Tough Conversations, Whole Hearts,
Vermilion: UK, Random House: US, 2018

[3] American Association of University Women, Barriers and Bias, The Status of Women in
Leadership, 2016

[4] Tomas Chamorro-Premuzic, (2019) Why are So Many Incompetent Leaders Male (and
how to fix it) *Harvard Business Review Press*

[5] Harvard business Review, 2015, How Emotional Intelligence Became a Key Leadership
Skill, Andrea Ovans

[6] Catalyst, The Gender Stereotyping Series

[7] The Economist, Editorial, Zanny Minton Beddoes, Editor-in-Chief, June 26th 2020

[8] Fetch, B., Poliner, J., (Un)Skirting the Issues: A Guide for the Well-Intentioned Man in
Today's Workplace, Lioncrest Publishing, 2017

[9] Glassdoor, Mission and Culture survey 2019, https://about-
content.glassdoor.com//app/uploads/sites/2/2019/07/Mission-Culture-Survey-
Supplement.pdf

[10] Gender Gap Report, World Economic Forum, 2018

[11] Black Panther, Eponymous American Superhero film of the Marvel comic hero, also

known as King T'Challa, 2018.

[12] King T'Challa's famous speech is regarded by many as a direct response to the "build a wall" plan of President Trump to create a border between the United States and Mexico.

[13] Dalai Lama and Desmond Tutu, The Book of Joy, (2016), Avery, *Penguin Random house: NY*

[14] Peer, Marisa, I am Enough: mark your mirror and change your life, 2018

[15] Brickman; Campbell (1971). Hedonic relativism and planning the good society. *New York: Academic Press.* pp. 287–302. in M. H. Apley, ed., Adaptation Level Theory: A Symposium, *New York: Academic Press.* The theory captures that as people gain economically, they continue to desire things, while their happiness levels stay relatively stable.

[16] Joshua Fields Millburn, (2013) Everything that Remains: A Memoir by the Minimalists, Asymmetrical Press